THE CIVILIZATION OF THE AMERICAN INDIAN SERIES

REDSKINS, RUFFLESHIRTS, AND REDNECKS

Indian Allotments in Alabama and Mississippi, 1830–1860

REDSKINS
RUFFLESHIRTS
AND REDNECKS

INDIAN ALLOTMENTS
IN ALABAMA AND MISSISSIPPI
1830–1860

MARY ELIZABETH YOUNG

NORMAN : UNIVERSITY OF OKLAHOMA PRESS

LIBRARY OF CONGRESS CATALOG CARD NUMBER: 61-15150

Copyright 1961 by the University of Oklahoma Press, Publishing Division of the University. Composed and printed at Norman, Oklahoma, U.S.A., by the University of Oklahoma Press. First Edition.

TO PAUL W. GATES

ACKNOWLEDGMENTS

IN PREPARING THIS VOLUME, I have lifted ideas freely from discussions with Professor John G. B. Hutchins of the Cornell School of Business and Public Administration; Professor Thomas H. LeDuc of Oberlin College; Peter Brannon, military archivist of Alabama; and W. C. Hare, attorney-at-law, Tuskegee, Alabama. Professor Paul W. Gates of Cornell University, by advice, assistance, and example, contributed essentially to my work. I am indebted to the staff of the National Archives, particularly to Marshall Moody, Roy Hart, and Maurice Moore.

The staffs of the Cornell University Library, Colgate University Library, the Library of Congress, the libraries of Duke University and Emory University, the Southern Historical Collection of the University of North Carolina, the William E. Clements Library of the University of Michigan, the Newberry Library, Chicago, the Burton Historical Collection of the Detroit Public Library, the Ohio State University Library; the Historical Societies of Chicago, Pennsylvania, Tennessee and Wisconsin; the Archives of Alabama, Georgia, Mississippi, and Louisiana State University; officials of the Bureau of Land Management and the Bureau of Indian Affairs, Department of the Interior; and county officers of Talladega, Russell, and Tuskegee counties,

Alabama; Muscogee County, Georgia; and Tunica, De Soto, Marshall, and Pontotoc counties, Mississippi, have all contributed material assistance.

Research and writing were financed by the Robert Schalkenbach Foundation, Cornell University, and Ohio State University. I owe a special debt of gratitude to my mother, Mrs. Mary T. Young, for research assistance in Alabama and Mississippi. Professors Paul W. Gates, Thomas LeDuc, and Foster Rhea Dulles have read the manuscript and made much helpful criticism, as have the editors of the *Mississippi Valley Historical Review* and the *American Historical Review*, where portions of this work have already appeared. Mrs. Ann Hall, Mrs. Margaret Weitzmann, and William Hartel typed the manuscript.

Columbus, Ohio   MARY ELIZABETH YOUNG
September 14, 1961

CONTENTS

xi

```
┌─────────────────────────────────┐
│                                 │
│         ILLUSTRATIONS           │
│                                 │
└─────────────────────────────────┘
```

TABLES

xiii

MAPS

GRAPHS

REDSKINS, RUFFLESHIRTS, AND REDNECKS

Indian Allotments in Alabama and Mississippi, 1830–1860

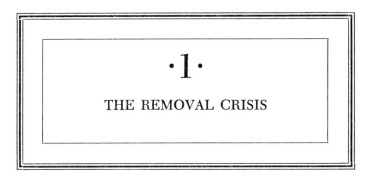

·1·

THE REMOVAL CRISIS

INDIANS AND INDIAN POLICY have not recently constituted a major theme in the definition of Jacksonian democracy. Yet to Jackson's contemporaries, Indian policy was a vital question. The growth of western states, the accessibility of their lands for settlement and speculation, townsite promotions, and internal improvement schemes—all depended upon cessions of land by Indian tribes. This in turn required the negotiation of treaties between the federal government and Indian "chiefs and headmen." The reluctance of tribal leaders to co-operate by ceding their lands promptly and cheaply confronted the Jacksonians with a practical and moral dilemma. For if they were avaricious, they were also "all honorable men." They recognized—and were from time to time reminded by the humanitarians among their constituents—that the Indians had some claim on the lands they occupied and that they should be divested of this claim only by a "free contract." Yet the lands must be obtained. It is not easy to reconcile avarice with honor or force with voluntarism, but the Jacksonians tried it. One aspect of their attempt was a series of treaties allotting portions of ceded lands to individual Indians and opening the remaining lands to settlement. The most important of these treaties were the Choctaw agreement of 1830,

3

the Creek, of 1832, and the Chickasaw, of 1834. The negotiation and administration of these agreements form the subject of this book.

Since allotment was later to become the basic feature of American Indian policy (from the Dawes Act of 1887 to the Reorganization Act of 1934), its earliest large-scale application by the federal government deserves attention. Furthermore, allotment was a land policy as well as an Indian policy. Its application offered unique opportunities for speculation, and affected the original distribution of landholdings over considerable areas. Finally, an account of the allotment policy as a part of the story of contact and conflict between white and Indian cultures offers instructive insights into the values and assumptions of the Jacksonian generation. Here we find commitments to private property, to freedom of contract, and to the rapid peopling of the earth and exploitation of its resources: values which, in practice, were often self-contradictory. One purpose of this book is to examine these values as sources of conflicting motives and modes of action in relation to specific problems of public policy.

At the time Andrew Jackson became President of the United States, Indians living in tribal communities still occupied parts of all the public domain states east of the Mississippi, as well as Georgia, North Carolina, and New York. These tribes had discarded the habits of scalping settlers, burning villages, and levying war against the United States. Substantial numbers of them devoted themselves to cultivating land, exchanging goods, and accumulating fortunes in the approved Anglo-American pattern. But this transformation did not make them more congenial neighbors. To most of Jackson's contemporaries, it simply demonstrated that homes were to be found and fortunes made on lands held by Indians; therefore, they reasoned, Indians should be removed from these lands so that white men might enjoy their resources.

The most notable instance of this "Indian problem" was the

situation of the four "civilized" tribes of the South—the Chickasaws, Choctaws, Creeks, and Cherokees—who comprised a population of nearly sixty thousand. Their domain, stretching from
the pine-scented foothills of the Appalachians to the swamps of
the Mississippi, covered twenty-five million acres. Thus, while
the southern frontier line had long ago crossed the Mississippi
and was pressing through Arkansas and Missouri, white settlements east of the river were interrupted by Indian tenure of
northeastern Georgia, Alabama east of the Coosa River and west
of the Tombigbee, and the northern two-thirds of Mississippi,
as well as enclaves in western North Carolina and southern
Tennessee.

Public opinion in the states affected demanded the immediate
opening of these Indian lands to white settlement and the removal of the aboriginal occupants across the Mississippi. But the
consequent determination of state and federal officials that the
southeastern tribes must emigrate was matched by an equal resolution on the part of tribal leaders that they would not be
moved. Treaties calling for the allotment of lands in severalty
to thousands of individual Chickasaw, Choctaw, and Creek
Indians were a product of this conflict.

These general allotment treaties and the methods by which
they were executed reflected contradictory policies. On one
hand, the Indians were expected to migrate west of the Mississippi; on the other, most of the adult tribesmen were given individual plots of land within the areas ceded to the United States,
presumably so that they might occupy and cultivate them.

The contradictory intentions of the allotment treaties reflected
a dilemma which has characterized American Indian policy
throughout our history: whether to try to assimilate the red man
into white society, or to segregate him from it. During the first
third of the nineteenth century, this dilemma emerged in the
contrast between the federal government's avowed policy of
removing eastern tribes west of the Mississippi, and the assistance it gave to groups and individuals whose mission it was to

bring "civilization" to the aboriginal heathen.[1] While government negotiators labored to relieve the tribes of their eastern
acres, traders, missionaries, and government agents encouraged
them to establish valuable farms, increasing the stake of leading
tribesmen in the lands they were asked to abandon. Furthermore, the government aided missionary efforts to turn Cherokees, Choctaws, and Chickasaws into literate Christians. The
well-publicized results of these efforts encouraged an influential
segment of the religious community in their belief that Indians
might rapidly be assimilated as ordinary citizens, and that their
imitation of Christian customs made them "deserving" of equal
treatment. The leaders of some tribes imitated American customs in forming centralized governments with written laws and
constitutions; this facilitated their efforts to form a "united
front" in opposition to further cessions of land.

In assisting the agents of "civilization," the government was
in some measure co-operating with a process it could not prevent.
Since their first contacts with Charleston and Augusta traders
in the late seventeenth century, the southern tribes had assimilated increasing portions of the white man's culture. The traders
introduced the tribesmen first to European goods and then to
European customs and ways of living. They brought with them
metal tools, horses, livestock, cotton cloth, and rum. In the
eighteenth century, Scottish, English, and French traders settled
in the Indian towns, taking native wives and fathering half-
blood children. They raised cattle and hogs, fenced their farms,
and employed Negro slaves to cultivate them. Gradually members of the tribe outside the trader's family came not only to
depend on his goods, but to imitate his methods of farming. This
process of imitation produced changes in patterns of living as

[1] The standard history of the formation and execution of the removal policy
is Annie H. Abel, "The History of Events Resulting in Indian Consolidation West
of the Mississippi," *Annual Report of the American Historical Association for
the Year 1906*, Vol. I, 269–75. The principal descriptive histories of the emigra-
tions are Grant Foreman, *Indian Removal: The Emigration of the Five Civilized Tribes of Indians* and *The Last Trek of the Indians*. George D. Harmon,
Sixty Years of Indian Affairs, 1789–1850, describes the government's effort to
"civilize" the tribes.

well as in agricultural practices. The southeastern Indians were agriculturists, but, except perhaps for the Choctaws, they gave little attention to cultivation, depending on hunting and fishing to supplement their diet. They planted their crops in common fields, keeping only small gardens around their houses as individual property. Among the Creeks, each family gathered its own crops, but contributed part of them to the common store used to carry the tribe through the starving times between harvests. Imitating the traders, Indian innovators began to use the plow, enlarge their fields, employ slaves, and plant cotton. Improvements in technique produced corresponding gradations of wealth, and the wealthier tribesmen fenced their improvements, settling out in separate plantations.

Wealth was not the only product of changing agricultural patterns. Under the traditional division of labor, women had tended the fields, owned the houses and gardens, and controlled the children. Perhaps because cattle and hogs were considered as game, the men of the family adopted stock-raising, and some undertook the responsibility for cultivating their fields. Generally the traders and their half-blood sons directed the work of their plantations, attended at least to the higher education of their children, and in some cases introduced inheritance of property through the male line.[2]

[2] Alexander Spoehr, "Changing Kinship Systems," Field Museum of Natural History, *Anthropological Series*, Vol. XXXIII (1947), 227–30; 201–204. Among the richest primary sources through which these developments may be traced are the published writings of the United States Indian agent, Benjamin Hawkins. See *Letters of Benjamin Hawkins, 1796–1806*, Georgia Historical Society *Collections*, Vol. IX (1916), and Hawkins' *Sketch of the Creek Country in the Years 1798 and 1799*, Georgia Historical Society *Publications*, Vol. III (1938). For the Cherokees, see especially Marion L. Starkey, *The Cherokee Nation*, and Henry T. Malone, *Cherokees of the Old South*. Angie Debo, in *The Rise and Fall of the Choctaw Republic*, discusses changes in Choctaw culture but gives little attention to agricultural developments. These can be traced in the incoming correspondence of the American Board of Commissioners for Foreign Missions, Choctaw Letterbooks, Houghton Library, Harvard University (hereafter cited according to catalog number, e.g., ABC 18.3.4). On the Chickasaws, see James Hull, "A Brief History of the Mississippi Territory," Mississippi Historical Society *Publications*, Vol. IX (1906), 542; Hawkins, *Letters*, 391–92; G. W. Long to Thomas L. McKenney, November 5, 1824, Chickasaw File 80, Records of the Bureau of Indian Affairs.

As new solutions were found to the problem of getting from dawn to dark and from January to November, the whole rhythm of life began to change. Traditionally the men of each village met daily in the town square to smoke, gossip, and discuss affairs of state. During most of the afternoon, outside the hunting season, members of the town regularly repaired to the square for ball playing and dancing. During the months following the harvest and again after the planting season, the whole tribe took to the woods in hunting parties. Such "idleness" and periodic roving was incompatible with the industrious pursuit of agriculture. One government agent explicitly encouraged the "settling out in villages" to wean his charges from "the old habits of indolence, and sitting daily in the squares, which seem peculiarly attractive to the residenters of towns."[3]

The activities of conscientious agents were not the government's only contribution to the civilization of the tribes. Treaty commissioners supported the work by including in payments for land cessions hoes and hogs and spinning wheels and appropriations for schools. Beginning in 1819, Congress appropriated $10,000 yearly to assist missionaries to the Indians.

Missionaries among the Chickasaws, Choctaws, and Cherokees maintained a number of stations and schools. Their objective was to combine agricultural and literary education with instruction in Christian doctrine. The larger mission "stations" were like great plantations, including schools where Indian children received "a good English education," training and work experience in farming and homemaking, and an introduction to the bracing discipline of the twelve-hour day.[4] Attempting to evangelize the natives, the missionary teachers and preachers exhorted young and old to abandon their heathen ball-plays and dances for camp meetings and the singing of hymns.

Many half-blood leaders co-operated with the missionaries

[3] Hawkins, *Sketch*, 45.
[4] Starkey, *Cherokee Nation*, and Debo, *Choctaw Republic*, give much information on the missionaries and their schools. Detailed plans of the American Board stations among the Choctaws may be found in the Choctaw Letterbooks, ABC 18.3.4.

and became enthusiastic converts to a variety of Anglo-Saxon habits, ranging from formal education and Methodism to constitution-making. These converts assisted in supporting schools, exhorted at camp meetings, and formed temperance societies. Among the Choctaws and the Cherokees, they substituted constitutions and written laws enforced by regularly appointed officers for retaliation or clan revenge, and officials elected for limited terms for hereditary or elective chiefs holding office for life. Under their laws, infanticide, polygamy, witchcraft, and other undesirable native practices were banned, together with such imported vices as the sale and consumption of whisky.

Clearly the missionary efforts, subsidized by the government and occasionally supplemented by the work of government agents, worked in opposition to the policy of removal. They gave birth to a group of leaders who owned valuable, improved property within the tribal domains, who prized their positions as leaders of their tribes and mediators between them and various representatives of the encroaching whites, and who in the end sought to stabilize their tenure of power within the tribes by organizing resistance to the uprooting of the natives from their accustomed homes. The establishment in the 1820's of government on the American pattern was an aspect of their attempt to concentrate their political authority. They intended to use this authority in offering effective resistance to further cessions of land. In addition, they perceived and exploited the fact that the progress of the tribes in civilization was frequently cited as evidence that they deserved to retain their lands.

In view of the difficulties which the "civilization" of the tribes raised for those who wished them removed, it is not surprising that advocates of removal became skeptical of the progress of the tribes in assimilating white culture. Chiefs and intermarried white men, these critics asserted, were becoming rich at the expense of the "common Indians." The fullbloods, on the other hand, were becoming daily poorer and more degraded by their contacts with the vices of white civilization. Observing that some of the tribesmen had emigrated voluntarily, the advocates

9

of removal assumed that emigration appeared to all the "real Indians" a desirable alternative to their present misery. Once freed from the tyranny of their chiefs, they would choose to emigrate west.[5]

A leading proponent of this view was Andrew Jackson. Both as general and as treaty commissioner, Jackson had extensive dealings with the southern tribesmen prior to his elevation to the Presidency. He equated the half-blood leaders who opposed emigration with the "aristocrats" among his political opponents: they were equally culpable of misleading the masses for their own profit. During the Cherokee negotiations of 1817, for example, Jackson observed of the anti-treaty party:

> These . . . are like some of our bawling politicians who loudly exclaim we are friends of the people, but who, when they obtain their views care no more for the happiness and wellfare of the people than the Devil does.[6]

There can be little doubt that some of the adverse reports of Indian "civilization" had substance. Recent studies of culture contact emphasize that uneven assimilation of alien habits, the degree of acculturation varying with social position and psychological idiosyncrasy, is the rule rather than the exception.[7] So far as the efforts of agents and missionaries to destroy their accustomed routines, their ancient religious beliefs and ceremonies, and the pattern of their family relations affected the "common Indians," they must have produced conflict and a corresponding sense of insecurity. It would be utopian to assume that all who were thus affected found immediate solace in the

[5] Wilson Lumpkin, *The Removal of the Cherokee Indians from Georgia*, I, 61–77; Thomas L. McKenney to James Barbour, December 27, 1826, 19 Cong., 2 sess., *House Doc. 28*, 5–13.

[6] Jackson to Colonel Robert Butler, June 21, 1817, in *Correspondence of Andrew Jackson* (ed. by John Spencer Bassett), II, 299.

[7] See for example Edward M. Bruner, "Primary Group Experience and the Processes of Acculturation," *American Anthropologist*, Vol. LVIII (1956), 605–23; SSRC Summer Seminar on Acculturation, "Acculturation: an Exploratory Formulation," *American Anthropologist*, Vol. LVI (1954); Spoehr, "Kinship, Systems," 216–26.

rewards of Christian and commercial civilization, or the native version of it. The pervasive problem of drunkenness is one indication.

But even if critics were often correct in believing that all was not well with the silent multitudes, they were led astray by their assumption that these people saw their alternatives in the pattern which appeared so obvious to interested white observers: extermination, assimilation, or removal. There is no ground for certainty that the majority of the Indians thought at all in terms of clear-cut alternatives. The mistaken assumption that they did think so lay at the root of many difficulties.

However mistaken the advocates of removal may have been concerning the implications of the uneven acculturation of the tribes, they recognized individual variations in "civilization" as a problem, which the allotment policy was first proposed precisely to meet. As early as March, 1816, Secretary of War William H. Crawford of Georgia suggested a plan for combining the assimilation of the "civilized" Indian leaders with the removal of the "savages." The tribesmen who had made separate improvements and wished to remain on them as farmers in the midst of a predominantly white population should be given allotments or, as Crawford called them, "individual reservations."[8] In the Cherokee treaty of 1817, this offer was combined with a plan calling on the remaining tribesmen to exchange their holdings east of the Mississippi for a district of equal size west of the river, where they might pursue their savage ways unmolested.[9] The amount of land ceded to the United States in exchange for lands in the west was to be proportional to the number who emigrated. The treaties did not stipulate that all who remained must take land in severalty.

Government negotiators considered the allotment feature of the Cherokee treaty as bait for securing the consent of the already numerous citizens of the tribe who had improved plantations and wanted to keep them after the cession of the tribal

[8] *American State Papers: Indian Affairs*, II, 27.
[9] *7 Statutes at Large*, 156–60.

lands. Governor Joseph McMinn, of Tennessee, one of the negotiators, observed further that one of the principal Cherokee
signers "must speculate a little to support his family," and believed that their main object in taking reservations was speculation.[10] Testimony later submitted to the War Department
showed that there was a good deal of trading in Cherokee reservations, McMinn being among the participants.[11]

However useful the granting of individual reservations may
have been in securing the consent of the chiefs and other prominent Cherokees to land cessions, the administration of the allotment feature of the treaty presented difficulties. McMinn, who
was responsible for assisting those who wished to emigrate, tried
to force the whole tribe to register either for emigration or for
allotment. Despite his efforts, the government had to renegotiate
the agreement, and under the treaty of 1819, boundaries were
drawn which left the Cherokees most of their eastern domain.
Three hundred and eleven of the tribe took reservations. Georgia and North Carolina resisted the granting of fee simple allotments within their limits since they were not public domain
states and therefore retained title to lands within their borders.
Eventually War Department agents had to buy the allotments
in Georgia and North Carolina and reimburse Cherokees who
had been forced to pay the state of Tennessee for the privilege
of keeping their lands. In Tennessee and Alabama, the reservees
had trouble with intruders, and the government went to considerable expense in hiring attorneys to defend Cherokee rights
in court.[12]

10 McMinn to Calhoun, April 12, 1818, Special File 131, Records of the Bureau of Indian Affairs; Same to Same, January 26, 1819, *American State Papers:
Indian Affairs*, II, 483. Return J. Meigs to Jackson, May 24, 1817, in *Correspondence of Jackson*, II, 295–96.

11 J. W. Wester to Calhoun, January 10, 1826, Cherokee File 64, Records of
the Bureau of Indian Affairs.

12 See Cherokee Reservation Book; "Purchase of Reservations of Indian Lands,"
Cherokee File 66; H. Montgomery to James Barbour, October 17, 1825, Cherokee File 39; William Roane to Hugh Montgomery, October 25, 1827, Cherokee
File 41, Records of the Bureau of Indian Affairs; James Barbour to the Speaker
of the House, January 23, 1828, *American State Papers: Public Lands*, V, 396–

The costs and controversies incident to this small-scale attempt at applying the allotment policy do not seem to have discouraged its proponents. Provisions for allowing allotments to all heads of families were written into the Choctaw treaty of 1820. Here, as in the case of the Cherokees, the tribe retained the lands where most of their villages were located, and therefore those who did not choose to emigrate from the ceded lands to the Choctaw Nation West did not need to take allotments.[13]

The practice of giving individual reservations to chiefs and half-bloods was common among treaty commissioners north and south in the first third of the nineteenth century. Sometimes the inclusions of reservations "under Indian cover" was necessary to obtain the influence of traders in support of land cessions. In other cases, they were required by chiefs or half-bloods who wanted to avoid emigration or obtain funds to pay tribal debts.

The unique features of the allotment treaties with the Choctaws in 1830, the Creeks in 1832, and the Chickasaws in 1834 were the large numbers of tribesmen who were to receive lands, and the donation of eastern lands to Indians whom the government expected to emigrate west. The deliberate adoption of this anomalous policy was the consequence of a crisis in the relations between the southern tribes and the federal and state governments, which made it imperative that the consent of the tribes to the cession of all their remaining eastern lands be immediately secured.

On the Indian side, the roots of the crisis may be found in the attempt of the southern tribes to consolidate a united front against further cessions of land to the United States. Half-bloods of the Choctaws and Cherokees formed constitutional governments to concentrate intratribal authority under their control. The Cherokees then secured pledges from the Creek leaders to join them in standing firm against cession, and the Choctaws

97; "Cherokee Reservations," Report of Mr. Greenwood, April 17, 1858, 35 Cong., 1 sess., *House Report 290*.

[13] 7 *Statutes at Large*, 210–14; Special Reserve Book A, Records of the Bureau of Indian Affairs.

made a similar agreement with the Chickasaws.[14] The murder of town chief William McIntosh of the Creeks for violating a tribal ordinance against further land cessions was a lively deterrent against further infringements of the agreements. Bribing a faction among the tribal leaders was no longer a workable method of securing further cessions of land.

Impatient for the removal of the tribes within their limits, the southern states, with the tacit concurrence of the federal government, began in 1828 the extension of state laws over the Indian tribes. Georgia led the way with a law of December, 1828, adding the lands of the Cherokee Nation within her borders to five frontier counties.[15] Alabama and Mississippi passed similar legislation in January and February of 1829.[16]

It was no coincidence that these states acted immediately after Andrew Jackson's election to the Presidency. Jackson had long held the view that dealing with the tribesmen by treaty instead of direct legislation was outmoded and unwise. Soon after taking office in March, 1829, the President through his secretary of war informed the tribes affected that the federal government was "unable" to prevent the extension of state jurisdiction.[17] In his first annual message (December, 1829), the President asserted that the "old states" already exercised jurisdiction over the tribes within their boundaries, and that "there is no constitutional, conventional, or legal provision, which allows [Alabama and Georgia] less power over the Indians within their bounds, than is possessed by Maine or New York. . . . A state cannot be dismembered by Congress, or restricted in the exercise of her constitutional power."[18]

[14] Campbell and Merriwether to Creek Chiefs, December 9, 1824, *American State Papers: Indian Affairs*, II, 570; John Crowell to Campbell and Merriwether, *ibid.*, 573; Clark, Hinds, and Coffee to James Barbour, November 19, 1826, *ibid.*, 709.

[15] Georgia, *Acts*, December 12, 1828.

[16] Alabama, *Acts*, January 27, 1829; Mississisppi, *Acts*, February 4, 1829.

[17] John H. Eaton to John Crowell, March 27, 1829, Office of Indian Affairs, Letters Sent, V, 372–73; Middleton Mackey to John H. Eaton, November 27, 1829, Choctaw Emigration File 111, Records of the Bureau of Indian Affairs; Jackson to Major David Haley, October 10, 1829, Jackson Papers, Library of Congress.

The President found his constitutional limitations convenient. As his old friend and adviser, John Coffee, put it with reference to the Cherokees:

> ... deprive the chiefs of the power they now possess, take from them their own code of laws, and reduce them to plain citizenship ... and they will soon determine to move, and then there will be no difficulty in getting the poor Indians to give their consent. All this will be done by the State of Georgia if the U. States do not interfere with her law. .... This will of course silence those in our own country who constantly seek for causes to complain—It may indeed turn them loose upon Georgia, but that matters not, it is Georgia who clamors for the Indian lands, and she alone is entitled to the blame if any there be.[19]

One of the principal aims of the extension of state laws was to undermine the political solidarity of the tribes and prevent the chiefs from exercising their authority to prevent emigration or the cession of land. Georgia required that after June 30, 1830, all the laws, usages, and customs of the Cherokees were to be null and void, and that no laws or regulations passed by the tribe in council might be given as evidence in a trial. Anyone who tried to prevent enrollment for emigration might be imprisoned for a term not exceeding four years. Anyone who attempted to deter a chief, headman, or warrior from meeting in council to cede land, or from ceding land, might be imprisoned for four to six years. Should a state official be resisted in enforcing these laws, the governor might call out the county militia to aid him.[20] Mississippi in January, 1830, provided a $1,000 fine and a year's imprisonment for anyone who exercised the office of "chief, mingo, head man, or any post of power" and deprived the Indians of all their rights under tribal laws.[21] The Alabama laws of January, 1832, followed the same pattern as those of

---

[18] December 8, 1829, 21 Cong., 1 sess., *Sen. Doc. 1*, 15–16.
[19] Coffee to Jackson, February 3, 1830, Jackson Papers, Library of Congress.
[20] Georgia, *Acts*, December 12, 1828; December 19, 1829; December 22, 1830.
[21] Mississippi, *Acts*, February 4, 1829; January 19, 1830.

Georgia and Mississippi in abrogating the customs of the Indians and the authority of their chiefs and in penalizing efforts to prevent enrollment for emigration and the making of treaties.[22]

A second objective of the extension of state jurisdiction over the tribes was to place on the tribesmen, most of whom were illiterate and spoke no English, the burden of compliance with state laws designed for an Anglo-American population. Under these laws the tribesmen might be sued for debt, although in Georgia and in some cases in Alabama, their testimony was not received in court. Mississippi guaranteed the tribesmen "all the rights, privileges, immunities, and franchises . . . enjoyed by free white persons . . . in as full and ample a manner, as the same can be done by act of the General Assembly." This meant that henceforth the Chickasaws and Choctaws would have to pay taxes, serve on juries, participate in road building, and muster with the militia. They might give testimony in court, but since the state constitution limited the franchise to white men, no Indian could vote.[23] The intent of these laws is betrayed by the fact that once the Chickasaws and Choctaws had signed removal treaties, Governor Brandon of Mississippi assured the President that the operation of the laws in the Indian country would be suspended until their removal, and directed collectors to suspend the collection of taxes assessed on Indian property.[24]

Alabama specifically exempted the Indians from taxation, jury or militia duty, and road work, but she went further than the other states in aiding her frontier citizens in their intrusions on the Indian domain. Her law provided that contracts for the purchase of Indian improvements should be legally binding. Before any treaty calling for the removal of the Creeks had been signed, she provided for the erection of county governments in the

[22] Alabama, *Acts*, January 27, 1829; January 16, 1832.
[23] Mississippi, *Acts*, January 19, 1830; *The Southern Galaxy* (Natchez), January 28, 1830.
[24] Jackson to Brandon, August 31, 1830; Brandon to Eaton, September 15, 1830, Mississippi Governor's Correspondence, E 13, Mississippi Department of Archives and History; Message of Governor Gerald C. Brandon, November 16, 1830, Mississippi *House Journal*, 1830; Brandon to Jackson, November 15, 1830, Mississippi Governor's Correspondence.

territory belonging to the Creek Nation.[25] This made it virtually necessary that white men reside within the new county borders, if only to vote for and serve as officers of the county governments. Many of the difficulties the federal government later encountered in the execution of its treaty with the Alabama Creeks arose from the state's policy of encouraging intrusions.

Since the tribal leaders believed that tribal sovereignty over the lands occupied by the Indians in Georgia, Alabama, and Mississippi was guaranteed them by their treaties with the United States, they had high hopes of assistance from the Supreme Court. The Cherokee leaders appealed two cases testing the constitutionality of the Georgia laws to the high court. In the first, decided in January, 1831, the Cherokees asked an injunction restraining Georgia from exercising her jurisdiction within their nation. The court dismissed their motion on the ground that the Cherokee Nation, not being an independent foreign power, had no constitutional right to bring suit in the Supreme Court. The court also held here that it was not within its competence as a judicial body to prevent the exercise of state jurisdiction. In *Worcester* v. *Georgia*, decided in January, 1832, the court determined that the Cherokees as a "domestic dependent nation" had a right of jurisdiction over their soil superior to Georgia's right. But it did not specifically reverse its decision that the court had no power to enjoin Georgia from exercising her jurisdiction.[26] Thus to implement the decision that the Cherokee sovereignty was "superior" would require the use of United States troops to expel Georgians from the Cherokee country. President Jackson and his War Department refused to enforce "John Marshall's decision."

Although there seemed to be no legal remedy available to the tribes to prevent the extension of state jurisdiction over them, the Indians were not without champions at the bar of public opinion. As soon as Jackson's laissez faire policies with regard to

[25] Alabama, *Acts*, January 27, 1829; January 16, 1832; December 18, 1832.
[26] *Cherokee Nation* v. *Georgia*, 5 Peters 1–2; *Worcester* v. *Georgia*, *ibid.*, 515–17.

the state laws became known, representatives of the American Board of Commissioners for Foreign Missions and their anti-Jackson correspondents in Congress began to mobilize opinion against the administration's Indian policies.

The board itself had a vested interest in the continuance of the tribes in their traditional location. By 1830, it had established eight schools in the Choctaw Nation, seven in the Cherokee Nation East, and four among the Chickasaws, giving instruction to a total of 514 Indian children. The board's twelve years of missionary endeavor in the Choctaw Nation alone represented an investment exceeding $100,000. In addition to the probable loss of these physical assets, the missionaries feared that the consequence of removal would be social disorganization and a "general lapse into barbarism."[27]

Besides conferring directly with opposition congressmen, the board carried out an extensive publicity campaign against the policy of permitting the encroachment of state jurisdiction over the Indian nations. Under the pseudonym "William Penn," Jeremiah Evarts, secretary of the board, wrote a series of impassioned articles in defense of Indian rights. During the winter of 1829, Penn's arguments were published in the Washington *Daily National Intelligencer* and circulated separately in pamphlet form.[28] Evarts also instigated a campaign among local clergymen for petitioning Congress to protect the Indians. As a consequence, Congress in February, 1830, received petitions from a number of northeastern communities calling for the enforcement of treaties guaranteeing the Indians possession of their lands.[29]

These timely remonstrances reached Congress in the midst of debate on a general Indian removal bill. The proposed legis-

[27] *Missionary Herald*, (Boston) August, 1830.

[28] *Essays on the Present Crisis in the Condition of the American Indians.*

[29] 21 Cong., 1 sess., *Sen. Docs. 56, 59, 66, 73, 74, 76, 77, 92, 96.* Probably not all these petitions came as a result of Evarts' work. Two are from Baptist groups. The Quakers also opposed the removal policy. A thorough account of Evarts' work is J. Orin Oliphant (ed.), *Through the South and West with Jeremiah Evarts in 1826,* 47–61.

President Jackson's first Secretary of War, John H. Eaton, negotiated the Treaty of Dancing Rabbit Creek.

Greenwood LeFlore, the Choctaw chief, led the half-blood faction in negotiations leading to the Treaty of Dancing Rabbit Creek.

lation called for a $500,000 appropriation to enable the President to arrange with tribes having lands within existing states or territories to exchange all or part of their holdings for districts west of the Mississippi. The federal government was to finance the emigration west and to feed, clothe, and house each tribe during the year following its removal.[30]

The bill provoked extensive debate between proponents and opponents of removal. The vital center of this debate was the status of tribal governments in the Indian nations and the obligation of the federal government toward them. Even opponents of the removal bill accepted the rationale behind white imperialism: they questioned only the methods the Jackson administration was using to achieve its objects. Theodore Frelinghuysen, senator from New Jersey and a regular correspondent of the American board, won through his leadership in the fight against the removal bill the title "Christian Statesman." Yet Frelinghuysen asserted that "when the increase of population and the wants of mankind demand the cultivation of the earth, a duty is thereby devolved upon the proprietors of large and uncultivated regions, of devoting them to such useful purposes. But such appropriations are to be obtained by fair contract, and for reasonable compensation."[31]

The fundamental condition of a fair contract, Frelinghuysen insisted, was recognition by the United States of the right of tribal governments to both ownership and jurisdiction over their lands. If tribal sovereignty were destroyed and encroachment on Indian lands encouraged by state law, the tribesmen would be placed in a bargaining position so weak that they had no choice but to cede their lands. Furthermore, the tribes had traditionally been respected as independent nations, and sovereignty over their lands guaranteed them by treaty. Legalistic arguments aside, the southern tribes "deserved" to be treated as coequal nations because their civilization was becoming so much like that of the United States. The Cherokees, with their written

[30] 4 *Statutes at Large*, 411–12.
[31] April 4, 1830, *Register of Debates in Congress*, VI, 311.

language, printing press, constitution, republican form of government, and schools and churches, bore the burden of this demonstration.

Proponents of removal, chief of whom was Representative Wilson Lumpkin of Georgia, contended that recognition of tribal sovereignty had been a matter of expediency and had never included jurisdiction with ownership of the land, that state jurisdiction over inhabitants within state limits was questionable and had never previously been questioned, that the progress of the southern Indians in acquiring civilization was a myth and that the true function of the tribal governments was to assist the rich to become richer at the expense of the poor. But just as the anti-removal faction agreed with the assumption that an agricultural civilization has a claim to lands ethically superior to that of a savage nation, the advocates of removal admitted that so far as the savages had become cultivators of the earth, they were entitled to the fruits of their labor. Lumpkin quoted, approvingly, John Quincy Adams' Plymouth Oration of 1802: "Their cultivated fields, their constructed habitations, a space of ample sufficiency for their subsistence, and whatever they had invested for themselves by personal labor, was undoubtedly, by the laws of nature, theirs."[32]

The removal bill became law on May 28, 1830. It had passed the Senate by a vote of 28 to 19, and the House by 103 to 97.[33] These margins were significant. Ratification of a removal treaty would require a two-thirds vote of the Senate, a larger proportion than the removal bill had received. Nor was the narrow margin in the House reassuring, should further appropriations be required for the execution of the treaties. It was therefore essential that the removal agreements be liberal and that they be designed to satisfy as large a proportion of the Indian tribesmen as possible. Protests against the ratification of unpopular treaties would be reflected in Senate votes against them.

The extent of opposition to Indian removal in Congress and

[32] *Ibid.*, 1031.
[33] *Ibid.*, 1135, 1110.

among the spokesmen of religious opinion made it necessary that treaties be "generous," so that tribal consent might be obtained with as little "force and fraud" as possible. Since both proponents and critics of the removal bill agreed that, legalistic arguments aside, the Indians deserved to hold their country in proportion to their skill in imitating Anglo-American civilization, especially as cultivators of the soil, land "allotments" or "reservations" covering the Indian improvements were logical forms of generosity.

· 2 ·

NEGOTIATIONS

IN DEALING WITH the negotiation of the removal and allotment treaties, we must consider the motives of the Indian negotiators as well as the purposes of the United States. Perhaps even more important, and certainly more clearly demonstrable, were the conceptions government agents had about the motives of the tribesmen. Tribal leaders were divided over the question of removal, and their differences played a significant part in treaty negotiations. It is highly improbable, however, that difference of opinion over the wisdom and necessity of emigrating west was the only factor involved in the important factional disputes within the tribes. The rapid changes in tribal life occasioned by the adoption of white customs also played a role in intratribal disputes. Related to these rapid changes was the competition among various tribesmen for leadership, in which the questions of "removal" and "civilization" became instruments for the alignment of groups behind one leader or another.

The Choctaw treaty offers the most clear-cut illustration of the role of tribal factionalism in the negotiation of a removal treaty. It also demonstrates how interpretations of factional divisions by government agents and other white men distorted their picture of the "desires of the Indians." Government nego-

tiators mistakenly assumed that resistance to removal represented only the half-blood point of view and that its psychological sources were principally megalomania and cupidity. Actually there were both fullbloods and half-bloods in all parties,
and it is doubtful whether most of the "real" Indians had either
knowledge or appreciation of most of the communications supposedly representing their point of view. Attitudes toward emigration as expressed in letters and petitions tended rather to
reflect the shifting beliefs of the leading men of the tribe regarding how the signing of a removal treaty and removal west would
affect their status in the tribe.

To explain the growth and composition of the factions involved in the negotiation of the treaty of 1830, we must examine
the progress of "civilization" among the Choctaws. The adoption
of agricultural innovations seems to have involved little stress
in Choctaw society. Except during periods of warfare when
their settlements were located on exposed frontiers, the Choctaws had never lived in compact towns. The dispersion of their
settlements and the wider separation of individual properties
were an easy accommodation of native patterns to an increased
emphasis on cultivation and the need for room to pasture livestock. Following the War of 1812, with the end of intertribal
warfare, many of the residents of the northwestern district of
the nation moved westward to cultivate plantations in the Yazoo
Valley. Apparently this settlement took place about the time
the first mission school was set up on the Yalobusha River, a
branch of the Yazoo, in 1818. A similar "frontier" movement
took place to the eastward in the Tombigbee Valley, near which
a second mission station was soon established.

The missionaries of the American Board of Commissioners for
Foreign Missions built these first stations. They continued the
effort initiated by traders and government agents to encourage
attention to cultivation and market-oriented agriculture; in addition, they concentrated on education and evangelism. The object
of their efforts was to accommodate native life to the ideal
pattern of New England. Wrote missionary Cyrus Byington,

"Where does society appear to better advantage than in New England? Why not introduce as many of the precious customs, practices & principles of our fathers, as possible?"[1]

In addition to the larger mission stations, the New Englanders set up small schools in the remoter parts of the nation, where young Choctaws might acquire an "English education" along with practical instruction and experience in agriculture and homemaking. These schools met with some resistance; yet on the whole, the missionary's "education" was in great demand. The schools took the children from the control of their mothers and uncles (mothers' brothers) who had had charge of their upbringing. The New Englanders' emphasis on strict attention to labor and their use of corporal punishment were new to the Choctaw children; it is not surprising that runaways and parental withdrawals were frequent. Yet the neighborhood schools were reportedly in great demand even among the "unenlightened" villages, and parents who impulsively withdrew their offspring also begged for the privilege of returning them. The lack of serious resistance to innovations in teaching may be explained in part by the decline of traditional methods of instruction, as well as by the Choctaw parents' appreciation of the value of an "English education."

In order to bring New England to pass in Mississippi, the missionaries found it necessary to attack more than the idleness and ignorance of the young. They threatened the authority of witch doctors by introducing American medical practices and attempting to suppress the execution of witches. They discouraged participation in "heathen dances" and ball-plays, especially since the latter were associated with gambling. Even such fundamental parts of the culture pattern as the native attitude toward death were to be speedily reformed. The Choctaws were notable among the southern tribes for their elaborate funeral customs, characterized by long periods of mourning with daily "cries" over the grave and a final ceremony in which poles erected over the grave were pulled down by men especially designated for

[1] Byington to Jeremiah Evarts, April 23, 1824, ABC 18.3.4.

24

the work. Dancing and feasting followed the ceremony. The missionaries felt that these carryings on expressed a sacrilegious attitude toward the workings of Providence and the future state of rewards and punishments. So "pole-pulling" entered the list with polygamy, infanticide, whisky-drinking, witchcraft, and obscene conversation as customs to be "put down."[2]

As a substitute for the pagan ceremonies, both the missionaries of the American Board and the Methodists who joined in their endeavors instituted the camp meeting. In October, 1828, a Great Revival began among the Choctaws, assisted by native preachers of the gospel. Many of the scholars and the captains of towns were found "among the anxious," and all the converts "manifested an unconquerable desire to sing."[3]

The missionaries enlisted the aid of "enlightened half-bloods" and white men in the nation. The most helpful of these were three traders' sons—John Pitchlynn, David Folsom, and Greenwood Leflore. Pitchlynn, son of a Tory merchant, was the eldest. He had grown to manhood among the Choctaws, and when factional differences arose, he identified himself with the fullblood chief Moshulatubbee. Despite this factional choice, Pitchlynn was no champion of the "Indian" way of life. He lived as a planter and trader and at one time contributed $1,300 to the support of missionary schools, the greater part of it in bonds of the Union Bank of Mississippi. Folsom was also an advocate of "English education"; during the revivals of the late 1820's he became an outstanding preacher. Leflore, the youngest of the three, was the son of a French trader and tavern keeper. Raised under his mother's control as an Indian child, he was later educated among his father's friends in Nashville, and took a white woman for his wife. In the late 1820's, he became the most active initiator of political reform within the tribe.

During most of the four years which preceded the signing of the Choctaw treaty of 1830, Folsom and Leflore were leaders

[2] Cyrus Kingsbury to (Jeremiah Evarts), January 28, 1829, ABC 18.3.4; H. S. Halbert, "Funeral Customs of the Mississippi Choctaws," Mississippi Historical Society *Publications*, Vol. III (1900), 353–66.

[3] Sarah Tuttle, *Conversations on the Choctaw Mission*, II, 50–56.

of the anti-treaty party. They tried to remodel the political organization of the tribe along Anglo-American lines in order to centralize power in their own hands. They were opposed by certain fullblood leaders, notably John Pitchlynn's ally Moshulatubbee. This alignment of forces tended to reinforce the government's assumption that cession and removal were opposed only by the wealthy half-bloods, and that once these men were somehow "taken care of," the emigration of the great majority of the tribe would be a foregone conclusion.

Early in 1826, Congress passed an appropriation for negotiating a treaty of cession with the Choctaws. In mid-April, following the appropriation, Folsom held an assembly of captains and warriors in Moshulatubbee's district. At this meeting, Folsom secured the deposition of the old chief and his own election as principal chief of the district. Leflore carried out a similar coup in the northwestern district, while Samuel Garland, a third half-blood, replaced Chief Tappanahoma in the southern district.

In August, 1826, Leflore held a council to draw up a constitution. This constitution called for the appointment of a committee of eight from each of the three districts of the nation, which was to meet quarter-yearly to examine and report on debts owed by individuals of the tribe. The committee was also to draw up and submit laws to a semiannual council composed of themselves plus the three principal chiefs, the captains of towns, and a member from each captain's company. The laws enacted by the council indicated its "reform" bias. In 1826 they provided for inheritance through the male line, defined the lawful enclosure of fields, prohibited trespasses, and discouraged polygamy. In 1828 the council abolished the custom of erecting poles in honor of the dead and prohibited the execution of witches without a fair trial.

The reorganization of the Choctaw government was intended also to assist the formation of a united front against further land cessions. In 1826, John Coffee of Alabama and Thomas Hinds of Mississippi were assigned to procure a cession of the eastern lands of the Choctaws and the Chickasaws. They found that the Choctaws had enacted a law severely punishing anyone who might sell his country in return for a bribe and had united with the Chickasaws in a resolution to cede no more. Although a few of the half-bloods, including Moshulatubbee's ally John Pitchlynn, favored the cession, they were silenced by the majority, and an offer of 300,000 acres in reservations for the "wealthy and enlightened" was insufficient to change the majority's resolve.[4]

Following the failure of the treaty negotiations of 1826, the government received a number of suggestions about how the removal of the Choctaws might be accomplished. All these suggestions were based on the assumption that the fullblood Indians and their leaders—the majority of the tribe—were willing to emigrate, but were deterred by the half-bloods.

In January, 1827, Edward Mitchell, a planter long acquainted with the Choctaws, recommended to the governor of Mississippi a variant of the allotment policy: the government should take a census of the tribe, assign each Indian his quota of the national domain, and allow him to lease it; Mississippi should then extend its laws over the Indian country. Mitchell estimated that at least half the Choctaws would be willing to sell their share of the nation's lands in return for sums sufficient to finance their removal.[5] William Ward, the Choctaw agent, preferred dealing with the tribal leaders, which was, after all, the legal procedure for obtaining Indian lands. Ward continued to predict that if the captains and chiefs of the tribe were offered sufficient bribes, they would remove, and the common people would follow.[6] John Pitchlynn suggested still a third alternative: instead of trying to bribe the half-blood leaders, the government should reinstate

[4] The Journal of the Commissioners is printed in *American State Papers: Indian Affairs*, II, 708–17. Coffee's copy of this journal, with addenda on the need for offering reservations, is in the Robert Dyas Collection of John Coffee Papers, Tennessee Historical Society.

[5] Edward Mitchell to Hon. William Haile, January 26, 1827, Mississippi Governor's Correspondence, E 13, Mississippi Department of Archives and History.

[6] William Ward to Hon. William Haile, January 29, 1827, *ibid.*

the old chiefs, who would be more amenable to proposals for emigration.[7] Apparently the War Department still chose to work through the formally elected chiefs and to follow the customary procedures of negotiation rather than interfere directly in tribal government or attempt to partition the Choctaw country among individuals without the formality of a treaty. Probably the department, like the resident agent, Ward, continued to have faith in the ambition and avarice of the half-blood leaders.

The Commissioner of Indian Affairs, Thomas L. McKenney, concentrated on appealing to Leflore and Folsom, outlining grand careers for them as governors of the Choctaw Nation West. Wrote McKenney to Leflore in January, 1828:

> It is the full intent of the Government to do great things for you and Folsom, by appointing you to office in the Government of the Indian Territory, or if you prefer it, give you handsome reservations here . . . .
>
> I almost wish I was a Choctaw, that I might take the lead in leading my people on to happiness.[8]

While the government turned its persuasive efforts on the half-bloods, the events of 1828 and 1829 increased the desire of certain fullblood leaders to emigrate. In October of 1828, the Great Revival began. The following February, Moshulatubbee and Bob Cole, the fullblood chiefs who had been displaced by Leflore and Folsom, offered to emigrate and take their friends with them, provided they might be allowed chiefs' salaries and be paid for their improvements. Once these men started a party, Agent Ward predicted, "the greater part of the full Bloods would follow, and the half breeds could be made full citizens."[9] The offer to emigrate coincided with a revulsion against revivalism on the part of some of the conservative Choctaws. In March, 1829, a missionary teacher reported that one Red Dog, formerly

[7] John Terrell to James Barbour, February 15, 1827, Miscellaneous File 348, Records of the Bureau of Indian Affairs.

[8] Office of Indian Affairs, Letters Sent, Vol. IV, 252–53, *ibid.*

[9] William Ward to Peter B. Porter, February 6, 1829, Choctaw File 112, *ibid.*

a Methodist, had become a bitter enemy of religion and had collected a party of captains who refused to have the gospel preached in their villages.[10]

The religious question was involved both in the controversy over removal and in the contest over tribal leadership. Folsom, hopeful for the backing of the missionaries and their allies in Congress, was active in evangelizing the Choctaws. John Pitchlynn described the chief's message as " 'Join the church and keep your country.' " In this, he commented, "There is plenty of rascality—but no religion."[11] To be certain of their leadership, the "conservative" chiefs must remove their people from the contaminating influence of the half-blood "hot-gospellers" and their missionary allies.

The extension of Mississippi's laws over the tribe in January, 1830, worked a near revolution in the views of the half-bloods. Shortly after the extension of these laws, Folsom announced his willingness to explore the country west of the Mississippi with a view to emigrating there if he found it satisfactory. Leflore, who had spent much time in Tennessee during the past summer and winter, was also converted to the removal policy and determined to turn it to his own advantage. On March 15 he convened the national council. The following day Garland and Folsom resigned, and Leflore was elected chief of the entire nation. Under the recent Mississippi law it was illegal for any person to act as chief, but since Leflore had been converted to removal, he presumed, correctly, that his action would not be punished. On the afternoon of his election, the council voted for emigration; and Leflore, Garland, Folsom, and two or three hundred "warriors" signed a treaty prepared by the Methodist missionary Alexander Tally, which provided that every head of a Choctaw family was to receive 640 acres of land in fee simple. The treaty was carried to Washington.

This treaty immediately became a pawn in the factional strife

[10] Harriet Wright to Captain Jared Bunce, March 19, 1829, ABC 18.3.4.

[11] John Terrell to John Coffee, September 15, 1829, Coffee Papers, Alabama Department of Archives and History.

between the fullblood and half-blood leaders. Leflore presented it to Moshulatubbee as a *fait accompli*. He informed him that he hoped for his co-operation, but could settle with him easily if he refused it. He also insisted that the treaty was in the best interest of the tribe as a whole:

> . . . any who would refuse to submit to the late council, can they do better for themselves than is done for them in the treaty? Can they make a better treaty for themselves, if they wish to go? And if they want to stay, the treaty secures them six hundred and forty acres of land to each family. . . . [12]

Since Leflore's treaty was written by a Methodist, Moshulatubbee interpreted it as a sign that the adoption of Christianity would lead the Choctaws to lose their country. In the southeastern district early in May, five captains friendly to religion were deposed; it was resolved that no professed Christian might be eligible to office and that ball-plays, dancing, and sports were to be encouraged rather than attendance at church.[13] Yet in his communications with the government, the old chief objected not to the removal feature of the treaty, but to the fact that it was designed to elevate Leflore at the expense of the legitimate leaders of the tribe. On April 16, Moshulatubbee and another fullblood leader, Nitaketchi, held a council which appointed them chiefs to replace Folsom and Garland. This council wrote to the Choctaw agent asking protection from the armed warriors Leflore had threatened to send among them should they refuse to submit to his leadership. They wrote the President asking that a commission be sent to the Choctaw country to treat with the whole nation, "where they can hear the general view of the people." This was a demand that the President deal with the fullbloods as well as Leflore; it was not a protest against removal. Moshulatubbee's and Nitaketchi's districts, Pitchlynn informed John Coffee, "are strongly determined to have a chief

---

[12] Greenwood Leflore to Moshulatubbee, April 7, 1830, Choctaw Reserve File 112, Records of the Bureau of Indian Affairs.

[13] *Missionary Herald* (Boston), August, 1830.

in each district and have a government of their own as usual."[14]

The President thought Leflore's treaty too generous and revised it substantially before sending it to the Senate. The Senate did not act on the revised treaty. Jackson invited the dissident chiefs to meet him at Franklin, Tennessee, in August to work out a more generally acceptable agreement, but the process of making up a delegation became so much involved in factional politics that Jackson had to leave for Washington without meeting the Choctaws. He then followed Moshulatubbee's suggestion by delegating John Coffee and John H. Eaton to deal with the tribesmen in their own nation.

Eaton and Coffee reached the Choctaw Treaty Ground between the forks of Dancing Rabbit Creek on September 15.[15] After some preliminary palaver, the pointed exclusion of the missionaries from the treaty ground, and a squabble over representation of the various factions, Eaton presented his terms: the chiefs and former chiefs, captains, and interpreters were to be provided with generous "individual reservations" of land; 150 sections of 640 acres each were offered to the few Choctaws who were expected to remain in the East. Fifty thousand dollars was to be divided among those with no reservations or improvements.

After these proposals were read and explained, the Choctaws held a council to consider them. Both the half-blood leader David Folsom and the fullblood town chief Little Leader advocated refusing to make a treaty, and so the council determined.[16] When their refusal was announced, Eaton made an angry half-hour speech, reminding the intransigents that this would be the government's last attempt to treat with them—that they would henceforth be left to themselves, to live without an agent, unprotected from state laws, and deprived of their potential asylum west of the Mississippi.

[14] John Pitchlynn to General John Coffee, May 3, 1830, Coffee Papers, Alabama Department of Archives and History.

[15] Except where otherwise noted, this account is drawn from the Journal of the Treaty Commissioners, published in 23 Cong., 1 sess., *Sen. Doc. 512*, 251–63.

[16] Kingsbury to Evarts, September 29, 1830, ABC 18.3.4; H. S. Halbert, "The Story of the Treaty of Dancing Rabbit Creek," *Mississippi Historical Society Publications*, Vol. VI (1903), 373–90.

Prior to this address a number of the tribesmen had left the treaty ground, assuming that no agreement would be signed. After the speech, however, a committee sponsored by Greenwood Leflore requested that Eaton remain and presented him with a series of counterproposals. These doubled the landed compensation for David Folsom, increased the special donations to a number of individuals, and provided for a vast increase in the number of general allotments. The Leflore committee proposals included the principal innovations adopted in the final draft of the treaty. They called for donations of 80 to 480 acres to heads of families who intended to emigrate, the amount of the donation to be proportional to the quantity of land the family had in cultivation. This category of allotments was intended not for actual settlement, but for sale to private persons or to the government. Thus these allotments were simply a substitute for the customary cash payment for abandoned improvements. More significant was the committee's second proposal: the government was to offer an unlimited number of allotments in fee simple to heads of families who would not emigrate, the size of the grant to be proportional to the number of persons in the family. These allotments were to enable all those averse to emigration to gain a freehold in the ceded lands.

On the morning following the submission of these proposals, the chiefs, captains, and headmen met the treaty commissioners in council, modifying details of the final agreement. The treaty was signed at one o'clock that afternoon—Monday, September 27, 1830. The following day a supplementary treaty was signed, giving further "special reservations" to several individuals. The beneficiaries included the "family connections" of chiefs and influential white men, with seventeen sections going to Leflore's relatives, ten to Pitchlynn's, and eight or nine to Folsom's.[17]

Returning home to Franklin, Tennessee, Commissioner Eaton wrote an account of the Choctaw treaty to his old friend John

[17] Kingsbury to Evarts, October 11, 1830, ABC 18.3.4; Same to Same, November 17, 1830, ibid.

Overton. In the letter, Eaton explained the intended consequences of the treaty he had negotiated:

> It is no grinding-starving treaty, but as it should be liberal . . .
> The Door to speculation is barred . . . . A section of land to each
> head of a family—half a section to each of his children over 10
> years and ¼ section to younger ones are allowed to those who
> determine to remain and become citizens—but to guard against
> fraud, they can receive no title on this account, until they have
> remained on the land for 5 years . . . .
> Indeed there are not more than 14 reservations which are
> floating and from laziness you know, Indians usually select the
> poorer lands—they will not cut down the heavy growth of rich
> lands . . . .
> This and the chickasaw [*sic*] country will more than meet all
> expenses of the treaty, and the costs of sale; if so, the country
> surely should be satisfied; but it will go beyond this, no doubt.[18]

The actual consequences of the treaty were quite different
from Eaton's predictions. The first error of prophecy to be revealed was the commissioner's overoptimistic estimate of public
reaction to the treaty. That portion of "the country" which
followed missionary opinion was far from satisfied. The missionaries of the American Board, angry because the treaty granted
no compensation for their expensive schools and mission stations, did not consider it generous in any respect. They regarded
the extensive reserves given to Indian leaders as mere bribes.
They deplored the scanty provision for emigrating tribesmen
whose improvements were small. They bitterly resented the
commissioners' misrepresentation of the way in which the agreement had been negotiated, for the missionaries insisted that
Eaton had used threats, although his report of the treaty denied it. Finally, they asserted that not five thousand, as Eaton
claimed, but perhaps one-tenth of that number were on the

[18] October 6, 1830, John Claybrooke Collection of John Overton Papers,
Tennessee Historical Society.

ground when the document was signed; that a majority of those present opposed it; that of 2,600 citizens of the Six Towns, the most "backward" of the Choctaws, only one man favored the treaty.[19] Thus, if the missionaries were correct, the negotiators' optimistic assumption that the statements of certain fullblood leaders favoring emigration represented the hopes of the majority of the tribe and of all the more "backward" tribesmen was not correct. If so, the number of Indians attempting to take advantage of the fee simple allotments provided in the treaty would be far greater than anticipated.

The objective of the missionaries, of course, was not to warn the government of problems to come, but to prevent the ratification of the treaty. The Choctaw agreement and the protests following it supplied grist for a new campaign against the administration's Indian removal policy. Already the Senate speeches against the removal bill had been printed and circulated and further petitions elicited. Their aim, as Henry Clay wrote Jeremiah Evarts, was "to defeat the execution of a bill, the passage of which could not be prevented."[20] After the Choctaw treaty had been presented to the Senate, Frelinghuysen and his allies in the House planned to propose the repeal of the removal act. As for the "liberal" Choctaw treaty, the Christian statesman wrote:

> What tremendous responsibilities rest upon our rulers.—To array against these helpless men all the terrors of wicked laws and abandonment on the part of those bound to protect them—to drive the many—to bribe their chiefs—& then worse (if possible) them all—tell us that arguments and persuasion were alone employed. When I reflect, my dear Sir, that God is the avenger of the friendless & that in dreadful righteousness he visits for national sins I tremble for my country.[21]

[19] Kingsbury to Evarts, October 17, 1830, ABC 18.3.4; Same to Same, January 1, 1831, *ibid.*; compare *Missionary Herald* (Boston), January, 1831.

[20] Clay to Evarts, August 8, 1830, Evarts Papers, Library of Congress.

[21] Frelinghuysen to Evarts, January 24, 1831, *ibid.*

Nevertheless, the Senate ratified the treaty, deleting only a preamble asserting the inability of the government to protect the Choctaws from Mississippi's laws.

The principal factor differentiating negotiations with the Creeks from those with the Choctaws was the lesser degree to which the Creeks had accepted and incorporated Anglo-American culture. Creek relations with the newer Americans were marked by a longer history of violence than those of any other major southern tribe. The Creek confederacy, an amalgam of the dominant Muskogee group with smaller tribes displaced by advancing pioneers, became a stronghold of cultural conservatism, resisting white encroachment both by warfare and by adherence to ancient ways.

From the close of the Revolution to the Florida Purchase of 1819, the Creeks occupied a marchland between the American and Spanish frontiers. The tribe attempted to preserve their territory as well as their trade by playing English, American, and Spanish negotiators against each other. The leading figure in these maneuvers was the half-blood chief Alexander McGillivray, son of a Scottish trader and an Indian woman of the most prominent clan of the Creek Nation. McGillivray, who died in 1793, combined the offices of trader, planter, and tribal leader in a way that became typical among the Choctaws, Chickasaws, and Cherokees.[22] Yet, though the resident trader and planter remained a familiar figure among the Creeks, none after McGillivray rose to high office in the nation. Where half-blood town chiefs exercised more than local influence, they wielded it through fullblood chieftains. Perhaps by necessity, their aims were not so broadly defined as those of the half-bloods of the other major tribes.

This political difference was symbolic of the tribe's resistance to embracing the white man's culture. Traders and agents, with apparent success, encouraged the Creeks to disperse their set-

[22] John R. Caughey, *McGillivray of the Creeks;* Arthur P. Whitaker, "Alexander McGillivray," *North Carolina Historical Review,* Vol. V (1928), 181–203; 289–309.

tlements, breed cattle and hogs, and plant and spin cotton. But they found that the men of the tribe, unused to the responsibilities of property ownership, frequently sold their surplus produce in the Georgians' whisky shops rather than using it to furnish their homes or educate their children. Missionaries attempting to introduce schools and churches made little headway, although one irately attributed his failure to an agent who thought preaching to unlettered savages was "fudge."[23]

Rejecting many of the white man's ways, the tribe yet failed to keep its aboriginal culture intact. We have noted their dependence on traders' goods and their willingness to follow the trader's pattern of settlement and cultivation. An acknowledged result of this imitation was the diminishing importance of the town as a center of social and especially of economic life. Furthermore, the Creek men faced two irresistible threats to their traditional status: the decline of warfare and the diminution of their hunting grounds. The Creeks, like the other southern tribes, had come (during the seventeenth and eighteenth centuries, at least) to define status according to feats of daring in war. After their defeat by Jackson in 1813–14, the tribe fought no more. This defeat entailed also a cession to the United States of the greater part of their domain—all of Alabama between the Tennessee, the Tombigbee, and the Coosa rivers, and the southern quarter of Georgia. With their gradual exclusion from Georgia in the late 1820's the tribal hunting grounds were still further diminished. The tribe's pursuit of the fur trade tended to exhaust the supply of game. Since the Creek men were deprived of their work as warriors and were decreasingly successful as hunters, it is not surprising that they became notorious for their drunkenness and "depravity."

Although they did not adopt the constitutional apparatus enacted by the Choctaws or accept formal leadership on the part of half-bloods of the tribe, the Creeks nonetheless became in-

[23] Report of Reverend William Capers to the Bishops of the South Carolina Conference of the Methodist Church, February 21, 1822, 19 Cong., 2 sess., *House Report* 98, 64–83; John Crowell to John C. Calhoun, March 18, 1824, *ibid.*, 48–55.

volved in the attempt of half-blood leaders of the other southern tribes to enforce sanctions against the cession of lands. Chief John Ridge of the Cherokees secured a resolution on the part of the Creeks to join with his tribe in refusing to make further cessions. His efforts were seconded by William Walker, a white trader married to the daughter of Big Warrior, principal chief of Tuckabatchee, the leading town among the upper Creeks. Walker's resolution, promising death to any chief who ceded tribal lands in return for a bribe, was enacted in council at Tuckabatchee in May, 1824.[24] In January, 1825, William Mc-Intosh, principal chief of Coweta town and speaker for Little Prince, head chief of the lower Creeks, violated the law by signing a separate treaty of cession for the lower Creek lands in Georgia. When McIntosh agreed to allow the Georgians to survey the ceded territory, the anti-treaty party dealt with lower Creek factionalism by a summary execution of the Tuckabatchee law. Early in the morning on Saturday the final day of April, more than one hundred warriors of the Okfuskee, Talladega, and Emukfau towns surrounded McIntosh's house and disposed of him and Estomme Tustunuggee, another signer, "by shooting near one hundred balls into them."[25]

The government annulled McIntosh's treaty and negotiated substitutes for it. The leading Indian spokesman in these negotiations was Opothleyahola, speaker of the upper towns. The cessions were not procured by the offer of individual reservations, although such offers had been standard practice in earlier negotiations with the Creeks. The treaties of 1826, 1827, and 1828, wherein the Creeks ceded their remaining lands in Georgia, were obtained in effect by coercion, since if they had failed, McIntosh's more inclusive cession would have been put into effect. Nothing so generous as a general allotment of the ceded lands was necessary, and the fate of McIntosh was sufficient

[24] Campbell to John C. Calhoun, January 8, 1825; Calhoun to John Crowell, January 13, 1825, *American State Papers: Indian Affairs*, II, 574–75, 577.

[25] Peggy and Susannah McIntosh to Colonel D. G. Campbell and William Merriwether, *ibid.*, 768; Campbell to Calhoun, January 8, 1825, January 11, 1825, *ibid.*, 574–76.

warning to those who might have demanded gratuities for themselves alone.

In the summer of 1830, the government appointed John Coffee
as an unofficial agent of the United States in the Creek country.
Coffee enlisted the aid of William Walker and other friends of
Opothleyahola to persuade the Tuckabatchee leader to cede the
remaining lands of the tribe in Alabama. Coffee asserted that
fifty landed reserves, given to the town chiefs, should be a sufficient inducement to procure their assent to the cession. Nonetheless, the Creeks refused to open negotiations. After their
refusal, in August of 1830 the President wrote irately that he
intended to withdraw the Creek agent and leave the tribe to the
jurisdiction of the state of Alabama.[26]

During the next year and a half, the Creeks remained steadfast
in their refusal to negotiate a treaty, concentrating their efforts
on petitioning Congress against Alabama's jurisdictional en-
croachments and the intrusions of her citizens. In January, 1832,
Alabama extended her legal interference in Creek affairs by
annulling the tribal customs and the powers of the chiefs. A
delegation of the tribe was then in Washington, demanding protection against the state. They met with the usual rejections and
decided that their cause was lost. At the same time, the former
Creek agent John Crowell proposed to the chiefs who had remained at home a way out of their dilemma: the Creeks should
cede their Alabama lands, but the entire tribe should take reservations in fee simple, which would enable them to remain
in their eastern territory.[27]

This proposal of Crowell's involved a substantial innovation
in government policy, since the administration had considered
the fee simple allotment or "individual reservation" as a boon
to the exceptionally civilized tribesman. Actually, however, a
similar arrangement had already been instituted by the state of
Georgia. In December, 1830, she had enacted a law calling for

---

[26] [Eaton and Jackson] to [Crowell], August 21, 1830, Creek File 192, Records
of the Bureau of Indian Affairs.

[27] Crowell to Lewis Cass, January 26, 1832, Creek File 178, *ibid.*

the survey and granting of her lands within the Cherokee country, but reserving to the Indians their occupancy rights: that is, the land they cultivated.[28] In effect, Crowell proposed that the government combine this policy of guaranteeing all the tribesmen possession of their improvements with the feature of the Choctaw treaty calling for a patent in fee simple and the granting of citizenship after five years' occupancy.

A delegation from the Creek country brought this proposal to Washington. Their "secretary" was John H. Brodnax, a white planter and trader in the nation. His presence suggests that the traders saw in the allotment provision the prospect of profit. That they did not suppose the Creeks would retain their reserves forever is shown by the fact that they proposed that an advisory commission be established to guard against fraud in the *sale* of the allotments.[29]

The Creek treaty, concluded in March, 1832, provided that each head of a family and each orphan child within the nation was to receive 320 acres of land. Each of the ninety chiefs was to receive 640 acres. The tribe's interpreter received 640 acres, including mills he had established in the nation. The chiefs were to have an additional 16,000 acres to sell for the benefit of the tribe as a whole. The proposed commission for supervising sales of the reserves was not established.[30] Nor did the treaty provide for the tribe's removal. Officially, the allotments were granted on the assumption that the tribe was undivided in its refusal to emigrate: actually, however, it remained the government's intention to get the Creeks out of Alabama as soon as possible. The real function the allotments were expected to perform was the segregation of individual "properties" from the remainder of the Creek lands in order to minimize clashes between Alabama intruders and the Indians.

Like the Choctaws, the Chickasaws were equipped with written laws, schools, churches, and half-blood planter-traders who

[28] Georgia, *Acts*, December 21, 1830.
[29] Brodnax to Cass, March 12, 1832, 23 Cong., 1 sess., *Sen. Doc. 512*, III, 258–59.
[30] 7 *Statutes at Large*, 366–68.

had political ambition and political influence. Although the full-blood "king" Ishetehotopa still reigned in the late twenties and early thirties, the leading politician of the tribe was the half-blood Levi Colbert. Wrote Commissioner McKenney, "Colbert is to the Chickasaws as the soul is to the body; they move at his bidding."[31]

Both the adoption of cultural innovations and the political ambitions of the half-bloods created conflicts within the tribe. In 1830 the Chickasaws had made considerable progress in the adoption of cattle and hog breeding, some of them had undertaken the culture of cotton, and the division of labor among the sexes had begun to approximate the white pattern. Yet as late as 1825, the Chickasaw agent had reported, "There is nothing like public spirit among them; they appear only to think for the moment. . . . They express no feelings of grattitude [sic] to the Gov't. for the efforts that have been made to better their condition. If one of their number conforms to the customs of the whites, even in dress, he is forced to abandon them or subject himself to frequent insult & have his influence amongst them completely destroyed."[32]

During the 1820's and 1830's, a factional conflict among the Chickasaws seems to have centered about the position and policies of Levi Colbert. Among the sources of opposition to Colbert's leadership was the well-founded belief that he and his relatives had profited from their role as negotiators with the United States government. In treaties of 1816 and 1818, Levi and his brother George had received valuable reservations within the ceded lands. When, in 1826, the government began negotiation for the cession of the Chickasaws' remaining Mississippi lands, the treaty commissioners were authorized to offer similar incentives to all the "enlightened half-bloods" of the nation. They met with a formal tribal resolution against any individual's receiving an allotment. A planter familiar with the tribe later

---

[31] McKenney to Eaton, June 27, 1829, Office of Indian Affairs, Letters Sent, VI, 28, Records of the Bureau of Indian Affairs.
[32] B. F. Smith to McKenney, October 6, 1825, Chickasaw File 80, *ibid.*

asserted that Levi Colbert feared to make overt propositions for removal because "his enemies" spread the rumor that his only object was to secure reservations for himself.[33]

The extension of Mississippi laws over the Indian country affected the Chickasaws much as it had affected the Choctaws, forcing the issue of removal despite factional opposition to the policy. The tribe sent a treaty delegation to Franklin, Tennessee, in August of 1830. There they concluded an agreement on the same model as the Choctaw treaty of Dancing Rabbit Creek, except that it provided simply for 600 half-section (320-acre) allotments to heads of families, who might either keep them or sell them, as they chose.[34] The ratification of this treaty was contingent on the tribe's acquisition of territory in the west to which they might migrate. The tribal leaders attempted to purchase lands from the Choctaws, but were unsuccessful. The Chickasaw treaty of Franklin was therefore never submitted to the Senate.

The extension of Mississippi laws brought hordes of intruders into the Chickasaw nation, making a cession of the lands on some terms imperative. Since the tribe could not emigrate until it had purchased a home in the west, it was determined to make temporary provision for its members by general allotment of a part of their eastern lands. In the spring of 1832, General John Coffee negotiated with the tribe an allotment treaty of unparalleled generosity. The Chickasaw lands were to be surveyed and sold "as soon as it can be done." If the tribe failed to obtain a "nation west" prior to the first sale of their lands, they were to select from the surveyed lands allotments for each single man and each family. Each single person might have 640 acres; families having five members or fewer, 1,280 acres; families of six to ten members, 1,920 acres; and larger families, 2,680 acres. An additional 320 acres was to go to each family with one to ten

[33] John D. Terrell to General John Coffee, September 15, 1829, Coffee Papers, Alabama Department of Archives and History.

[34] The treaty, signed August 31, 1830, is in Chickasaw File 82; the Journal of Proceedings at Franklin is filed with the Choctaw Treaty of September 27, 1830, in the Ratified Treaty File, Records of the Bureau of Indian Affairs. See also *Daily National Intelligencer* (Washington), September 13, 1830.

slaves. If the family's improvements were on land fit for cultivation, the allotment must include them; otherwise it might be selected from any unoccupied land in the cession. The tribe was to receive the net proceeds of the sale of the unreserved lands, after the cost of survey, sale, and emigration had been met. At least three-fourths of this revenue was to be invested in a trust fund on which the tribe was to receive the interest. After the Chickasaws emigrated west, their allotments were to be offered at public sale at a minimum price of three dollars per acre, creating a fund from which individuals might be paid the appraised value of their improvements and of all their lands actually in cultivation.[35]

Despite its generosity, this agreement became a bone of contention among tribal factions. A number of half-bloods, led apparently by Levi Colbert, were bitter at not being allowed to sell their lands individually. They combined with would-be land speculators in an attempt to defeat the ratification of the treaty. When that attempt failed, they tried to block its execution, and ultimately were successful in forcing a renegotiation of their own terms.

The role of white land speculators in this controversy is suggestive. John Terrell, a planter of Marion County, Alabama, had long served as a "special agent" to propagate a spirit of emigration among the Chickasaws and Choctaws. Henry Cook was a Tuscumbia, Alabama, merchant who later speculated heavily in Chickasaw allotments. On October 10, 1832, Terrell informed Cook that Levi Colbert was completely dissatisfied with the treaty, since Coffee had refused to listen to any Chickasaw proposals. He asked that Cook be present at a meeting to be held at the Monroe County courthouse the first Monday in November, 1832, where a formal protest against the treaty would be prepared. "I know you have the confidence of Levi," Terrell exulted. "Nothing can be lost but much can be gained. . . . I gave Coffee rope. Now let us draw it up."[36]

[35] Coffee to Cass, October 26, 1832, Ratified Treaty File, *loc. cit.*; 7 *Statutes at Large*, 381–89.

Terrell and two white men residing among the Chickasaws got up a delegation to Washington which included the brothers Levi, George, and Pitman Colbert and Chief Tishomingo. According to G. W. Long, another "Indian countryman" and critic of Colbert, the delegation had "clothed their objects in mystery and darkness," so that few in the nation knew what they were about.[37] Although the delegation failed to achieve its objects, the opponents of the treaty were undismayed. A number of them proceeded to lease their improvements to planters, giving the lessee the option of purchasing the allotment should they be given the right to sell it.[38]

In October, 1832, missionary T. C. Stuart wrote that the nation was divided between half-bloods and "Reds," the former demanding large fee simple allotments and the latter holding out for national ownership of their diminished domain. Stuart remarked that "it is now thought reserves will be given all who wish, of every color."[39] Stuart did not indicate who might be the leaders of the "Red" faction, but apparently some half-bloods and white men sided with the Chickasaw agent in approving the original version of the treaty.[40]

In the spring of 1834, the Colberts visited Washington and were successful in having the treaty refashioned to meet their demands.[41] The reserves provided in the 1834 treaty were given in fee simple and additional special reserves were supplied to the Colberts and several others. As a compromise with those who felt that the Indians generally could not profitably manage their own property, a committee of seven (including the old King, the three Colbert brothers, and some of their erstwhile opponents) was given authority to determine the competence

[36] Terrell to Cook (copy), October 29, 1832, John D. Terrell Papers, Alabama Department of Archives and History.

[37] Long to Coffee, December 15, 1832, Coffee Papers, *ibid.*

[38] *Lewis* v. *Love and Lane,* 1 *Alabama Reports,* 335; *Pettit's Administrator* v. *Pettit's Distributees,* 32 *Alabama Reports,* 288.

[39] T. C. Stuart to Daniel Green, October 14, 1833, ABC 18.4.4.

[40] G. W. Long to Coffee, December 15, 1832, Coffee Papers, Alabama Department of Archives and History.

[41] 7 *Statutes at Large,* 450–57.

of each individual to sell his reserve, and to act in effect as agents for those who were deemed incompetent. In addition to protecting the unsophisticated, this commission gave the half-blood leader a potentially profitable control over the sale of reserves— a convenient combination of individual and national interest. Further innovations in the renegotiated treaty included a provision giving allotments to single women and orphan children of the tribe, permission to the Chickasaw agent to sue intruders at tribal expense, and graduation of the selling price of unallotted lands in proportion to the time they had been on the market.

The allotment treaties negotiated with the Choctaws, Creeks, and Chickasaws represented a series of compromises. The government negotiators wanted to appropriate the Indians' domain and open it to legal settlement; the tribesmen wanted to keep the lands. Therefore the land was divided between them, according to what the white men thought the Indians needed or deserved to retain. In the case of the Choctaws, the provisions for Indian retention of land were governed by the white men's belief that the "civilized" tribesmen with their stores, farms, and ferries were the only ones indissolubly wedded to the soil. With the Creeks, the chieftains' stubborn insistence that none of their people would go west won out, and every man had his homestead. The Chickasaws received allotments far larger than those of the Creeks, but with the explicit understanding that they would soon sell out and abandon them.

All the treaties contained inducements to ease the avarice of the influential, or, in the view of the beneficiaries, legitimately to fill their special needs. Special reservations crowded the "supplemental articles" of the Choctaw and Chickasaw treaties. These may have served the particular function of healing the breaches of faction among the tribal leaders by persuading all that their advantage lay in forwarding the government's removal policy and convincing the skeptical that the government played no favoritism among the leading men of the tribes. Even the Creek town chiefs received twice the quantity of land their tribesmen were entitled to, and their traders had $100,000 to divide among themselves, appropriated by treaty to pay the debts of the tribe. At the same time, provisions of allotments or money compensation for the less wealthy and less influential tribesmen were expected to stifle their indignation over the favored treatment given the tribal aristocrats and discourage attempts to align them against the signers of the treaty.

But the essential conflict between the white man's intent to remove the tribesman and the Indian's determination that he should not be moved was not resolved by the allotment provisions. These articles offered to the tribesman the hope that he might keep his lands, since it was theoretically up to him whether he should remain as a landholder or sell his allotment and emigrate. To the treaty negotiators they offered the expectation that the Indians, freed of the tyranny of "interested" chiefs and halfbloods, surrounded by white settlers, and tempted by purchasers, would see his real interest, sell out, and depart.

This specious compromise was perhaps affected by the belief, shared not only by state legislators and treaty commissioners but also by missionaries and political opponents of the administration's Indian removal policy, that to treat an Indian "fairly" was to treat him as though he were a white man. This, in the peculiar definitions of the state governments and the Jackson administration, meant freeing him of the tyranny of tribal chieftains, giving him land, the sovereign means of support, and leaving him to take care of himself under the white man's laws. Once the contract was signed and the Indian became a freeholder and a free agent, what he "chose" to do, in the grip of intolerable confusion and under the spur of "legitimate" coercion, was his own business and need not trouble the conscience.

Once this big lie was signed and sealed into the supreme law of the land, no effort on the part of the government to secure the proper execution of its promises could avail. To see that every Indian got the land he was entitled to, or equitable compensation for it, became impossible. Most of the government's efforts

45

to secure "just" compensation to the tribesmen simply played into the hands of one or another group of rival speculators in Indian allotments. Only in the case of the Chickasaws, where neither side supposed that the reserves were anything other than a station on the way west and where the government profited from earlier mistakes in implementing its policies for the disposal of allotments, was an allotment treaty executed without serious harm to the supposed beneficiaries.

· 3 ·

THE CHOCTAW SPECULATION

THE CHOCTAW TREATY, negotiated in a moment of crisis as a measure for clearing central Mississippi of its Indians, complicated, rather than solved, the problems of Indian removal and the sale and settlement of the Choctaw lands. The agreement was conceived and executed on the false presumption that the great mass of the tribesmen welcomed the opportunity to go west. Acting under this misconception, the Choctaw agent refused to register many legitimate claims, and the government was faced with the problem of providing the Indians compensation for the lands they lost. Furthermore, the Indian allotments had first priority in the lands of the cession. But in its haste to thrust the Choctaw lands on the market, the government sold or permitted settlement on areas later claimed by the tribesmen according to their treaty rights. The resulting contest among rival speculators, in which all sides were represented by attorney-speculators with political influence, delayed Indian removal and upset titles in many parts of the Choctaw cession for as much as a generation following the signing of the treaty.

The treaty signed at Dancing Rabbit Creek provided for three main varieties of allotment.[1] Under the nineteenth article, heads

[1] 7 *Statutes at Large,* 333–41.

47

of families received 80 to 320 acres surrounding their improvements. The size of these allotments depended on the quantity of land the family had in cultivation; they were known as "cultivation claims." Owners of these claims sold them to pay their debts or to finance their pioneering operations in the Choctaw Nation West. "Special reservations" ranging from 320 to 2,560 acres went to Indians, white men, and half-bloods whose services, needs, or influence gave them particular claim on government generosity. The most valuable of these special allotments were floating claims which could be located anywhere in the Choctaw cession. Their owners might keep them or sell them, at their discretion. Most of the owners sold out, often to townsite promoters. Finally, an unlimited number of allotments, including improvements where possible, were provided under the fourteenth article of the treaty to heads of families who wanted to remain in the ceded area. After the claimant had lived on his allotment for five years, he was to get a patent for his land and become a citizen. Each head of a family was allowed 640 acres, with an additional 320 for each child over ten and 160 for each child under ten.

Altogether, 334,101.2 acres of the 10,423,139.69-acre cession were used directly to satisfy claims under the treaty. An additional 702,320 acres of land were covered by scrip ultimately issued under the fourteenth article of the treaty to those who were unable to establish claims before their improvements were sold. Of this scrip, 169,402 acres were located in the Choctaw cession. Although the treaty contemplated that as many as 1,600 persons might acquire land under the nineteenth article, only 748 actually benefited from its provisions because an unexpected number of the emigrating Indians had improvements of only two to twelve acres. For owners in this size classification, only 350 allotments were provided. In the larger size classifications there were too few farms to fill the established quotas.[2]

[2] 36 Cong., 1 sess., *Sen. Report 283*, 6–10; E. B. Merritt to Robert J. Enochs, November 17, 1926, Choctaw File 315 (1915) No. 69324, Records of the Bureau of Indian Affairs; 21 *Court of Claims Reports*, 74.

The nineteenth article "cultivation claims" and the special reservations went on sale soon after the treaty was signed. A number who took land under the nineteenth article sold their claims to the government for fifty cents an acre, for they emigrated west before they could find private purchasers. Those who waited found their best customers among the citizens of the upper Tombigbee settlements in Monroe County, Mississippi, and adjacent parts of Alabama. Prominent among the purchasers were George S. Gaines, Reuben H. Grant, Daniel W. Wright, John H. Hand, and John C. Whitsett. These men had long served the tribe as doctors, lawyers, or traders; Gaines Grant, and Wright claimed an important role in promoting the treaty of cession.

The principal difficulties which arose in connection with the nineteenth article claims concerned their location. The Choctaw villages were situated in a part of Mississippi where clay hills meet swampy flatwoods on the north and rich limestone prairies on the south. Furthermore, tribal settlements were located near stream beds or river bottoms running through otherwise unfertile country. Therefore, as a contemporary put it, "a man may in very many cases stand with his feet on very fertile land and toss a biscuit on land not worth owning."[3] Most of the allotments had to include improvements and adjacent lands, taken in legal subdivisions of not less than forty acres. To obtain fertile land and avoid that "not worth owning," purchasers had to employ ingenuity in locating their claims. Their skill was equal to the task. Where good land was uninhabited, cabins and token improvements could be built. A 320-acre reservation might be located in 80-acre tracts "adjacent" only at their corners, thereby covering a lot of ground.

Thus settlers beginning their farms a mile from any Indian improvement sometimes found an Indian claim, legally prior to their own, sweeping down to rest on their clearings. The variety of claims and the nearness of Indian improvements to one an-

[3] Chapman Levy to Joel R. Poinsett, June 19, 1837, Choctaw Reserve File 139, Records of the Bureau of Indian Affairs.

other occasioned frequent disputes among rival speculators, as well as between settlers and speculators. It was more than a generation before all the conflicting claims were settled. Compared with the extent of the cession, the number of these conflicts was small, but the location of allotments on or near towns and other early settlements gave them a nuisance value disproportionate to their quantity.

More important in number and influence were the so-called "contingent claims" produced under the fourteenth article. This provision of the treaty proposed, in effect, to create a group of Choctaw homesteaders by allowing land and citizenship to those who registered their claims and remained on their improvements five years following the ratification of the treaty. As a result of fraudulent administration of the registration procedure, it gave birth instead to a body of claims whose history exemplifies both the opportunities and the limitations of land speculation in the "Age of Jackson."

The fourteenth article was itself a product of the ambiguous intentions joined in the negotiation of the Choctaw removal treaty. Those who proposed it appear to have expected its beneficiaries to be a relatively small group, principally half-bloods, so far advanced in the arts of cultivation and civilized living that they might settle down as citizen planters in the midst of a white community. This belief was based on certain rationalizations of the government's Indian removal policy: most of the fullblood Indians absorb the "vices" of civilization but in the short run at least are impervious to its benefits; they would prefer to isolate themselves by emigration, but are restrained by their selfish leaders; a few Indians, and more half-bloods, having shown themselves capable of living as white men do, deserve to remain where they are; the government should provide the funds to remove those who cannot remain and the means of making a living to those who can; those who stay in the East will be few, but they will be those best able to follow Anglo-American patterns of living.

These assumptions served the purpose of rationalization well

Portrait by George Catlin

Moshulatubbee, district chief of the Choctaws, was leader of the fullblood faction during negotiations of the Treaty of Dancing Rabbit Creek.

From McKenney and Hall, *The Indian Tribes of North America*

Paddy Carr, a half-blood Creek trader, acted as interpreter for white speculators.

enough, but as guides to the attitudes of the tribesmen they were misleading. Although certain fullblood leaders advocated emigration, the course of treaty negotiations in September, 1830, indicated that the leaders of towns whose members were least "civilized" were among those most anxious to remain in Mississippi. Certainly the half-blood chief Greenwood Leflore was aware of their opposition to removal, and it was probably due to his prompting that the limitation of fourteenth article registrants to 150, originally proposed by the treaty commissioners, was dropped in the final version of the agreement. Interested parties later secured testimony to prove both that the "common Indians" did not hear, or did not understand, the provisions of the fourteenth article and that the inclusion of this article was the one aspect which made the treaty acceptable to them.[4] Probably each contention was true—of different Indians.

At any rate, it is clear that the Choctaw agent frustrated the attempts of a number of the fullbloods to provide a permanent home for themselves in Mississippi by registering for land under the fourteenth article. After the treaty of 1830 was signed, leaders in the three districts of the nation held meetings at which those who wanted to register gave their names to half-bloods, who reported them to the United States agent, William Ward. In addition, captains of the remoter towns collected bundles of sticks indicating the number of their people who wanted to take allotments. The agent accepted and recorded less than one hundred names; on the register he submitted to the War Department, only eight of the registrants were marked as fullblood Indians.[5] Ward himself later testified that when "upwards of two hundred persons from one section of the country" applied for registration at a council in June, 1831, he "put them off," believing that "they were advised to that course by designing men

---

[4] Compare affidavits of William D. King, September 17, 1836 and Thomas Young, October 14, 1836, *ibid.*; Charles Fisher, "The Claims of Certain Choctaw Indians . . ." enclosed in letter of July 16, 1834, Choctaw Reserve File 134, *ibid.*

[5] There was more than one copy of Ward's register. Part of it was destroyed and the remaining copies were not identical. One copy, with notations on the race of each registrant, is in Choctaw File 133, *ibid.*

who were always opposed to the Treaty."[6] In the fall of 1834, attorneys for the Indians submitted testimony that Ward, who was often drunk and careless in his methods, rejected or destroyed a large number of applications, telling the applicants they should emigrate.[7] As the agent saw it, he was carrying out the intent of the government, and the government was long in contradicting him.

Naturally no claims could be located on maps of the district and reserved from sale until they were registered. Public sales of lands in the cession took place before many of the claims could be registered and confirmed. The original deadline for registering claims was August, 1831, but the surveys of the cession were not sufficiently complete to permit their location to begin until June, 1833. The locating agent, George W. Martin, was instructed to reserve from public sale only those claims which appeared on Ward's register. Those whom the agent had excluded remained landless. In September, 1833, the agent in charge of Choctaw emigration reported ominously, "Strange as it is, it is also true, that there are a large party who seem almost determined to remain, not one of whom have a foot of land. This is owing to some three or four leading Captains, who themselves are entitled to land."[8]

The President proclaimed 112 townships in the Choctaw cession for sale in October and November of 1833. Martin received notice of the sales September 8. The General Land Office, which had never dealt with Indian allotments on so large a scale, was unprepared to supply the locating agent with plats of the sur-

[6] Ward to Hamilton, June 21, 1831, Choctaw Emigration File (1826–31), *ibid.*

[7] Deposition of Adam James, Gabriel Lincicum, and Reuben H. Grant, inserted in Charles Fisher to Lewis Cass, August 22, 1834, Choctaw Reserve File 134, *ibid.* These depositions are printed in *American State Papers: Public Lands,* VIII, 629–33, 691–93. The Board of Choctaw Commissioners ultimately admitted 1,293 persons to the list of those who attempted to comply with the registration provisions. E. B. Merritt to Robert J. Enochs, *op. cit.*

[8] William Armstrong to George S. Gibson, September 14, 1833, Choctaw Emigation File 124, Records of the Bureau of Indian Affairs. Armstrong estimated the number of recalcitrants at 400; Secretary of War Lewis Cass, in his annual report (1833), estimated the number at 1,500 to 3,000.

veyed townships. Martin was forced to locate the Indian claims by reference to maps in widely separated land offices, riding "like a post-boy . . . at least one thousand miles through a wilderness, having, in part, to pack my provisions, & sometimes compelled to sleep in the woods."[9] In addition to having to play the raw frontiersman, the former planter and cotton merchant found his troubles multiplied by attorneys who took up unregistered Indian claims and insisted on having them located. Following the sales of public land in October and November, further complaints came from the Indians, but President Jackson determined that all claimants not on Ward's register must seek relief from Congress.

Since Congressional relief might be long in arriving, and since the sales of Choctaw lands were speeded along as fast as the surveys would allow, the plight of the Choctaws was critical. Just prior to the second auction of Choctaw lands, in the fall of 1834, however, the Indians gained valuable allies among the area's active and enterprising land speculators.

While the importunate Choctaws had waited, their lands had begun to acquire a widespread reputation. The public sales of 1833 and 1834 brought to the cession a crowd of land-lookers and land-buyers. A few of these men saw in the Indian claims a means of acquiring carefully selected lands at noncompetitive prices. They hired themselves out as attorneys for the complaining Indians, and it is likely that in their enterprising search for clients they may have increased the number of complainants.

Among the attorney-speculators were two influential Democrats—Charles Fisher and William M. Gwin. Gwin was United States marshal for the northern district of Mississippi and brother of the register of the Chocchuma, Mississippi Land Office; Fisher, who later served as congressman from North Carolina, was working in Mississippi primarily as a land agent. The two attorneys admitted to partnership three local traders and lawyers whose acquaintance with the Indians made them useful allies.

[9] Martin to Cass, December 6, 1833, *American State Papers: Public Lands,* VII, 4–5.

Their contracts with the Choctaws required them to defend the claims in return for a half-interest in the lands to be acquired. If the Indians chose, they might exchange the remaining half of their claims for other lands, "to be taken in a body."[10]

Gwin, a personal friend of Jackson, persuaded the President to order Martin to register all the Choctaw claims reported to him, locate them on the township plats, and have the locations suspended from sale pending Congressional action. This order went out in October, 1834, just prior to the second offering of Choctaw lands. In December and January, Martin transmitted lists of claims, with supporting evidence, to the War Department. The department submitted the claims to Congress; in February, 1835, a bill was reported calling for their satisfaction.[11]

Even after Martin's report, the production of claims continued. Since in many cases the Choctaws' improved lands had been sold, the contingent claims were transformed into floats, which might be located anywhere in the Choctaw cession. The attorneys naturally saw to it that the "floating claims" were located on carefully selected lands.

This migration of claims brought forth a protest from William Gwin's brother Samuel, who as Register of the Land Office was carrying on a colorful war with "speculators" on many fronts: "There is no justice in their *floating* from the poor pine lands, east of the Yala Busha, to the richest river lands on the Mississippi. . . . I have seen enough to know that anything can be proved where *rich river lands* are in view."[12] Gwin's description was exaggerated. Approximately half the contingent claims were located in the plateau and prairie lands in Eastern Mississippi, in the vicinity of the Choctaw villages. To the west, claims were settled on the loess lands near the Big Black River, the

[10] This clause gives color to the later assertion by Choctaw officials that "five or six thousand" of the tribesmen wanted to stay in Mississippi and form a colony. Compare Power of Attorney to William M. Gwin, September 24, 1834, 28 Cong., 1 sess., *Sen. Doc. 168*, 118; "Memorial of the Choctaw Nation," March 18, 1870, 41 Cong., 2 sess., *Sen Misc. Doc. 90*.

[11] Martin's report is in *American State Papers: Public Lands*, VII, 641 ff.

[12] Samuel Gwin to Commissioner of the General Land Office, May 7, 1835, *ibid.*, VIII, 394–95.

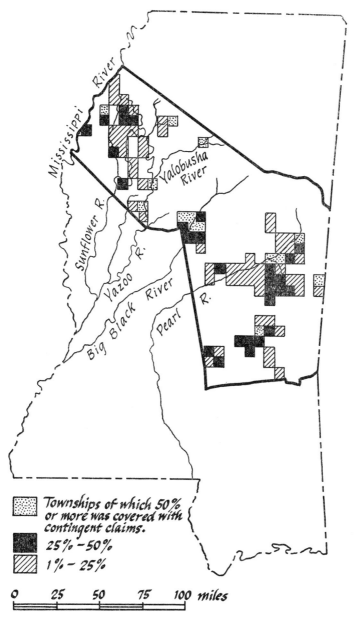

MAP 1. Location of Choctaw Contingent Claims (Mississippi)

valley of the Yalobusha, and the Delta lands near the Sunflower and the Yazoo. Most of the Mississippi bottom had been on the market since the fall of 1833; the best lands there had been taken before the contingent claims became available.

Nevertheless, these claims pre-empted a significant proportion of the lands which had been surveyed but had not yet been offered at public sale. By the time of the third offering of Choctaw lands in December, 1835, prospective buyers reported that their access to desirable lands was barred by contingent claims. There was, in fact, close correspondence between the areas most heavily covered by the claims and those offered for sale in 1835.

Frustrated speculators at the public sales combined to petition Congress in protest against the machinations of the Choctaw attorneys. This petition, which reached the Senate on January 11, 1836, traced the "history" of the fourteenth article claims and concluded:

> A few active, enterprising, and intelligent speculators, discovering the opening which was thus presented for the acquisition of large fortunes ... have caused to be set apart for them the choicest lands in the country, sweeping over large districts inhabited and cultivated by persons who settled the public lands on the faith of the policy of the government indicated by the passage and renewal of the pre-emption laws at almost every session of congress, that their homes would be given them at a reasonable price, unexposed to the heartless grasp of the voracious speculator.[13]

Simultaneously, Stephen Cocke, of Columbus, a state senator and agent for northern investors at the land sales, provoked an investigation of the Choctaw claims by the Mississippi legislature. The legislature transmitted the testimony that had been collected to Congress.[14]

Thus the satisfaction of the Choctaw claims became a political question, involving not simply the rights and wrongs of the

[13] "Application of Inhabitants of Mississippi . . . ," *ibid.*, 337.
[14] Compare Cocke to Nicholas Biddle, July 19, 1835, Biddle Papers, Library of Congress; James D. Lynch, *The Bench and Bar of Mississippi*, 167; "Application of Inhabitants of Mississippi," *loc. cit.*

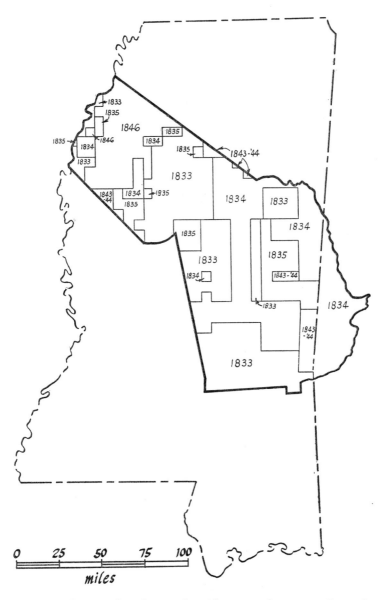

MAP 2. Public Land Sales in the Choctaw Cession, 1833–46

Indians, but also the ambitions of rival speculators. Furthermore, the Choctaw contingent locations interfered in some cases with those of Mississippi's frontier settlers, so that the conflict over the validity of the Indian claims became a three-cornered battle among representatives of the Indians, speculators at the public sales, and settlers.

In the long run, conflicts between Indian claims and settlers' claims—both parties were, of course, represented by attorneys with a speculative interest in the lands involved—gave birth to the bitterest rivalry. Rapid migration into the Choctaw cession had begun within a year after the treaty was ratified. By its terms, settlements made before September, 1833, were illegal. In response to the requests of Choctaws who were anxious to accommodate buyers of their allotments, the War Department was pleased to condone the intrusions. Wrote Secretary Cass, "The President is happy to find . . . that he is not called upon to execute the provisions of the treaty."[15] Settlers in the cession acquired the legal right of pre-emption—purchasing their lands at the minimum price before they were offered at public sale—by a law of June 30, 1834. This law allowed an occupant who had cultivated any part of the public domain in 1833 to buy 160 acres at the minimum price of $1.25 per acre in advance of the public sales. It revived an act of 1830 which assumed that settlements might be made before the chosen lands were surveyed. Since this sometimes led to conflicts of title to particular legal subdivisions, the law of 1834 provided "floating" pre-emptions. If the surveys showed that two or more settlers occupied the same quarter-section, the later occupants gave up their claim to the original 160 acres, receiving in return the right to locate 160 acres at the minimum price anywhere in the land district.[16] These floating claims multiplied nearly as easily as the Choctaw floats, and the poor settler, like the poor Indian, became the object of lawyers' charity.

---

[15] Cass to Plummer, May 23, 1832, *American State Papers: Public Lands,* VII, 611.

[16] 4 *Statutes at Large,* 421, 678.

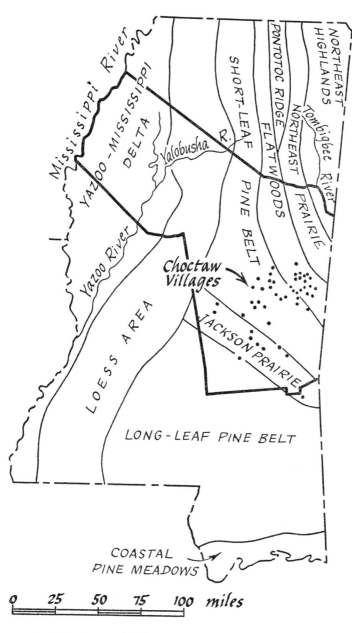

MAP 3. Soil Regions of Mississippi

Where the owners of Choctaw claims came into conflict with settlers, they often promised them title to their lands at a special price. William M. Gwin contracted to sell "actual settlers" their quarter-sections at the government minimum price of $1.25 per acre. Others were apparently less generous: none, of course, could guarantee title. In various forms, the contest between holders of pre-emption rights and promoters of the Indian claims lasted more than a decade. Ultimately, despite the influence at their command, the Choctaw speculators lost out.

The first effect of the contest over claims was to delay action on the determination of Indian rights. It was not until February, 1837, two years after the first bill for satisfying the Indian demands had been submitted, that Congress established a commission to receive evidence and report on the validity of the Choctaw claims. In pursuance of this act, land covered by Choctaw contingent claims was reserved from pre-emption entry. The pre-emption law of June 22, 1838, contained a similar requirement. This law also required the President to reserve from sale, pending Congressional action on the commissioners' report, enough unimproved land in the Choctaw cession to satisfy unlocated claims. Accordingly, the General Land Office postponed the public sales which had been proclaimed for October and November, 1838, and closed the entire Choctaw cession to private entry until Congress or the President should direct otherwise. Pre-emption entries were allowed, but with the warning that they would be void if an Indian established a right to the tract entered by the pre-emptor. The settlers, however, won an election-year victory in the law of June, 1840, which declared that pre-emption claims could not be impaired by "any contingent Choctaw location." Immediately the General Land Office sent instructions that the Choctaw cession lands be opened to pre-emption entry.[17]

[17] 5 *Statutes at Large*, 252; "Notice of Postponement of Public Sales and Private Entry within the Limits of the Choctaw Cession," July 22, 1838; Copy of instructions to Registers and Receivers, August 4, 1838, Choctaw Reserve File 140; Circular to Registers and Receivers of the United States Land Offices, June 30, 1840, Choctaw Reserve File 145, Records of the Bureau of Indian Affairs; 5 *Statutes at Large*, 382.

The pre-emption laws of 1830–40 "forgave" settlements made prior to their enactment; but to qualify for a claim under such laws, the settler must have made his improvement before the law was passed. In September, 1841, Congress enacted the first law providing for claims which might be occupied after the law was passed. To give this law effect in the Choctaw cession, it was only logical that the reservation of unsold and unimproved lands from entry to satisfy claims under the Dancing Rabbit Creek treaty be repealed.[18]

The repeal of prohibitions on pre-emption entry seemed to the Indian attorneys to threaten their interests in the lands of the Choctaw cession. In November, 1841, one *Justitia et Humanitas,* of Jackson, Mississippi, addressed the Commissioner of Indian Affairs:

> The last pre-emption law has thrown open the lands reserved for sale for those Indians to settlers, and for the last three months they have been spreading themselves all over those lands that are worth settling. . . . More than ten years have elapsed without any relief to those suffering Indians. The last ray of hope fled with the passage of the late pre-emption law. . . . A great number of suits have been brought for the recovery of the lands which rightfully belong to them, but which, for ten years, have been occupied and cultivated by purchasers from the government. This is a tedious and expensive process, and many will probably abandon their claim from despair.[19]

The steady encroachment of settlers on the Choctaw lands spurred the attorneys to new efforts to have the Indian locations validated. The commission of 1837–38 had reported on only a fraction of the claims. The attorneys therefore sought to have another commission appointed and bent all their efforts toward getting Congress to dispose of the claims on terms favorable to the Indians. The work of a paid lobbyist, memorials from the

[18] *Ibid.*, 453–58.
[19] November 25, 1841, Choctaw Reserve File 143, Records of the Bureau of Indian Affairs.

Mississippi legislature and the "Choctaw citizens of Mississippi," letters to Congressmen from interested parties, and William Gwin's services as congressman from Mississippi combined to further the Choctaw claims. Yet the law of August, 1842, embodied just those proposals least desired by the speculators. Where land surrounding the Indian improvements had been sold, the Indians were to have scrip, receivable only for public lands open to private entry in Alabama, Mississippi, Arkansas, and Louisiana. Thus, only pre-emption claims and land remaining unsold after it had been offered at auction could be entered with Choctaw scrip. Furthermore, any Indian claim assigned to an attorney before the five-year period of residence required by the treaty had expired was to be void.[20]

Once this act for the settlement of claims went on the books, there was little reason for further conflict between holders of Indian "contingent claims" and other investors or settlers who wished to establish title to land in the Choctaw cession. Successful Indian claimants were to receive title to scrip, rather than to specific parcels of land. After 1842 conflicts over the Indian claims reflected principally the rivalry of various individuals and groups of speculators interested in the claims themselves.

The speculators' first frustration came from divisions within the new Choctaw Claims Commission, which delayed final action on the claims for more than two years. Ironically, the principal architect of this delay was Commissioner J. F. H. Claiborne, who owed his position on the board to the influence of speculator William M. Gwin.

Immediately after the law establishing the commission was passed, Gwin secured the appointment of Claiborne, a Mississippi Democrat, to the Board of Choctaw Commissioners. Gwin and his partner, Abram A. Halsey, owed Claiborne $30,000. They depended on the proceeds of their Choctaw scrip to cover the debt. They promised Claiborne 32,000 acres of land out of the first proceeds of their claims.[21] Since Claiborne, a vocal cham-

---

[20] 5 *Statutes at Large*, 513–16.
[21] Gwin to Claiborne, March 19, 1842, Claiborne Papers, Library of Congress.

pion of the rights of the settlers, had opposed the Choctaw claims in Congress, his appointment gave a tone of impartiality to the commission. His peculiar stake in the scrip speculation was expected to insure swift and sympathetic action on the claims in which Gwin was interested.

The Board of Choctaw Commissioners convened at Hopahka, Mississippi, in December, 1842. Despite Claiborne's forthright opposition to critics, protests against the validity of the claims gained a hearing before the commission. Reuben H. Grant, a trader whose testimony in 1834 had favored the Indian claimants, now maintained that claims had been created far in excess of the number of Indians actually entitled to them. He asserted that most of these claims had been assigned before the five-year-residence period had expired, and were therefore void under the law of 1842. The Office of Indian Affairs ordered an investigation of Grant's charges, which exposed many contracts made by Fisher, Gwin, and their agents prior to the expiration of the five-year-residence period. Claiborne thereupon demanded that all proceedings be stopped until fuller examination could be made to uncover fraudulent contracts.[22] Since he had been appointed to the board to insure the execution of just such contracts, it is unlikely that their discovery was the actual reason behind his change of front. In their communications with the Indian Office, the enraged speculators provided him with a variety of less creditable motives. Among those borne out by Claiborne's private memoranda and correspondence was the growing conviction that Gwin did not mean to have him paid out of the proceeds of the scrip, or to allow him any interest in a proposed contract for the removal of those Choctaws who remained in Mississippi.[23]

[22] Claiborne to Crawford, May 20, 1843; Reuben H. Grant to Crawford, June 3, 1843; Crawford to Choctaw Commissioners, July 6, 1843; Thomas J. Word to Board of Choctaw Commissioners, August 16, 1843; Claiborne to Ralph H. Graves, August 25, 1843, 28 Cong., 1 sess., *Sen. Doc. 168*, 57–63, 83, 78–88, 107–108, 108–11; Deposition of Reuben H. Grant, December 23, 1834, *American State Papers: Public Lands*, VII, 629.

[23] John D. Freeman to Claiborne, November 21, 1842; William M. Gwin to Claiborne, March 1, 1843; Claiborne's note, "to be delivered to my wife," No-

Claiborne levied war against Gwin on many fronts. He bombarded the Indian office with demands that no claims be allowed or scrip issued without further investigation. He attacked the Choctaw speculators in the *Vicksburg Sentinel,* his articles serving the double purpose of embarrassing Gwin and providing hot copy for a newspaper in which he was interested. In return, the speculators protested his membership on the board, forced it to dissolve, and issued Claiborne a series of invitations to "coffee and pistols for two." Eventually the controversy led to the dismissal of Claiborne and Ralph Graves, his principal opponent on the board.[24]

Having so auspiciously begun his career as a trumpet of righteousness, Claiborne carried on. On April Fool's Day, the *Sentinel* promised its readers an entire history of the Choctaw claims, "with sketches, biographical and political, of all the leading characters concerned. These articles alone will be worth more than the subscription price of the *Sentinel.* They will contain more of life, intrigue, and secret history, more that will be at once startling and amusing, more of the machinery of management and government, than any publication issued in the last ten years."[25] Claiborne followed through with the promised reports, and for full measure, started a movement in the Mississippi legislature adverse to the Choctaw claims. Finally Gwin capitulated and compromised the debt; Claiborne's agitation ceased.[26]

Meanwhile the reconstituted Board of Choctaw Commissioners proceeded with its work. The attorneys saw to it that no more "fraudulent" contracts could be found, and it was decided

---

vember 20, 1843; "Biographical Notebook, 1843–44, Memorandum, Choctaw Business"; Freeman to Claiborne, January 1, 1844, Claiborne Papers, Library of Congress. Same to Same, February 2, 1843, Claiborne Papers, Mississippi Department of Archives and History; Affidavit of Benjamin Jacoway, February 27, 1844; Charles Fisher to Ralph Graves, March 5, 1844, Choctaw Reserve File 151, Records of the Bureau of Indian Affairs.

[24] The *Oxford Observer* (Oxford, Mississippi), November 25, 1843, quoting from the *Vicksburg Sentinel.*

[25] *Vicksburg Sentinel,* April 1, 1844.

[26] Claiborne to Gwin, March 15, 1845 (draft), Claiborne Papers, Library of Congress.

that most of those which had been discovered were not technically fraudulent after all. In December, 1844, the board adjourned to Washington, where six months later it made a final report. Under this report and the findings of the earlier commission, 143 heads of families and their children received land, and 1,150 Choctaws and their 2,683 children became entitled to payment in scrip.[27]

Half the scrip to which the Choctaws were entitled was never issued to them. Instead, the government "funded" it for them; that is, it promised to pay the claimants 5 per cent yearly on the total value of their scrip, estimated at $1.25 per acre. This action was taken in response to the petition of the western Choctaw leaders, who feared the impact of pauper immigrants on their nation's territory.[28]

The acquisition of the remaining scrip was fraught with difficulties for the speculators, mainly because of their internecine rivalry. By the time the scrip was issued, the Choctaw claims had undergone a process of subinfeudation characteristic of the land business of the period. Approximately one-fourth of the claims were represented by Colonel John F. Forrester, another fourth by John Johnston, Sr., and the remaining half by Gwin and Fisher, who shared an interest in 113 claims with their agents and interpreters. On November 19, 1835, they had sold their entire interest in the Choctaw claims to a group of capitalists and land agents, including Moses Lewis, Thomas Herndon, Franklin Shaw, Robert Jamison, Henry Anderson, and Edward Orne. These men paid $100,000 for 100,000 acres of claims and pledged to pay one dollar an acre for any additional land that

---

[27] Thomas H. Crawford to William Tyler, March 16, 1844, Office of Indian Affairs, Letters Sent, XXXV, 48; Thomas J. Word to Messrs. Gaines and Rush, September 6, 1844, Choctaw Reserve File 147; Tyler, Gaines and Rush to the President, May 1, 1845, Choctaw Reserve File 153, Records of the Bureau of Indian Affairs; Commissioner of Indian Affairs, *Annual Report*, November 24, 1845, 29 Cong., 1 sess., *House Exec. Doc. 1*, 451; E. B. Merritt to Robert J. Enochs, *op. cit.*

[28] Nathaniel Folsom, James Fletcher and Isaac Folsom to William Armstrong, February 1, 1844, Choctaw Emigration File 129, Records of the Bureau of Indian Affairs; 5 *Statutes at Large, 777*.

might be acquired, up to 256,000 acres. Immediately following this transaction, Anderson and Orne, both agents of New York and Boston joint-stock land companies, sold $5,000 worth of their claims to R. F. Houston; $10,000 worth to Richard Bolton, agent of the New York and Mississippi Land Company; and $7,500 worth to Daniel Saffarans, a Tennessee merchant and land dealer. In January, 1836, they sold 35 per cent of their 50 per cent interest in the claims for $35,000 to a company of Georgians, including Sterling Neblitt, Roscoe Cole, Daniel W. Bragg, Eli S. Shorter, and James C. Watson.[29]

Even though he had sold his "entire interest" in the Choctaw claims in 1835, Fisher in November, 1843, sold 50,000 acres' worth of Choctaw scrip (in potentia) to Elisha Riggs of New York for $12,500. At the same time, he entered into agreement to embark on the purchase and sale of Choctaw scrip with Corcoran and Riggs, Washington bankers; the mercantile firms of Peabody, Riggs and Company of Baltimore and Riggs, Son and Paradise, of Philadelphia; and Elisha Riggs.[30] This agreement need not have come into conflict with his other obligations, had he realized more than 256,000 acres' worth of scrip. Unfortunately, he acquired only a fraction of that amount, and the conflicting interests he had promised to serve made the execution of his contracts impossible.

Fisher was an inspired architect of speculations, but there was more of prophecy than reason in his calculations. In presenting the project of a scrip speculation to the Riggs group, he asserted that at least 1,820,000 acres' worth of scrip would be issued. He expected that most of it would be thrown on the market as soon

[29] Copy of agreement between Fisher, Lincecum, Young and Wright, December, 1834; Memorandum of Agreement, Gwin and Fisher, November 27, 1834; Fisher to Elisha Riggs, November 19, 1843, Riggs Papers, Choctaw Agency, Library of Congress. Vice Chancery Court, Northern District of Mississippi, Final Record, Vol. M., 219, 222–23, 243, 244, Chancery Clerk's Office, Holly Springs, Mississippi.

[30] Copy of assignment by Fisher to Riggs, November 7, 1843; copy of agreement, November 7, 1843, Riggs Papers, Choctaw Agency, Library of Congress. Except where otherwise noted, the account of the Fisher-Riggs speculation is drawn from the Choctaw Agency File, the Paradise Letterbook and Account Book, and the Letters Received, 1846, in the Riggs Papers.

as it was delivered to the Indians, selling "greatly below its value" at twenty-five to fifty cents per acre. In three years' time, "the whole of it [could] be converted into cash at not less than 95 cents in the dollar. The process of converting it [would] commence immediately, & in less than one year the capital [might] be returned."[31]

It is apparent from this outline that with the enactment of the law promising the Choctaws scrip rather than land in satisfaction of their claims, the character of the "speculation" had changed. Originally it had been Fisher's aim to use his half of the Choctaw rights to pre-empt choice land that had not been offered for sale. Now he seems to have expected profit not so much from the location of the scrip, as from the opportunity to act as middleman in buying and selling it. In addition, he expected to obtain some of the scrip at half-price by virtue of the contracts in which his Indian clients had promised him half their lands. The change in his outlook on the speculation is symbolic of the evolution of the nature of the Indian claims: no longer did anyone expect that many of the Indians would become homesteaders on lands obtained under the fourteenth article; what the government "owed" them became simply an equivalent for the value of the lands they had lost, an equivalent which most of them were expected to exchange for money or goods to assist in their emigration west.

Fisher's objective in the scrip speculation was to obtain as nearly as possible a monopoly of the market as a buyer—selling, of course, on a competitive market to prospective purchasers of government land. The story of his Choctaw business and that of his "partners," the Riggs group, illustrates some of the hazards encountered by the would-be monopolist in an economic world still cluttered with competitors.

The Riggs group organized as the Choctaw Company to invest $20,000 in the purchase of Fisher's interest in the Choctaw claims and goods to be sold the Indians and their agents in

[31] Charles Fisher, "The Choctaw Claims," n.d., Riggs Papers, Choctaw Agency, Library of Congress.

return for scrip. W. S. Paradise, a young nephew of Romulus and Elisha Riggs, was charged with handling the business. He was expected to show a profit by exchanging goods at high prices for scrip at low prices, obtaining as nearly as possible a monopoly of the scrip, and selling it at a much appreciated price. Riggs, Son and Paradise made their first shipment to the Choctaw country in December, 1843. For three years following, Paradise supplied the attorneys who played the roles of Indian traders for the benefit of their clients. But while suspenders, shawls, soap, tobacco, claret, castor oil, and acres of blue, bleached, and striped domestic passed over the counter, Paradise accumulated little in return but bills receivable. Finally, in the spring of 1846, the Choctaw Company began receiving scrip; actually, the issuance of scrip only complicated their situation.

The Riggs' hope of profit depended on three unreliable contingencies. They must collect the scrip owed them by the various Indian attorneys, Fisher's debt being the largest. They must corner the market in scrip by buying from the Indians and the attorneys at low prices. Finally, they must sell the scrip at a considerable advance over its cost. The company swung three times and struck out.

Their first failure was their attempt to acquire scrip cheaply. The effort of the various attorneys to persuade the Choctaw emigration agent to force his charges to abide by their contracts was only partly successful. A host of competing buyers entered the market, and for three years following the first issue, the scrip never sold at prices as low as those Fisher had predicted. Finally a new emigration agent made an arrangement allowing the attorneys to buy scrip at 31.75 cents per acre, while outside competitors had to pay 75 cents.[32] The Choctaw Company's main competitor was Daniel Saffarans, who represented several of those to whom, in the mid-thirties, Fisher had sold his "entire interest" in the Choctaw claims. Eventually Fisher compromised with Saffarans, to the Choctaw Company's cost, but competition

[32] Hugh McDonald to Fisher, June 11, 1848, Fisher Papers, Southern Historical Collection, University of North Carolina.

from other sources continued. Furthermore, the attorneys contended not only for scrip, but also for contracts to remove the Indians to the Choctaw Nation West. This competition, interrupted by a series of imperfect reconciliations, delayed both emigration and the issuance of scrip.

Marketing the scrip raised equal problems. The attorneys hoped to create a market among the settlers of the Choctaw cession. Much of the Grenada district, in the northwestern part of the cession, had never been offered at public auction. In March, 1846, the Choctaw speculators secured an order proclaiming the unoffered lands of the Grenada district for sale the following June. The interval between proclamation and sale was unusually short, and the attorneys anticipated that settlers would find it hard to get the means of paying for their pre-emption claims before the sale. They anticipated that competition among pre-emptors for scrip to pay for their lands would bring its value close to the governmental minimum of $1.25 an acre. They even projected a time entry business, taking lands for settlers in Paradise's name and selling it to them on credit for $1.50 to $2.50 an acre. But despite their influence in securing the proclamation, the speculators were foiled. Local protests elicited an order postponing the sales until fall.[33] Nearly all the autumn sales—which totaled only 49,003.10 acres—consisted of pre-emption entries paid out in Choctaw scrip.[34]

Thus the ultimate result of the Choctaw claim speculation in Mississippi was to delay the offering of a million and a half acres of land for six to eight years; settlers could take up lands and hold them free of charge for as long as eight years, then enter them with scrip, for which they paid less than the government minimum price. Prices mentioned in the Riggs correspondence averaged about one dollar an acre. Although in other

[33] *The Guard* (Holly Springs), May 8, 1846, quoting from the Jackson *Mississippian; ibid.*, April 17, 1846; James Shields to Register and Receiver, Grenada, Mississippi, May 6, 1846, Letters Sent to Registers and Receivers, n.s., Vol. XX, 102, Records of the Bureau of Land Management.

[34] Abstract of Cash Entries, Grenada Land Office, 1846, *ibid.;* 30 Cong., 2 sess., *House Exec. Doc. 12,* 229.

states where the scrip was used, relatively little of it was paid for pre-emption entries, the overwhelming proportion of it was located by individuals who bought only 80 or 160 acres. None of the Choctaw attorneys made large-scale entries of land, and only a few individuals bought more than a section or two using scrip.[35]

Indeed, the scrip seems to have been more effective as a means of reducing prices paid by small entrymen than as a source of profit to the Choctaw speculators. There were two principal outlets for the sale of scrip: the cotton commission houses and money brokers of New Orleans, and the local land offices in Mississippi, Alabama, Louisiana, and Arkansas.[36] The delays in its issue meant that by the time dealers received the bulk of the scrip, they were forced to sell in competition with the flood of military-bounty land warrants issued to veterans of the Mexican War. The harassing delays, the competition incurred both in buying and selling the scrip, and the perfidiousness of their debtors involved the Choctaw Company in heavy losses. When they closed their agency in 1849, they had received not more than half of their original investment.

In his chronicle of the "Flush Times of Alabama and Mississippi," Joseph Baldwin produces an apt obituary on the Choctaw speculation. He tells of a young Virginian, Tom Edmundson, who came to Mississippi with a ten-thousand-dollar patrimony. After investing half in "cigars, Champagne, trinkets, buggies, horses, and current expenses . . . He invested the balance, on private information kindly given him, in 'Choctaw Floats'; a most lucrative investment it would have turned out, but for the facts: 1. that the Indians never had any title; 2. the white men who kindly interposed to act as guardians for the Indians did not have the Indian title; and 3dly, the land, left subject to entry, if the Floats had been good, was not worth entering."

Thus the Choctaw land speculation entered into the golden

---

[35] Choctaw Scrip Patent Books, Vols. I–XII, Bureau of Land Management, Department of the Interior.
[36] *New Orleans Commercial Bulletin*, 1847–54, *passim*.

legend of the "flush times." Like the ingenious legal practices and the imaginative credit systems of the pioneer period, it was surrounded by an aura of audacious rascality which lends piquancy, if not precision, to historical memory. In this sense, the speculation may be viewed as a kind of tragicomedy of unintended consequences. The Choctaw claims, promoted as a boon to the Indian and opposed because they were to enrich the "speculator" at the expense of the settler, operated in each case in an opposite manner. The fourteenth article allotments failed to create a corps of Indian homesteaders. Instead, the claims produced a band of wanderers, increasingly dependent on attorneys and traders not only for their dealings with other white men but even for food and clothing. The small community of Choctaws who remained in Mississippi became itinerant agricultural laborers and ultimately achieved the status of sharecroppers. Furthermore, if the Choctaw Company is exemplary, the claims cannot have enriched "speculators." The evidence here is far from complete, but when the cost of maintaining Indian claimants, buying influence, and ultimately buying scrip is compared with the depressed price of scrip selling in competition with military-bounty land warrants, it seems unlikely that any large-scale operation in Choctaw claims could have been profitable. As for the settlers, the uncertainty and conflict surrounding the "contingent locations" of Choctaw claims may have discouraged many; but the long-term limitation of entries in the Choctaw cession to settlers with pre-emption claims and the impact of scrip issue on the price of land probably benefited many more.

This tale of casual cruelty and calculated righteousness does not simply illustrate the truism that people sometimes do not get precisely what they bargain for. The story of the Choctaw claims also exemplifies many of the conditions of land speculation in the "Age of Jackson." The primary factor governing speculation in lands was the national government's willingness to dispense liberally from the public domain. In the administration of the land system, political influence and access to capital operated often on the side of the speculator. Even actions supposedly taken to benefit the poor and homeless in fact operated to the equal or greater benefit of the land dealer. The picture of the "actual settler" or the "poor Indian" may be in considerable measure one of those images of small men which persist because large men can make use of them. Yet in the end, the practices of the "large men" were self-limiting. The rapid sale of public lands enabled speculators to acquire land at low prices in advance of settlement; the sale of Indian allotments to speculators made such acquisitions easier. Similarly, the issue of scrip to Indians—and many others—who could not use it tended to concentrate floating claims in the hands of capitalists who could. At the same time, the government's liberality in offering new lands for sale and its wholesale production of assignable claims, such as the military warrants, outran the capital available to any one group for their purchase. The machinations of the Choctaw speculators illustrate abundantly that at every step of connivance, purchase, and sale, the "capitalists" failed to maintain the kind of co-operation which monopoly requires. Furthermore, as the pre-emption laws and postponements of land sales demonstrate, power was sometimes on the side of the people—who, after all, could vote. The Indian allotment policy of the 1830's offered unique opportunities for speculation, but as in the case of the public lands, the division of the spoils was still an open game.

·4·

THE CREEK FRAUDS

THE CREEK TREATY OF MARCH 24, 1832, differed from the Choctaw treaty in that it was not ostensibly a removal agreement.[1]
It provided allotments of 320 acres to each head of a family,
with 640 acres to each of the tribe's "chiefs and headmen." The
individual reserves were to be located so that members of the
same town could live together on a compact body of land which
would include their improvements. The treaty guaranteed the
tribe against instrusions on its lands and against forcible removal.
Returning from their Washington negotiations, the treaty delegation informed their followers that they had not really sold
the tribal lands but had made each individual his own guardian,
and that the tribesmen "might take care of their own possessions,
and act as agents for themselves."[2] Presumably white settlers
might ultimately occupy the unallotted lands, but the allotted
lands were to provide a permanent home for all the Creeks who
did not choose to sell their allotments.

Yet even more than in the Choctaw case, the story of Creek
allotments exhibits the ironic contrast between the declared

[1] 7 *Statutes at Large*, 366–68.
[2] John S. Scott to Lewis Cass, November 12, 1835, Creek File 193, Records of
the Bureau of Indian Affairs.

purpose of the allotment policy and its actual operation. Instead of giving the tribesmen a more secure title to their individual holdings, the allotment of their lands became an entering wedge for those who would drive them from their eastern domain. This displacement by intrusion and purchase was supposed at least to promote competition among the buyers of reserves and, as a consequence, to bring profit to the Indians. But more significant, both in fixing the price of lands and in hastening the removal of the Indian owners, was the competition for influence on the Indians and on government officials and politicians in Washington. The situation was further complicated by competitive connivance at fraud and the exposure of fraud.

The government executed its obligation to allocate the lands with scrupulous regard to the letter of the treaty. Census takers, appointed two months following the treaty's ratification, made certain that all qualified Indians were registered for reservations. Within a year they submitted returns showing that 6,557 Creeks were entitled to 320-acre allotments. Additional grants to chiefs and orphans brought the total to 6,696 separate locations, embracing an estimated 2,187,200 acres of the approximately 5,000,000 acres of the cession. A special commission, employing many assistants, completed the work of locating the allotments according to the federal land surveys in January, 1834.

It was in dealing with potential buyers of Creek allotments and intruders on the ceded lands that federal officials violated both the letter and the spirit of the treaty. Their aim was to accommodate white settlers and speculators while at the same time forwarding what they regarded as the interest of the Indians. Unfortunately, these aims were incompatible, and the officials' actions made a fair administration of the treaty impossible. The truth of this conclusion becomes evident by an examination of the course of speculation and settlement in the Creek cession.

Just across the Alabama border in the six-year-old Creek cession of western Georgia, a community of merchants, planters, and lawyers was building the city of Columbus. Here, at the falls

of the Chattahoochee River, the cotton of the eastern part of the
Alabama cession would find its inland market, and here lived the
proprietors of the banks, warehouses, wharves, and steamships
required to get the staple to its destination in the metropolis of
Liverpool. Before the first Indian had given his name to a census
taker, the capitalists of Columbus had laid plans for assuring
that the Creek lands, as well as their produce, might pay them
tribute.

On April 5, 1832, twenty men of Columbus agreed to con-
tribute five hundred dollars each to the capital of the Columbus
Land Company, "that as extensive purchases shall be made as
possible of lands in the Creek Territory from Indian Chiefs and
heads of families."[3] The company appointed two of its number
as purchasing agents. The partnership was to continue for not
more than six years, and when its business was closed, each member was to have an equal share of the land and a refund of the
money he had invested.

The Columbus Land Company was one of many which began
operating in the Creek cession shortly after the treaty was ratified. These associations sent agents into the territory with stores
of goods and whisky. By allowing the Indians to buy from them
on credit, they were able to get in return, as security, bonds for
title to the Indian lands. Unwittingly, the census takers helped
them by insisting, contrary to Creek usage, that the men of the
tribe were the heads of families and therefore entitled to own
the reserves. Unaccustomed to owning landed property, many
of the Creek men were easy prey.

The speculators used Negro slaves as interpreters and paid
them bonuses to hunt out the owners of unsold allotments and
importune them to sell. Thus the speculators owned the people
who might be able to give evidence against them in case of
fraudulent purchases. One government agent reported that these
Negroes were encouraged "to hunt the reservees down like male-
factors or wild beasts, and to follow them incessantly whereso-

---

[3] Articles of Agreement, Columbus Land Company (copy), April 5, 1832,
Creek File 219, *ibid.*

ever they might retreat to avoid importunity and persecution, and never cease hampering them, till from mere disgust, not a few have committed suicide, and many more have sold for very inadequate prices."[4] In response to an inquiry of the Creek agent regarding the propriety of such sales, the commissioner of Indian Affairs gave his opinion that the Indians were "unwise" to dispose of their rights before the allotments were located. But, to facilitate speedy removal, they should be encouraged to execute powers of attorney to agents who would sell for them.[5]

In addition to the sale of allotments, a second inducement to Indian emigration was the intrusion of settlers on Creek lands. Like the speculators, the intruders had reason to believe that their behavior would be acceptable in the sight of officials of the federal government. The principal pressure forcing the tribe to a cession of its lands had been the extension of state law over its territory, with the acquiescence of the federal government. This extension had encouraged intruders. The treaty of cession obliged the federal government to remove them, but settlers whose improvements did not interfere with Indian rights were to remain long enough to harvest their growing crops.

Immediately federal officers began to extend the category of legal settlement. Secretary of War Lewis Cass asserted in his instructions to the United States marshal and in his correspondence with members of the Alabama delegation in Congress that those living on the public domain might remain until January, 1833. Of settlers on Creek improvements, only those who failed to get the owner's permission were to be removed. The marshal was as lenient as possible in carrying out instructions. Where the Indians were willing to lease their improvements to settlers, he encouraged them to do so. But in the part of the nation between Montgomery, Alabama, and the Chattahoochee "the extreme hostility existing between the Indians, & these Intruders,

[4] Return J. Meigs to Cass, September 26, 1834, "Report on Sales of Indian Reservations," 24 Cong., 1 sess., *Sen. Doc. 425*, 180–82.

[5] Elbert Herring to John Crowell, October 15, 1832, Office of Indian Affairs, Letters Sent, Vol. IX, 297, Records of the Bureau of Indian Affairs.

forbad a compromise of any kind taking place, nothing but absolute expulsion [of the settlers] would do them."[6]

The Indians had been induced to let the intruders remain and gather their crops, on the ground that the improvements to be abandoned by them would make valuable selections for those Indians who took reservations. The project, however, brought trouble. The Indians who tried to include settlers' farms in their selections were threatened with death, and even those Indians who extended their own improvements met with violence. The first serious clash came in July, 1832, at the white settlement of Irwinton, located on the Chattahoochee in the midst of the Indian town of Eufaula, where the marshal expelled settlers and burned their cabins. The settlers returned under arms, escorting the sheriff, who tried to serve writs on the marshal and on the officer who, with troops from Fort Mitchell, was carrying out the marshal's orders, as well as on the Indians who had repossessed their improvements. The settlers reported indignantly that the officer in command of the troops "refused to have the warrant served and ordered one of his soldiers to bayonet the sheriff which he Did and has sevearly wounded one of the best Citerzens of that County[.] the sherriff is a man of Good Reputation and the Ground is stained with his blood."[7]

Despite the bloodshed, the following December Cass informed the Alabama delegation in Congress that since the surveys were nearly completed, those settlers not in conflict with the Indians might remain until the allotments were located and that they would then need to move only if they were on land selected for the tribesmen. Since the settlers might then be able to buy the Indian reserve, this looked like a blanket permission for settlements which did not involve forcible dispossession of Indian owners.

[6] Crawford to Cass, August 31, 1832, Creek File 177, *ibid.* Cass to Robert L. Crawford, April 5, 1832, and Cass to Samuel W. Mardis, May 17, 1832, 23 Cong., 1 sess., *Sen. Doc. 512*, II, 806–807, 833.

[7] Henry Irwin to Cass, July 30, 1832, Creek File 177, Records of the Bureau of Indian Affairs. See also John Crowell to Cass, August 3, 1832, and Crawford to John Robb, September 15, 1832, 23 Cong., 1 sess., *Sen. Doc. 512*, III, 413, 453.

The Alabama Legislature was already at work to entrench the settlers still further. In December it erected nine counties in the Creek cession. In January, on receiving from the delegation in Congress assurance of the federal government's liberal interpretation of settlers' rights, the legislature proceeded to authorize the judges of the county courts and commissioners of roads and revenue to take a census of the counties. Commissioners were appointed to locate sites for county seats and let contracts for buildings. Other county officers were to be elected the first Monday in March, 1833.[8]

By the late summer of 1833, however, Indian complaints and the reports of the marshal and his assistants made it clear that the indulgence granted the settlers had become intolerable to the Indians. Cass, showing a more rigorous attitude than he had earlier, directed the marshal to remove all settlers as soon as they had harvested their crops and ordered the United States district attorney at Mobile to prosecute all who resisted removal.

Cass's stiffening attitude was indicative of the growing disagreement on Indian policy between the federal government and the state of Alabama. The trouble was aggravated in the summer of 1833 by the killing of Hardeman Owen, a commissioner of Russell County. Owen was a particularly violent and obnoxious intruder on Indian improvements, and while resisting expulsion from an Indian cabin in August, 1833, he was shot and killed by soldiers from Fort Mitchell. The soldiers were indicted for murder at the October term of the Russell County Circuit Court. Following the killing, Governor John Gayle appealed to the Secretary of War to "refer the complaints of the Indians, to a tribunal less objectionable than the Marshall with an armed soldiery." He suggested that since the laws of Alabama and the jurisdiction of her courts were now in force in the former Creek Nation, trespassers could be expelled by summary proceedings before a justice of the peace. Since the only justice of the peace in Russell County, where Owen was killed, was an intruder with

[8] Alabama, *Laws* (1832–33), 8–11, 30–33, 48–51. Governor John Gayle to the Alabama Senate, January 7, 1833, Alabama Legislature, *Senate Journal* (1832–33), 150.

78

a large plantation, this mode of protecting Indian rights did not recommend itself to federal authorities.[9]

In behalf of the settlers the Governor argued that large numbers had been encouraged to begin farms within the Indian nation through the federal government's known record of granting retrospective pre-emption rights to intruders on the public domain, its acquiescence in the extension of state jurisdiction over Creek lands, and its earlier indulgence of settlers in the Creek cession. Perhaps twenty-five thousand were already within its limits. Many had come a long way and had sold their horses and wagons to obtain food and shelter during the first lean year of pioneering. Their removal would cause great and unjustifiable hardship.[10]

By September, 1833, volunteer companies were forming to resist the removal of the settlers. Officers at Fort Mitchell, anticipating that "a General rupture between the State and the General Government" would issue from the conflict between federal troops and volunteers, sent to the Augusta arsenal for additional supplies of ammunition.[11] To avoid such a rupture, the War Department sent Francis Scott Key, district attorney for the District of Columbia, to Montgomery. Key worked out a compromise whereby the Alabama authorities agreed to drop the prosecution of Owen's "murderers," and the federal authorities promised to make no further removals until all the Indian reserves had been located and then to expel intruders only from allotments. In January, 1834, the Alabama Legislature enacted a law providing that anyone who trespassed on an Indian reserve without contracting to buy or lease it would be fined from $250 to $1,000 or sentenced to three months in jail.[12]

---

[9] Gayle to Cass, August 20, 1833, 23 Cong., 1 sess., *Sen. Doc. 512*, IV, 529–30; Cass to Gayle, September 5, 1833, and Francis Scott Key to Cass, November 13, 1833, Creek File 178, Records of the Bureau of Indian Affairs.

[10] H. H. Wyche to the Secretary of War, October 1, 1833, and Clement C. Clay to Cass, October 8, 1833, Creek File 178, *ibid.;* Gayle to Cass, October 2, 1833, Creek File 179, *ibid.*

[11] Crawford to Cass, September 23, 1833, and J. S. McIntosh to Crawford, October 15, 1833, Creek File 178, *ibid.*

[12] Alabama *Laws* (1833–34), 42.

The compromise agreement committed the War Department to a course of inaction substantially the same as the one Secretary Cass had originally promised the Alabama delegation in December, 1832. It was clearly a violation of the Creek treaty, which called for the removal of *all* settlers as soon as their 1832 crops were harvested. But by his earlier indulgence of settlers and acquiescence in the extension of state laws, Cass had put himself in a position where such violation appeared to be the only alternative to civil war. The delicacy of the War Department's position was indicated by the advice Cass received from General Winfield Scott, commander of the army's Eastern Department. The use of federal troops to put down an intruder's insurrection, Scott predicted, would "excite the sympathies and inflame the passions of Virginia, North Carolina, South Carolina, Georgia and Mississippi, and thus give a wider spread to the heresies of nullification and secession."[13]

In the midst of the difficulties between the Indians and the intruders, the War Department indicated an important change of policy by seeking to purchase the Creek allotments in order to eliminate friction and expedite the process of removal. But in this effort it met with resistance from the Columbus speculators, who had advanced considerable sums in return for bonds for title from the Indians. The Columbus Land Company, through their agent, John S. Scott, had procured title bonds to at least seven hundred allotments. Since the government had removed its own agent from the nation, the Indians depended upon the traders, who were generally agents of land companies, for advice. Naturally, the Indians were advised to refuse to cede their reserves. The Columbus company also threatened to retard emigration, if the allotments were ceded, by suing all the Indians who owed them money.

Negotiations for the purchase of the Creek allotments by the government, held in late June and early July, 1833, were un-

---

[13] Winfield Scott to Cass, November 20, 1833, Creek File 179, Records of the Bureau of Indian Affairs. Less than a year earlier, the President, supported by Cass, had taken this risk to prevent South Carolina from enforcing her nullification of a tariff law.

successful. Following the failure of the negotiations, Eli S. Short-er, a leading speculator, offered to sell to the government at 62.5 cents per acre those reserves on which he had procured title bonds.[14] John J. Abert, one of the agents assigned by the government to negotiate the purchase of allotments, favored indemnifying the speculators, on the ground that they might try to enforce their contracts in court and thus prevent emigration. "The case is a choice of evils," he asserted, "between a small fraud and uninterrupted prosecution of its declared policy, or a large fraud, embarassments to its policy at every step, and finally being obliged to forward the views of the very speculators It is anxious to defeat." Abert's associate, Enoch Parsons, wrote President Jackson that by paying a high price for the reserves and giving "some fifty or hundred perhaps of *Special Reservations* [presumably to influential Indians], and possibly some [to] *White Men* under the guise of *Indian Covering*," an agreement might be made. Jackson forwarded this suggestion to the War Department with two marginal notations: "No concession will ever be made by me in favor of *such men*—A. J." and "A pure government cannot, nay, ought not to be influenced by such corruption—A. J."[15] And so the Creeks kept their allotments, the companies retained their bonds, and the Creek lands passed into the hands of Shorter and other "*such men.*"

The location of allotments to the Indians proceeded rapidly following the Key compromise, and agents for approving contracts of sale began work in the late winter of 1834. Their instructions required them to approve no contracts for the sale of allotments which called for the payment of less than $1.25 an acre, unless sworn appraisements indicated that lands were worth less than that amount. Almost immediately reports of fraud began to issue from the Creek country. The principal complaints were that the Indians were paid in overpriced goods or were forced to return money they received and that when

---

[14] Eli S. Shorter to Cass, July 11, 1833, 24 Cong., 1 sess., *Sen. Doc.* 425, 77–79.
[15] Abert to Cass, June 9, 1833, Creek File 202, Records of the Bureau of Indian Affairs; Parsons to Jackson, September 21, 1833, Creek File 178, *ibid.*

an owner refused to sell his allotment, another Creek was hired to impersonate him before the officer in charge of certifying contracts. Secretary Cass wrote to the three agents responsible for approving Indian deeds, asking for reports on the means taken or to be taken to prevent fraud.

Leonard Tarrant, who worked the northern counties of Coosa, Tallapoosa, Talladega, Randolph, and Benton, described his requirements for certifying a sale. The land had to be valued and described if its price was under the $1.25 government minimum. Two disinterested men had to swear to its value before a justice of the peace, and the purchaser had to swear that he would not require the return of his money. John W. A. Sanford, in charge of Russell and Barbour counties, wrote that he required an oath concerning the identity of the Indian reservee, but that he doubted whether fraud could be prevented by oath-taking. "Nothing exceeds the artifice but the casuistry of the times, and *both* appear to have found here an appropriate field for their indulgence." Robert McHenry, who supervised sales in Macon and Chambers counties, suggested that if the Indians could be required to deposit in the Columbus banks one-half or one-third of the proceeds from their sales, they would be less likely to be swindled out of them. Like Sanford, he implied that the reported frauds were in fact widely practiced.[16]

Since the Creek contracts required Presidential approval, the War Department on receiving the deeds from the certifying agents prepared them for the President's signature. When the department received Sanford's and McHenry's letters, the preparations and approvals were suspended. Abert, who had been recalled to Washington to supervise the review of contracts, advised his friend Sanford that it would be well to temper his reports. He should specify cases where he could prove fraud but should not cast doubt on the validity of all contracts. If a purchaser lost his land as a result of unfounded allegations,

---

[16] Leonard Tarrant to Cass, March, 1834, Creek File 204, *ibid.*; Sanford to Cass, March 7, 1834, Creek File 203, *ibid.*; Robert McHenry to Cass, March 12, 1834, Creek File 203, *ibid.*

Abert warned, his remedy would run against the agent.[17] Sanford replied immediately that Abert's views were precisely his own. He was convinced of the *"utter* futility" of trying to prevent the occurrence of frauds.[18] Abert took Sanford's letter to the Secretary of War, who submitted it to the President, and orders were given to resume the preparation of contracts for presidential approval.

At the same time, the War Department sent Return J. Meigs, a Tennessee lawyer and grandson of a famous United States Indian agent, to investigate possible methods of preventing frauds. Meigs suggested that agents be appointed to value the reserves and to sell them at public auction, using half the proceeds to pay the owner's debts and paying the remaining half to the owner after he had reached the new Creek home in the West. Cass replied that the government could sell the reserves only if it first bought them from the Indians. Meigs rejected this contention. The Creek allotments, he averred, were being subjected to the same kind of combination among buyers that depressed the prices of public lands, with the usual result that settlers were deprived of the right to buy them. The government's duty was to obtain a fair value for the Indians and a fair chance for the settler to compete with the speculator on something like equal terms. This could be done if the lands were auctioned at an appraised minimum price. Prior contracts of Indians with speculators need not stand in the way. A court of equity would refuse to decree a specific performance of them on the ground that the prices they called for were inadequate.[19]

Cass's reply to these arguments was evasive. He realized that if the Indians were allowed freedom in selling their reserves, fraud was inevitable; but the treaty guaranteed them that freedom. "All that could be done would be," he said, "by a wise system of administration, to circumscribe such proceedings within

---

[17] Abert to Sanford, March 26, 1834, J. W. A. Sanford Papers, Alabama Department of Archives and History.

[18] Sanford to Abert, April 5, 1834, *ibid.*

[19] Return J. Meigs to White, May 7, 1834, Creek File 193; Meigs to the President, September 3, 1834, Creek File 204, Records of the Bureau of Indian Affairs.

the narrowest limits." He seemed to realize the ambiguous character of "freedom of contract" when applied to Indian affairs. "It is exceedingly difficult," he added in a later letter, "to draw a practical line between their right to act for themselves under the treaty, and the arts of designing men, who are desirous of dealing with them."[20]

Abert encouraged Cass in his decision, arguing that if the aim of the government was to promote the sale of all the reserves, it would be unrealistic to insist on securing for the Indians the government's minimum price for their lands. Public lands elsewhere sold too slowly at this price to expect the whole of the Creek lands to be purchased at their maximum valuation.[21]

The approval of contracts continued, and the approved contracts were forwarded to their owners. An important clue to the methods the speculators used to secure approval of contracts was provided by a meeting of the Columbus Land Company on November 3, 1834. At this meeting, Congressman Seaborn Jones, who had given the War Department much unsolicited advice favorable to the interests of the speculators and had served as agent in forwarding the approved contracts to the company, was voted five hundred dollars for his services. This incensed Agent Sanford, who passed on his observations to Abert: "What! a member of Congress paid for the indiscriminate defence of a landjobbing co. thro right and thro wrong.—paid, Sir, to tell or disguise the truth, to disclose or discolor facts so as to misguide one of the Departments of Government in its investigations."[22]

In view of Abert's role as adviser to the War Department, his reply is interesting:

> The desire to grow rich, and to grow rich rapidly, are the besetting sins of our country. . . .

[20] Cass to Meigs, October 31, 1834; Same to Same, November 13, 1834, 24 Cong., 1 sess., *Sen. Doc. 425*, 23.

[21] Abert to Cass, November 11, 1834, *ibid.*

[22] Sanford to Abert, November 7, 1834, Sanford Papers. For letters of Seaborn Jones to the Secretary of War, see Creek Reserve Files, 1833–35, *passim*, Records of the Bureau of Indian Affairs.

In a government or community which bestows no mark of distinction, but such as are awarded by the common consent of the community, these become the prize for which ambition seeks, and with a commercial people, that distinction is wealth. Even ambition, therefore, high toned, high minded ambition sees in wealth so important an auxiliary that all its efforts are lost without its aid . . . and therefore with the many, if one is only successful, the means of acquiring it are not looked into, and if not too glaringly dishonest are rarely condemned. Look around you in the world and see what a crime it is to be poor.

The world will have its way and he who sets up to reform it, will rather find himself like the renowned knight, tilting against windmills. It must be done by the opinion of the mass, if done at all. All one can do is to keep oneself "unspotted" and the day will come when that "unspottedness" is properly estimated.[23]

Two days after writing this unofficial credo, Abert refused a proffered interest in the Creek land speculations.[24]

Encouraged by the government's impotence, both the Columbus group and other speculators enlarged their operations. By January, 1835, their business with Indians in the towns along the Chattahoochee in Russell and Chambers counties was nearly finished. Indians in the upper towns, located farther west on the Coosa and Tallapoosa, were more reluctant to sell. The center of resistance, both to sale and to emigration, was in their principal town, Tuckabatchee, located on the Tallapoosa River in Macon County. In this town, Opothleyahola, speaker of the nation and an outstanding opponent of removal, was a rising power. His principal white advisers were among the Alabama speculators who opposed the operations of the Columbus group.

The solution which Columbus speculators found for this problem was to substitute willing Indians for the unwilling. The "land-lookers" studied the roll of locations, selected tracts, and hired a group of "their" Indians to impersonate the owners. These hired Indians then went before the government agent and

[23] Abert to Sanford, November 20, 1834, Sanford Papers.

[24] Abert to David Hubbard, November 22, 1834, George W. Campbell Papers, Library of Congress.

acknowledged the conveyance of the tracts to the company. Once one group from Columbus began this practice, the other had to adopt it or lose all chance of obtaining land. Eli Shorter was distressed by the competition and handicapped because his agent, John Scott, married to an Indian woman, refused to participate in the fraudulent land transfers. In exasperation, Shorter wrote: "When I see such men with so few advantages getting so much valuable land at $10 per tract & see how much *we* have paid out, the *power* we have had, & see how the *quantity* and *quality* of land we have received, & particularly when I think of the *reason* why these things are so, I can almost tear my hair from my head. There is yet time to do something, but I almost despair of its being done. If Scotts Indian wife was at the Devil, I should have some hope." Shorter's partner, Elijah Corley, joined him in urging the agents to be "up and doing while it lasts." As for their competitors in Columbus, he said, "they have rogued it and whored it among the Indians, until I fully believe that, for the purpose of getting a piece of land, they would swear to Almighty God that the Indians in Russell County were located in Coosa. . . . The harvest is nearly over, and perhaps there will never be another such a one."[25]

When news of the spectacular frauds reached the Indian Office, the War Department took immediate steps to stop them. About a year earlier, on receiving reports of fraud in land dealings, the department had temporarily suspended the preparation of contracts for presidential approval. Now, in April, 1835, it directed its agents to cease certifying contracts for the sale of allotments. Immediately the approving agents began investigating contracts and, where they found them to be fraudulent, recertifying the land to new buyers. On May 19 the Alabama speculators, who had apparently not participated in the frauds, formed a company for the purpose of repurchasing reservations. This group of speculators, centering about Robert J. Ware,

[25] Shorter to Scott, Elijah Corley, and the Cravens, March 1, 1835; Corley to Scott, Craven, and Craven, March 25, 1835, 24 Cong., 2 sess., *House Exec. Doc. 154*, 21–24.

Thomas M. Cowles, and Clement Billingslea, of Montgomery, brought into its orbit some of the Georgia speculators who had operated independently of the Columbus group and a number of "Indian countrymen"—white traders whose long residence in the Creek Nation gave them great influence with the Indians. On May 20 several members of the newly formed "Ware, Dougherty, and Company" participated in a meeting of the citizens of Macon County which memorialized the President, asking that all contracts certified after January 10, 1835, be annulled. Advising against this course, Agent McHenry wrote, "The struggle is white man to white man in many Instances, and the interest of the Indian not much at hart."[26]

At the President's suggestion, the War Department appointed another special agent to investigate and report on the Creek frauds. The man appointed was John B. Hogan, of Mobile, who was currently charged with superintending the removal of the few Creeks willing to emigrate beyond the Mississippi. Hogan started work first in Macon and Chambers counties, conducting his investigations in the Indian town squares. He encouraged the tribesmen to come forward and give testimony if their lands had been sold by persons other than their true owners. Although he gave notice to the land dealers whose interests were involved —many of them associated with the Columbus group—they found the prospect of entering the Indian villages too dangerous and did not appear to defend themselves. Instead, they protested to the Secretary of War against *ex parte* investigations and the acceptance of Indian testimony as evidence. Growing louder in their complaints as the investigation proceeded, they asserted that the clamor about frauds had its origin in the "loose, general, and unintelligible" allegations of their Alabama rivals. Among the complainants were Indians who may have been impersonating the true owners of the allotments. Memorials begging the President not to put their homes in jeopardy came from "honest and innocent" planters of Russell and Barbour counties, who held title under the speculators. In writing to Secretary Cass,

[26] McHenry to Cass, May 23, 1835, 24 Cong., 1 sess., *Sen. Doc.* 425, 281–82.

Shorter insisted that the annulment of contracts "upon the naked denial of any Indian or number of Indians" was "a palpable violation of all law, & a total subversion of every principle of civil government."[27]

The aggrieved speculators also used pressure upon their representatives in Congress. Pointing out that Ware, Cowles, and Billingslea had been prominent supporters of South Carolina during the nullification controversy, Luther Blake, an Indian countryman who belonged to the Columbus Land Company, wrote Congressman George W. B. Towns of Georgia: "I think I can answer for many others—who were supporters of union men . . . our property is left at the whim of a prejudiced agent and a d——md set of nullifiers. If you are a partaker I am your friend no more."[28] Towns rushed to the Secretary of War to secure proof that he had in no way supported the investigation of the frauds.

During the investigations the discouraged chiefs of the upper towns finally resolved to emigrate. Immediately following their decision, a contract for their removal was made by the government with a company of men from Columbus. John W. A. Sanford, the government's former certifying agent, was nominal head of the company, but its membership consisted largely of a number of the principal land dealers of the Columbus group, including Alfred Iverson, nephew of Secretary of State John Forsyth. This company quickly came into conflict with Hogan when it charged that his investigations offered the Indians a specious hope of recovering their lands and therefore retarded emigration. Hogan believed, on the other hand, that the speculators in their role as emigration agents were attempting to remove the Indians so that Creek testimony adverse to the fraudulent contracts could not be obtained.

The controversy was resolved by an outbreak of hostilities between some of the Creeks and the whites in March, 1836.

[27] Shorter to the Secretary of War, October 16, 1835; Same to Same, November 10, 1835, *ibid.*, 347–51, 361–66. A. B. Dawson *et al.* to the Secretary of War, February 20, 1836, Creek File 210, Records of the Bureau of Indian Affairs.

[28] Luther Blake to George W. B. Towns, February 9, 1836 (copy), *ibid.*

Several people accused the Columbus speculators of instigating the conflict, and it seems certain that the land frauds figured among the irritations which led the Indians to resort to violence. While it is possible that some of the speculators may have encouraged the hostilities, no direct evidence of this encouragement was produced. Many of the towns where the worst frauds were perpetrated never joined the hostile activities, and since the plans of the warriors included burning the city of Columbus —which was not done—it is fairly certain that the speculators had little control over them.

In any case encouragement was unnecessary. The first allotments sold to incoming farmers had been those containing the Indian improvements. The tribesmen therefore had no crops to provide them with subsistence after they had bargained away their lands. Even those who received fair sums of money for these lands enriched the saloonkeepers rather than the farmers and grocers. By the spring of 1836, they could live only by stealing, and the resulting conflicts with the settlers led to war.

On May 19, Secretary Cass ordered General Thomas S. Jesup to proceed with United States troops to the Creek country. Although the contract with the emigration company was not abrogated, the removal of the Indians was made a military operation. The government discontinued the investigation of frauds. The hostiles were readily defeated and removed in chains to Mobile for embarkation to the West. The remaining tribesmen were taken off in large parties during the following summer and fall. Informing the Secretary of War in midsummer that peace had been restored, General Jesup wrote uneasily: "I would prefer to fight all the Indian warriors in the Creek Nation to have [sic] any agency in settling the difficulties between the land speculators of this country."[29]

Instead, he had an agency in unsettling them. The defeat of the hostile Creeks had been accomplished with the aid of friendly Indians under the direction of Opotheyahola. To secure their services in a campaign being planned against the Seminoles,

[29] Thomas S. Jesup to the Secretary of War, July 15, 1836, *ibid.*

General Jesup allowed the friendly chiefs to reclaim the lands which Agent Hogan had listed as fraudulently purchased from them and to resell them en masse to a company from Columbus including men who had participated both in the frauds and in the removal contract. On August 28 the chiefs sold this land for $75,000 to James C. Watson and Company, giving that company also an option of buying all their unsold lands at appraised prices.[30]

The original members of Watson's company were James C. Watson, president of the Insurance Bank of Columbus; John Peabody, of Columbus; Edward C. Hanrick, a Montgomery merchant; Peter C. Harris, a wealthy planter of Macon County, Alabama; and William Walker, an "Indian countryman" and trader who had married the daughter of Big Warrior, late principal chief of the Creek Nation. Watson, Harris, and Walker had purchased extensively of Creek lands; they were also members of the Alabama Emigrating Company, successor to J. W. A. Sanford and Company in the business of removing the Creeks.

The Watson contract came under the scrutiny of yet another set of investigators into the Creek frauds. Appointed by the War Department, pursuant to a House resolution of July 1, 1836, Alfred Balch and T. Hartley Crawford set up office in Macon County in September and notified all parties claiming tracts under Creek contracts to file memorials giving evidence of the validity of their claims within forty days.

The Indian Office referred the Watson contract to Commissioners Balch and Crawford. During their investigation of the contract in early November, 1836, several persons and companies filed memorials against its ratification. Irvin Lawson, James S. Calhoun, and others from Columbus alleged that the contract was made "in a private room, and after the hour of midnight" without due notice either to competing purchasers or to the Indians supposedly benefited. Ware, Dougherty and Company, whose entire investment was in "recertified contracts"—

---

[30] Jesup to Cass, August 30, 1836, Creek File 182, *ibid*. The original contract is in Creek File 221, *ibid*.

second contracts for the purchase of land for which previous contracts had been rejected on account of fraud—asserted that the Indian chiefs had no right to sell for their people and that the Watson contract was therefore invalid.[31]

The commissioners, following the line of reasoning laid down by Ware, Dougherty and Company, recommended that the Watson contract be rejected. Crawford estimated that under the contract Watson's company would receive about 201,600 acres for slightly more than 37.5 cents per acre. Balch pointed out that members of the company held large numbers of fraudulent contracts which the ratification of the Watson agreement would, in effect, confirm. Witnesses testifying favorably to that contract were also interested in contracts which War Department investigators had recommended for reversal on grounds of fraud.[32]

Following the rejection, Watson appealed to the Secretary of War, asking that the company be allowed to try to obtain the assents of individual reservees entitled to lands covered by his contract. Carey A. Harris, commissioner of Indian Affairs, reported favorably on this appeal. The commissioner's report is of special interest since it is highly probable that he himself held a share in the Watson company.[33] The President approved his report, and the contract was finally sustained with the proviso that the company must obtain the consent of the Indians whose lands were involved.

The approval of the contract did not in itself determine how much land Watson's company might receive. A great number

[31] Memorial of Irvin Lawson *et al.*, November 12, 1836, Creek File 208, *ibid.*; Memorial of Ware, Dougherty and Company, November 12, 1836, *ibid.*

[32] Opinion of T. Hartley Crawford, December 1, 1836; Opinion of Alfred Balch, December 7, 1836, *ibid.*

[33] Carey A. Harris to Butler, February 17, 1837, Creek File 183, *ibid.* Harris was dismissed as Commissioner of Indian Affairs for participating in Indian land speculations. He received a loan from Watson of $1,500 and one for an equal amount from Daniel McDougald, a member of the Watson company, making $3,000, the price of one-half share in the company. Compare Andrew Jackson to Martin Van Buren, July 6, 1838, Van Buren Papers, Library of Congress; Cave Johnson to James K. Polk, April 29, 1842, Polk Papers, Library of Congress; Russell County Deed Book, Vol. E, 14, Probate Office, Courthouse, Phenix City, Alabama.

of the more valuable tracts for which fraudulent contracts had been made, and then rejected by the War Department, had been resold. Some of the second sales had been certified by government agents and some had not. Since the President had not had the opportunity to approve or disapprove the rejection of the first contracts and since the recertification process had been interrupted first by direction of the Indian Office and then by war, the status of the second contracts was dubious. Yet these second contracts were largely untainted by fraud; the manner of making them was more nearly in line with the treaty than the manner in which the Watson contract was made, and it was still entirely possible that they might be sustained, leaving Watson's company holding only such lands as had been fraudulently purchased but not resold.

The Watson company's first move following the conditional ratification of its contract was therefore to include within its membership as many holders of second contracts as it could. For this purpose it held a meeting in Columbus in April, 1837, admitting a number of new members and increasing the number of shares in the company to twenty. All shareholders were to execute relinquishments to the company of any of their lands included in the area covered by the Watson contract.

Except for the Shorter group, which had reached a separate compromise with the Watson men, and a few dissidents, such as Lawson and Calhoun, the Watson company included all the principal Columbus speculators, their Alabama allies, and a large proportion of the influential Indian traders. Many of its members had been active participants in the making of fraudulent contracts. They had operated within loose and overlapping partnership arrangements, constructed largely on the motive of putting down competition. The Watson company represented the culmination of their co-operative efforts, aimed at recouping the assets originally obtained by fraudulent purchases. Their principal opponents in this effort were the same group of speculators who in 1835 had organized Ware, Dougherty and Company to repurchase "stolen" lands.

By July, 1837, the Watson company had procured the assent of the Indians whose lands were embraced in the Watson contract. Evidence of this assent was forwarded by the company to the War Department in November. The holders of conflicting contracts hired Thomas J. Abbott and Joseph Bryan as attorneys to represent their claims in Washington. Abbott and Bryan enlisted the support of the Alabama delegation in Congress, directing their efforts first to the defeat of Commissioner Harris' ruling in favor of Watson and against the holders of recertified contracts. The ruling, they claimed, was directly contrary to the criteria proposed by Crawford and Balch and was undoubtedly dictated by the commissioner's partiality to the Watson contract. The attorneys proposed that the War Department investigate the manner by which the Watson company had obtained the assent of the individual Indians to their contract. Commissioner Harris opposed this suggestion; the Alabama congressmen then proposed that patents be issued to those Indians involved and the whole controversy settled in court. This multiplication of issues and solutions tended to obscure the question of whether any of the purchases—regardless of the identity or interest of the purchaser—had been made in pursuance of the treaty and for adequate consideration. It is likely that this obfuscation was deliberately produced. On July 12, 1838, Alfred Iverson, a member of Sanford's original emigration company, wrote to Sanford: "I am 'busy as a bee in a tar barrel' attending to the emigrating business and the Watson contract, all of which is at present in the most desirable confusion."[34]

Finally Joel R. Poinsett, President Van Buren's secretary of war, decided on an investigation of the validity of the statements of assent which reservees had given to the Watson contract. The inquiry was first entrusted to Crawford, but he was unable to serve because of subsequent appointment as commissioner of Indian Affairs. In December the department appointed a substitute. In April, 1839, attorneys Abbott and Bryan secured additional time to file evidence before the special investigator.

[34] Alfred Iverson to Sanford, July 12, 1838, Sanford Papers.

Perhaps because this evidence promised to discredit the Watson Company's proceedings or because the members of the company decided that they could no longer sustain the expensive litigation, a compromise was reached in May. On the condition that no further investigation would be made, patents to all the lands in question were to be issued to the Watson company. By relinquishment from that company, Ware, Dougherty and Company were to obtain all the land for which they had contracted. With other contesting parties, the company generally settled on a half-and-half basis.[35] Although the compromise made no provision for ascertaining whether the Creeks had been properly paid for their lands, Poinsett recommended its approval. The Creek chiefs themselves had petitioned on behalf of the contract, he reported to the President, and their agent had assured the department that Creek assent had been obtained without fraud. "Nor, so far," he added, "are the United States concerned in either interest or duty to oppose an arrangement by which an excited community will be composed, floating interests rendered stable, and the settlement of Alabama advanced."[36]

Thus approximately 209,920 acres, nearly one-tenth of the lands covered by the Creek allotments, were partitioned among the speculators. The disposition of the remaining lands was for a considerable period subject to dispute, but from a different source.

The Watson contract had covered only those lands for which the contracts of purchase had been rejected. There were many more contracts whose validity was at least doubtful. Investigators Balch and Crawford had recommended the rejection of contracts in several categories. Some were objected to because they were merely "informal"; that is, they lacked a signature, a date, or some other item, the absence of which probably indi-

[35] Aside from affidavits produced by opponents of the contract the department in March received a letter from an apparently independent witness stating that the assent of the reservees had never actually been obtained. Charles F. Betton to the Secretary of War, March 23, 1839, Creek File 219, Records of the Bureau of Indian Affairs. Copies of the compromise agreements are in the same file.

[36] Poinsett to Van Buren, July 18, 1839, Creek File 218, *ibid.*

cated carelessness rather than fraud. A large group of contracts described the allotments purchased as "pine lands," calling for prices well below the $1.25 minimum, but the commissioners asserted that a more detailed description and an attestation of the value of the lands were necessary to justify the low price. Most significant and most productive of controversy was the commissioners' recommendation to reject all contracts made by persons who had been accused of fraud in depositions taken before their investigating commission.

Nearly all the contracts recommended by the commissioners for rejection were eventually sustained by the Secretary of War and approved by the President. With regard to the "informal" contracts, there had never been serious suspicion of fraud. With regard to the "pine lands" contracts, Sanford, a witness on whose word the department habitually relied, assured the President that "pine lands" was a term generally used in Georgia and Alabama to denote lands of inferior quality. Furthermore, it was argued, prices of land were much higher in 1837 when the commissioners conducted their investigation than in 1835 when the land was purchased.[37] As for the persons accused of committing frauds, there could be no doubt that some of them were guilty in some instances. But the witnesses who testified to the fraud were themselves interested in companies which were in competition with the persons whom they accused. The case of Shorter and his partners was different, since their own letters bore witness against them. But for Shorter and his associates, as well as the others, the department's final decision was to approve the original contracts except in those specific transactions where fraud could be established. Since the speculators had brought hundreds of Indians to the agent's office each day and the only witnesses available were incompetent because of interest, it would have been nearly impossible to prove fraud in specific cases. But to reject contracts wholesale on the basis of general allegations of interested witnesses would have been a violation

[37] Sanford to the President, February 4, 1839, Creek File 220, *ibid.;* Samuel P. Bascom to Harris, August 21, 1838, Creek File 216, *ibid.*

of due process and would not necessarily have done greater justice than would the sanctioning of frauds already committed.

Since many of the speculators were also local politicians, it was inevitable that some of the decisions made by the War Department on their operations would be influenced by political considerations. Usually the chain of communication was through the members of the Congressional delegation, whose re-election depended upon their ability to promote the interests of the stronger elements among their constituents and to whom in turn the national authorities looked for support in the implementation of policies. In the early stages of the Creek land controversy the Alabama delegation in Congress unquestionably influenced Secretary Cass's decision of 1832 in the interest of the settlers. In an intermediate stage the speculators offered special inducements (as in the case of Seaborn Jones) or used pressure (as in the case of Towns) on individual congressmen to gain their support. Some of the speculators were sufficiently important politically to present their case directly to the War Department and the President. While the department was forming its decisions on the company contracts during the late summer and early fall of 1839, for example, Alfred Iverson, who was deeply interested in the fortunes of the Columbus speculators as well as a power in the Democratic party in Georgia, wrote to Secretary Poinsett and to President Van Buren, urging rapid settlement of the land claims. The Georgia election, he explained, would take place in October, and it was highly important to the party that the Secretary's decisions be known, especially if they were favorable. "I know," he said, "that it would have a very important influence upon the election in the county where I reside & as the parties in the State are very equally divided, a single county may turn the scale."[38]

The story of the Creek frauds is a record of political influence and personal intrigue, but it is not enough simply to say that the government failed to fulfill its treaty obligations or that it gave

[38] Iverson to Poinsett, August 2, 1839, and Iverson to Van Buren, October 20, 1839, Joel R. Poinsett Papers, Historical Society of Pennsylvania.

aid and comfort to selfish men who sought their fortune by way of chicanery and violence. Fundamentally the higher government officials sought to apply the principles dictated by the conscience of the Americans of their generation with respect to the Indian problem, but because they were caught in the grip of motives that could not be compromised, their every act of conscience seemed to foster greater corruption and misery. While the American people generally were convinced in the 1830's that it was the destiny of the Indian to be removed from the path of the white man's advance, they believed with equal conviction that he must be fairly treated. The allotment policy was the instrument through which these incompatible convictions were to be reconciled, and its failure was the inevitable failure of self-deception—a self-deception both implemented and complicated by that generation's failure to define equity as respect for the ideas or customs sacred to the Creeks. Rather, its conception of fair treatment involved principally the protection of the individual's right of property in the land he had improved as well as protection of his right of freedom of contract. Although dispossession was necessary, it must satisfy these conditions of propriety. The Indian must be allowed to retain his improvement. If he could not do that, he must be paid for it—paid a stipulated price in a currency he hardly understood for a "right" of ownership equally foreign to his conceptions. Once paid, he must be free to dispose of his mess of pottage as he saw fit. And when this, too, passed into the hands of his exploiters and the Indian faced starvation, he could still not be forcibly removed. He could only be provoked into war which would give "justification" for his forcible removal.

As for those who gained homes and fortunes at his expense, they too were supposed to proceed according to the forms of propriety. The settler must be allowed to enter the Indian nation; but he must not be permitted to disturb the tribesmen in his improvement—until the settler was so well entrenched that he could not be evicted without civil war. As for the speculator, the architect of fraud, a pure government may never make concession to such men; conscience, and competitors, must be satisfied by examination after examination into their nefarious activities. But since the Indian must be removed and must be permitted to sell his allotted portion freely, the speculator must be encouraged to buy until he, too, was so far entrenched that the whole truth about his activities might never be known, that justice could not be done, and that expediency, the omnipresent handmaiden of the powerful, ruled by default.

·5·

THE BUSINESS
OF CREEK LAND SPECULATION

THE CONTESTS OF SPECULATORS among themselves and with the federal government are only a part of the story of speculation in Creek allotments. Investment in Indian lands was a business as well as a sport. In this chapter we shall examine the business of Creek land speculation.

The companies of speculators who monopolized the purchase of Indian allotments exercised an effective right of pre-emption to the choice lands of the Creek cession. Allotment locations took precedence over both cash sales and settlers' pre-emption rights, and the business of buying these locations was easier for a large-scale investor than for a settler. The land dealers' influence on interpreters and Indian traders gave them an essential "inside track" in buying from a people almost wholly dependent on these agents for the conduct of their business in a white man's world. Furthermore, the leading speculators, by virtue of their personal fortunes or financial connections, enjoyed superior access to ready capital. Eighty-seven per cent of the Creek allotments went to purchasers of two thousand acres or more, nearly all of whom presumably bought land for investment rather than for cultivation.

The purchasers of Indian claims were not completely uninhibited in locating the allotments. The War Department dictated that members of the same Creek town must be located in a single area, within prescribed limits. Those heads of families who had made improvements were limited to the 320-acre half-section including their houses and fields. But the exceptions to these regulations proved more important than the rules. Unmarried Indians were allowed floating claims which might be located anywhere within the general town limits. The Creek extended family included several nuclear "families" as defined by the federal locating agents. The members of these extended families generally settled so close together that a number of "heads" of the nuclear families had to take allotments apart from their improvements so that each might have a half-section. The principal government locating agents attempted to place the floating allotments so as to preserve neighborhood groupings. But a large number of the assistant locating agents were also members of land companies, and for them the important consideration was the quality of the land on which the allotment was settled and how well its location would satisfy the needs of white planters. To place an Indian's allotment far from his own neighborhood was actually advantageous to the speculator, for it meant that the Indian would be willing to sell his claim more cheaply. Furthermore, the Creek population was concentrated in the neighborhood of the best lands. The speculators had no irremediable difficulty in covering the choice spots with allotments.

The chosen lands were located mainly in the southern part of the cession. The areas contested between the Watson company and their Alabama rivals, for example, were predominantly in Macon and Tallapoosa counties, where the eastward extremity of the Black Belt intrudes upon the red and yellow soils of the coastal plain. The entire coastal plain area, with its gently rolling topography and easy access to river transportation, was popular among the land-lookers, but the prize locations within the area were the alluvial terraces above the Chattahoochee in Russell and Barbour counties. Other popular spots were southern Chambers County, which contained some of the richest soils of the

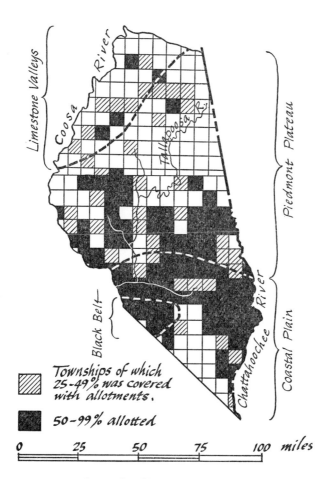

MAP 4. Location of Creek Allotments (Alabama)

Alabama piedmont, and the limestone valley of Talladega County, which gave early promise of offering "a home to the opulent, fashionable, & Gay."[1]

The fact that opulent lands were engrossed by speculators does not mean that the investors established a long-term pattern of large absentee estates. The principal object of most of the investors was rapid turnover; furthermore, many of them had em-

---

[1] Hugh Barclay *et al.* to Cass, July 31, 1833, Creek File 179, Records of the Bureau of Indian Affairs.

barked on a variety of speculations and during the panics and depression of the late thirties and early forties had to liquidate their holdings in order to pay their debts. The evidence on this point is incomplete, but what there is indicates that the largest holders of land made sizable sales immediately upon receiving title and that within twenty years most of the major operators had sold out nearly all of their speculative holdings.[2] The outstanding exception is an investor whose lands were kept off the market not as a deliberate policy but as a consequence of his bankruptcy.

The land companies operating in the Creek cession were not conceived as enduring associations. They were mainly joint-venture partnerships of men of capital, Indian traders, and land-lookers. Their membership is so overlapping that it is impossible to disentangle the precise quantity of land in which a given individual was interested. (See Table 1.) The object of organizing the companies was the pooling of influence, information, and capital and the reduction of competition. They aimed at joint purchase, followed by immediate sale or partition of the lands among the individuals interested.

The companies' capital was supplied principally by citizens of Columbus and Montgomery who had ready access to banking accommodations. Eli S. Shorter was president of the Farmer's Bank of the Chattahoochee, Columbus; James C. Watson, of the Insurance Bank of Columbus; Seaborn Jones, of the Bank of Columbus; and Daniel McDougald, of the Planters' and Mechanics' Bank of Columbus. A number of other members held large quantities of stock in the Columbus banks. Of the Alabamians, Edward Hanrick and Robert J. Ware enjoyed large accommodations at the banks of Montgomery and Mobile. Direct participation on the part of northeastern capitalists is rare, though easterners were heavy stockholders in at least two of

---

[2] Administrator's notice on the estate of William Walker, *Macon Republican* (Tuskegee), January 16, 1851; Appraisement of the estate of Alexander J. Robinson, February 10, 1834, Journal of Returns of Estates, Muscogee County, Vol. N, 241–42, and the report of his administratrix, March 2, 1868, *ibid.*, Vol. P, 479, Courthouse, Columbus, Georgia.

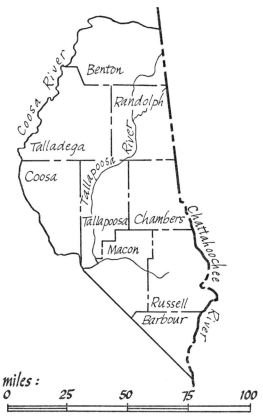

MAP 5. Original Counties of the Creek Cession

the Columbus banks, and Hanrick and McDougald derived a part of their capital from eastern merchants. In the northern part of the Creek cession, where desirable lands were more scattered and most of the allotments were sold after the frauds had run their course, smaller companies predominated. These derived their capital from wealthy settlers and their business correspondents in a number of Alabama and Georgia towns. Around the principal capitalists were grouped a constellation of lesser speculators, including the half-bloods and Indian countrymen who acted as interpreters, purchasing agents, and land-lookers in return for a share in the profits.[3]

[3] Georgia, *House Journal*, 1833, Appendix,, 106; *ibid.*, 1835-36, 360-62;

A few cases may illustrate these generalizations. The affairs of Eli S. Shorter, a planter and lawyer of Columbus, show the complexity of the speculators' business arrangements. Shorter was a member of the Columbus Land Company. In addition, with his brother James, Elijah Corley, Benjamin P. Tarver, James S. Moore, and John S. Scott, he belonged to E. Corley and Company. Shorter and John S. Scott each had a half-interest in the lands purchased by Scott in the name of Shorter and Scott, although some of the lands purchased in the name of this firm were intended for the Columbus Land Company. Shorter included Scott, an Indian countryman, in two other companies: Hill, Shorter and Company (Shorter and James H. Hill) and E. S. Shorter and Company. Then there were Shorter, Moore, and Company (Shorter, James Moore, and Milton J. Tarver); Shorter, Tarver, and Shorter (Eli S. and James Shorter and William H. Tarver); and E. E. Bissell and Company, in which the firm of Shorter, Tarver, and Shorter had an "interest."

Shorter's affairs were extricated from those of his various partners in the following manner. The Columbus Land Company and E. Corley and Company both held an early division of their lands. Shorter bought out the interests of his brother James and of James H. Hill. In 1836 he died, and his estate made a division of lands with the estate of Benjamin Tarver. His administrators settled John Scott's interest in the companies by paying Scott's estate $2,500, the extent of Scott's earlier withdrawals from com-

---

Nicholas Biddle to James C. Watson, May 2, 1837, Biddle Papers, Letterbook I, 188, Library of Congress; 11 *Georgia Reports*, 461–539; Chancery Court, Montgomery County, Final Record, Vol. K, 770–73, Courthouse, Montgomery, Alabama; Edward Hanrick to F. S. Lyon *et al.*, July 14, 1846, Hanrick Papers, Library of the University of Texas; Deed of Daniel McDougald and Alexander J. Robinson to Robert C. Connell, receiver of the Lafayette Bank, New York, November 19, 1842, Talladega Deed Book, Vol. D, 353, Courthouse, Talladega, Alabama; 8 *Alabama Reports*, 372 ff.; 16 *Alabama Reports*, 600 ff.; 17 *Alabama Reports*, 32–36; Chancery Court, Talladega County, Final Record, Vol. IV, 601–99; Vol. IX, 355–484, Courthouse, Talladega, Alabama; Articles of Agreement, Columbus Land Company, April 5, 1832, Creek File 219, Records of the Bureau of Indian Affairs; Petition of Clement Billingslea in *Billingslea* v. *Ware and Cowles*, Chancery Court, Montgomery County, Final Record (1856–57), 34–35, Courthouse, Montgomery, Alabama.

TABLE 1

DISTRIBUTION OF ORIGINAL PURCHASES OF CREEK ALLOTMENTS

James Abercrombie (Talladega); Clough; Michael J. Bulger (Tallapoosa)	11,304
Howell Rose (Wetumpka)	11,534
John Sims & Co. (Columbus, Georgia)	11,674
John Erwin and John Milton (Chambers)	12,160
William Vann, et al. (Cherokee Nation)	12,928
J. J. Fannin; Fannin & Howell (Columbus, Georgia)	14,080
Malcolm Gilchrist (Lawrence)	15,534
Alvis Q. Nicks (Talladega); Thomas Goodwin; James D. McCann	16,527
Isaac Estill; Jesse Diren (Benton); William H. Hogan (Talladega)	16,867
William McGhee	16,960
Mark E. Moore (Coosa); John Smith	19,840
John J. Worsham (Russell); James S. Calhoun (Columbus, Georgia)	21,979
Eli E. Gaither (Wetumpka); Wilie W. Mason (Wetumpka); Bird and Benjamin Young	23,598
John J. Williams, et al.	24,034
William H. Moore; James Hall (Talladega); Gideon Riddle (Talladega)	26,674
Arnold J. Seale (Macon); Gilder; John J. Williams	30,770
Robert G. Haden, et al. (Macon)	34,915
Stewart, Fontaine, & Hargroves (Columbus); W. Williams; John H. Hudson (Columbus)	41,118
C. D. Strange (Macon); Peter C. Harris (Macon); Thomas S. Woodward (Montgomery); Seaborn Jones (Columbus); John W. Freeman	46,608
Jacob T. Bradford (Talladega); William Winslett (Coosa); Joseph H. Bradford (Montgomery)	53,074
Samuel W. Mardis; Walker Reynolds; John Goodwin (all of Talladega)	59,475
Ethan Stroud; William Dougherty (La Grange, Georgia); Charles McLemore (Chambers); James Islands (Creek	

Nation); Nimrod Doyle (Creek Nation); Robert J. Ware, Thomas M. Cowles, and Clement Billingslea (all of Montgomery) 131,686

Eli S. Shorter (Columbus); Benjamin P. Tarver (Columbus); Job Taylor; Michael W. Perry (Columbus); Corley and Co.; Columbus Land Company 312,574

Alexander J. Robison (Columbus); Daniel McDougald (Columbus); Luther Blake (Creek Nation) Columbus Mills (Cheraw, S. C.); Edward Hanrick (Montgomery); Peter C. Harris (Macon); James C. Watson (Columbus) and James C. Watson and Company; William Walker (Creek Nation). 477,089

────────

1,443,002

Size:	Acreage:
160–1,999	250,536
2,000–4,999	175,603
5,000–9,999	101,183
10,000 +	1,443,002

────────

1,970,324

Note on sources and method: Creek Patents, vols. 1–11, Bureau of Land Management, Department of the Interior, must be supplemented by a list of approximately 1,000 unpatented reserves, printed in Public Lands Committee, House, Title to Creek Indian Lands in Alabama, Hearings before Committee and Subcommittee, January 10 and 16, 1912, on H 16,661 (Washington, 1912). Both these sources give the name of the first alienee and the date of the original deed. Information regarding residence is derived from Indian and General Land Office correspondence and from standard biographical sources (see Bibliography). The acreages assigned to each group represent the purchases of the named members individually, plus the purchases of various partnerships to which they belonged. Membership in interconnecting partnerships is the basis on which individuals are assigned to the same group. Where the partnerships were very large, only the members who were most active—as trustees or as individual entrymen—are listed. It is not intended to imply that each of these aggregates was managed as a whole. Since, however, it was impossible to determine the amounts of individual interests in the partnership purchases, the next best criterion seemed to be apparent community of interest in the buying of land. The total acreage of allotments given here is smaller than that usually cited for the Creek cession. The usual figure was constructed simply by multiplying the number of heads of families in the Creek census by 320, the standard acreage of a half section. A considerable number of Indians were later stricken from the list of eligibles, generally because they were not heads of families. A number of the tribesmen selected fractional half sections. These two facts probably account for the discrepancy between the 2,142,720 acres usually cited, and the total above.

pany funds being in dispute.[4] Information on these divisions indicates that Shorter himself owned more than fifty thousand acres in the Creek cession.

His investments did not lead to deliberate, long-term withholding of lands from the market. Of 38,400 acres for which we can definitely account, he himself sold 23,040 before his death in 1836, receiving an average price of $4.12 per acre. According to his administrator, this represented a net profit of $26,294.32 on an investment of $42,230.68, or 62 per cent in two years or less. In the panic times of the late thirties and early forties, his administrators succeeded in preventing a premature auction of the Alabama lands. They persuaded creditors of the Shorter estate to exercise patience by intimating that only bankruptcy could issue from trying immediately to settle their debts out of "Tallapoosa lands or some such out of the way and unsociable property."[5] With the improvement of the land market in the mid-forties, the administrators began selling. They disposed of 5,760 acres between 1843 and 1849 at an average price of $1.93 per acre. The post-1850 sales in Russell County, where the better lands were located, averaged $2.85 per acre. By 1857 the holdings of the estate had been almost completely liquidated.[6]

[4] Information on Shorter's associations is derived from *Iverson, admr.* v. *Urquhart, admr.*, Chancery Court, Russell County, Final Record, Vol. G, 299–336, Courthouse, Phenix City, Alabama; Articles of Association of E. Corley and Company, Talladega County Deed Record, Vol. B, 74–77, Courthouse, Talladega, Alabama; and Alabama Patents, Vol. 505, pp. 211–12, Vol. 509, p. 412, Vol. 506, p. 45, Vol. 512, p. 278, Bureau of Land Management, Department of the Interior.

[5] James H. Shorter to John P. King, May 19, 1844, Chancery Court, Russell County, Final Record, Vol. F, 446, *loc. cit.*

[6] Figures for the period before 1850 compiled from the testimony of Shorter's administrator in *Iverson* v. *Urquhart, loc. cit.* Urquhart filed a settlement of Shorter's Alabama estate on June 16, 1859, his return indicating only one tract as "unsold." Russell County, Records of Annual and Final Returns (1859–62), 190–95, Courthouse, Phenix City, Alabama. Statistics on Russell County sales after 1850 compiled from Russell County Deed Records, *passim.*

The case of Daniel McDougald, another Columbus speculator, illustrates the combined effect of financial panic and accumulated debt on the administration of landholdings. McDougald's most important financial commitment was to the Planters' and Mechanics' Bank of Columbus, of which he was both president and stockholder. This institution was organized in the early spring of 1837 when the stockholders paid in their 25 per cent installments on its capital stock with specie certificates issued by the Bank of Columbus. In the fall of 1837 the bank began business by making loans to its stockholders, up to the amount they had paid for the purchase of stock. Then in February, 1838, with less than $1,000 cash in its vault, the Planters' and Mechanics' Bank issued nearly $300,000 in bills. At this time, McDougald owned 2,289 shares of the bank's stock, each share having a face value of $100. Through its excessive lending the bank became completely insolvent and forfeited its charter. At the time of the forfeiture, its obligations, amounting to $230,000, were held by the Bank of Columbus. When that bank in turn failed, Edward Carey, its receiver, sued the stockholders of the Planters' and Mechanics' Bank. The Georgia courts held that they were responsible for its debts in an amount equal to the face value of the stock for which they had failed to pay—and each stockholder still owed the bank 75 per cent of the price of his stock.[7]

Nor was his obligation to the Bank of Columbus McDougald's only debt. Most of the lands he disposed of prior to his death were assigned to New York creditors. Finally, in 1846 he executed to Seaborn Jones and Robert F. Alexander a deed for trust for the payment of his remaining obligations. The items listed in this deed indicate the variety of McDougald's enterprises. They include lands in Alabama, Georgia, and Mississippi, including town lots in Columbus, Geneva, Cusseta, and Girard; an interest in the Choctaw claims; a brick store, steam press, and

[7] *Columbus Inquirer* (Columbus, Georgia), February 16, 1842; 11 *Georgia Reports*, 461–539, 550 ff.; 18 *Georgia Reports*, 411 ff.; 24 *Georgia Reports*, 17.

wharf property in Apalachicola; several Negroes; 2,565 shares in the Insurance Bank of Columbus; and claims against other land dealers amounting to $208,149.48.[8]

McDougald died in the fall of 1849 with the trust unexecuted. In January, 1851, his administrator applied for permission to sell his Alabama lands. Carey, the Bank of Columbus receiver, obtained an injunction against the sale on the ground that the property had already been assigned under deed of trust. The estate was then declared insolvent, and McDougald's administrator was assigned the job of hearing the claims of the creditors. Thus the sale of approximately 30,880 acres, much of it apparently well-located river land in Russell and Barbour counties, was postponed until the late 1860's while the creditors of the estate wrangled over who was to have first claim on the proceeds.[9]

McDougald had been a member of most of the land companies whose operations culminated in the formation of James C. Watson and Company. In its organization and functioning, this company occupied a transitional stage between the joint-venture partnership which characterized most of the land business in the Creek cession, and the New York and Boston joint-stock associations which operated contemporaneously in buying land in the Chickasaw cession. The unique feature of the Watson company's organization was that its twenty-four members assigned their interest in the company lands to James C. Watson as trustee. Therefore, although many members of the company became insolvent, its lands were not levied on to satisfy their debts.

Like the joint-venture groups, however, the Watson company sought a rapid turnover of its lands. By Watson's death in 1843, the company had sold at least 167¾ sections—in round figures, 107,360 acres. The rapid sales were exceedingly profitable. The company's total investment up to 1843, including expenses, did not much exceed $110,000. An incomplete listing of the prices

[8] Russell County Deed Record, Vol. F, 714 ff.
[9] Chancery Court, Russell County, Final Record, Vol. F, 1–180; Probate Court, Russell County, Minutes (1863–66), 496–98, (1866–68), 39, 166–67.

it received shows that it had sold 120 of the 167¾ sections on credit for $204,330.70, or an average of $2.66 per acre plus interest.

One reason for the rapid sales was that the company's operations were dictated by a few controlling members—Watson, Mc-Dougald, Joseph Fitzpatrick, Peter C. Harris, and Alfred Iverson. Probably most of these men were financially embarrassed and promoted swift sales of the lands in order to recoup their losses. Instead of keeping the notes of the company's debtors in a general fund, the agents who sold company land assigned the notes to a few influential stockholders. Ostensibly, this was to pay them for their advances to the company, but the sum of the assignments considerably exceeded the total quantity of money advanced. The contribution of the twenty-four stockholders totaled $90,000. By 1845 the notes and lands assigned McDougald, Harris, Fitzpatrick, Watson, and Peabody equaled $110,563 plus interest from the date of each note. In addition, Alfred Iverson had received $20,025 for his services as the company's attorney in Washington. Other payments for services and expenses totaled $21,213.56; payments to minor stockholders, $8,-750. Thus, of the known profits only $43,779.14 can be presumed to have been put into the general fund of the company. These figures do not reveal the amount or disposition of all the company's returns. They do indicate that the venture was profitable, although the profits were channeled mainly into the pockets of insiders.[10]

The Watson company's Alabama rivals also attempted to liquidate their investment rapidly. A central figure in this group was Robert J. Ware of Montgomery, a former physician who

[10] In *Collins* v. *Merrill, Hanrick, et al.*, Chancery Court, Macon County, Final Record, Vol. C, 522–56, Courthouse, Tuskegee, Alabama, the sales of 120 sections are recorded and the disposition of the notes indicated. Apparently this record also listed further sales, but the last six pages have been obliterated. In *Hanrick and Harris* v. *Peabody and Walker*, Chancery Court, Montgomery County, Final Record (1840–46), 525–32, Courthouse, Montgomery, Alabama, further lands are listed as sold, although no record of the grantee, time of sale, or price is given. Both these cases, which were tried in 1845–46, indicate that the sales began in 1839 and continued until Watson's death in 1843.

had forsaken the practice of medicine and "directed his energies of both body and mind to the accumulation of property." During the period of his Creek land speculations, Ware derived his capital from the profits of his plantation on the Tallapoosa, loans at Montgomery and Mobile banks, and the funds of a minor brother. In partnership with Thomas M. Cowles and Clement Billingslea, of Montgomery, he invested $17,248.09 in the purchase of twenty-nine and one-half sections. Within twelve years he had sold twenty-four and one-half sections, realizing from the sale and rental of these lands a net profit of $37,725.31, or about 18 per cent a year. In addition, he derived an income from the joint cultivation of two hundred acres of a plantation formed out of his Creek purchases. Another profitable speculation was the joint purchase by Ware, Cowles, Billingslea, and thirteen associates of fifteen sections sold by the Creek chiefs at auction in 1835. This land cost the group $35,000; by 1838 they had managed to resell it for $75,000.

Ware's associations in the land business were typically complex. He had a one-third interest in the firm of Brodnax and Coker, a one-sixth interest in each of the firms of Brodnax and Kidd, Brodnax and Whitaker, and T. W. Coker and Company, and an undefined interest in the lands of S. M. Hagerty and Company. He was a leader in the organization of Ware, Dougherty and Company and ultimately bought out the shares of several of its members. Hagerty and Company did not settle their business until 1851, at which time they had sold all but three sections of their lands. Ware, Dougherty and Company, on the other hand, auctioned off their remaining lands at a public sale in Dadeville, county seat of Tallapoosa County, in 1840. Some testimony implies that these last speculations of Ware's were unprofitable; exact figures are not available.[11]

---

[11] Petition of Robert Ware in *Ware v. Cowles*, Chancery Court, Montgomery County, Final Record, Vol. K, 770–73, Courthouse, Montgomery, Alabama; *Billingslea v. Ware and Cowles, ibid.,* (1856–57), 34–131; *Hardaway v. McGehee and Thomas*, Chancery Court, Macon County, Final Record, Vol. C, 317–21, Courthouse, Tuskegee, Alabama; Report of John B. Hogan on sales of Chiefs'

None of the investors we have considered seem to have been anxious to withhold their lands from market, and the subsequent fate of the lands indicates that this attitude represented intelligent business judgment. The settlement of the Creek cession, having begun even before the treaty of 1832, was sufficient to create a booming market for land from 1834, when the speculators began making their sales, until as late as 1839, when the Watson company unloaded the majority of its holdings. It is probable that the original speculators realized most of their profits during this period. For several years following the panic of 1839, the land market was poor indeed. If we may judge by figures obtained for Shorter's sales, lands sold during the forties and fifties brought only about enough to pay their cost plus interest and expenses. It may be, of course, that the lands which sold at later dates were inferior in quality or location to those sold earlier.

The policy of rapid sale, however, does not mean that all the speculative holdings were sold immediately to settlers, since secondary speculators took a considerable share in the buying. But it does mean that the lands were available to settlers who were willing to offer three or four times the government minimum price in the thirties or 50 to 150 per cent of the $1.25 minimum in the forties and fifties. The high prices charged for lands in the boom period, as indicated by Shorter's and Ware's returns, may have contributed to the failure of a number of land buyers. This would be hard to demonstrate, since the transaction by which the settler transferred his bond for title to another buyer—or back to the seller—was not usually recorded in the deed books. An advertisement like the following is suggestive:[12]

Cotton Lands for Sale

The subscribers offer for sale 22,000 acres of land, lying mostly in different parts of Macon County, Alabama. They comprise almost

Lands, October, 1835, Creek File 205, Records of the Bureau of Indian Affairs; Peter Brannon, "Old Ware P. O.," *Montgomery Advertiser*, October 9, 1933.

[12] *Columbus Enquirer* (Columbus, Georgia), July 24, 1844.

every variety, and some of them are as good cotton Lands as can be found in the State. A portion of these lands were selected by one of the subscribers in the very first settlement of the country, and are very desirable. Among them are lands which were purchased and improved by persons who were embarrassed and failed to pay. Of this class are

5 plantations of 640 acres each;

2   *"*   of 1,280   *"*   *"*

2   *"*   of 320   *"*   *"*

in a high state of cultivation, with all necessary appurtenances. . . .

James Dent

Homer Blackman

George Stone.

The partition of the Creek allotments among speculators apparently established no permanent pattern of huge landed estates. A number of the speculators owned large plantations within the cession, but original land speculation was not the primary means of establishing them. Both the land companies and the holding of large acreages were intended to be temporary. Land speculation enters in only as one of many short-term ventures by which enterprising businessmen might turn credit into profit. Like other such ventures, it produced both fortunes and bankruptcies. Both were produced at the expense of the supposed beneficiaries of the allotment policy—the Indian and the settler.

·6·

CAPITAL
IN CHICKASAW SPECULATION

IN THE PRECEDING CHAPTERS we examined the course and consequence of speculation in Choctaw and Creek allotment claims. Dealings with both tribes were marked by bitter conflict within the speculative fraternity and by frauds which the government found it impossible to prevent. Speculators also acquired most of the Chickasaw allotments; but in this instance conflicts among investors were relatively insignificant, and the Chickasaws received what were deemed "fair" prices for the lands they sold.

The more orderly execution of the Chickasaw treaty may be attributed to the hard lessons the government learned among the Choctaws and Creeks. There was little hypocrisy in the Chickasaw agreement. The tribesmen were to have allotments, but only as temporary homes from which they were committed to remove as soon as possible. For this reason, there was no opening for serious disagreement over registration procedures, no invidious distinction made between those who "intended" and those who "did not intend" to emigrate. Furthermore, since the Chickasaws were committed in advance to emigration, there was no need for special finagling to force them to bargain away their allotments. From the beginning they were expected to sell them, and the government could therefore turn all its attention

From McKenney and Hall, *The Indian Tribes of North America*

Speaker of the upper towns of the Creek Nation, Opothleyahola was a leading figure in negotiations leading to the Treaty of Washington, 1832; later he led the friendly Creek warriors in the Creek War of 1837.

From McKenney and Hall, *The Indian Tribes of North America*

The execution of Creek Chief William McIntosh for signing the Treaty of Indian Springs in 1825 warned other tribal leaders against further cessions of Creek lands.

to assuring them a fair return on the sale. Even the fiction of the individual Indian as a rational, economic man was abandoned, and a committee of the more sophisticated tribesmen supervised the sale of lands belonging to those thought "incompetent" to manage their own affairs.

Perhaps even more important than modifications in governmental practice was the abundance of capital available for investment in the Chickasaw lands. This abundance reflected the upward trend in the business cycle during the mid-thirties, especially the rapidly rising price of cotton.

In April, 1835, a retired New York merchant with a shrewd eye for business conditions observed in his diary: "Money is plenty, business is brisk, the staple commodity of the country (cotton) has enriched all those through whose hands it has passed, the merchant, mechanic, and proprietor of land all rejoice in the result of last year's operations."[1] Philip Hone was recording the beginning of a business boom which lasted from the second quarter of 1835 to the third quarter of 1837. Cotton, the chief export, brought steadily higher prices. From enterprising British importers of the staple, New York merchants acquired "open credits" to finance their growing export trade. These merchants invested not only in cotton, but also in cotton lands.

They were encouraged in their investment by the government's policy of opening new areas for sale and settlement as quickly as possible. The land boom of 1835–37 was a general phenomenon. Not only in Mississippi and Alabama, but also in Illinois, Indiana, Michigan, and Wisconsin, the offering of government lands and the establishment of new farms, cities, banks, and railroads seemed to promise generous returns to the venturesome capitalist. In northern Mississippi, the government offered at public sale between 1837 and 1838 nearly half the area of the state. Public land sales in the peak year, 1836, totaled 3,267,-299.33 acres. (See Table 6.) Even this figure understates the extent of the Mississippi land boom, for in 1836, title to the

[1] *The Diary of Philip Hone, 1828–1837* (ed. by Allan Nevins), I, 154.

greater part of more than two million acres of Chickasaw allotments passed into the hands of speculators.

These speculators were more concerned with security of title than with minimizing the prices they paid. The lands being offered in Alabama, Mississippi, and Arkansas in the 1830's were believed to be among the last well-located cotton lands in what was then the public domain. Capitalists invested in these lands with the expectation that they might be resold immediately at five to ten dollars an acre, and that, with the exhaustion of older lands, they would continue to appreciate in value. With these prospects, they were willing to pay the Chickasaws the $1.25 an acre which the government deemed a fair price—or even twice that amount.

As in the case of the Creeks, the capitalists of the Chickasaw cession found it advantageous to ally with the Indian traders, using them as middlemen in their dealings with the tribesmen. Indeed, the Indian traders were the first to venture into the game of buying from the Chickasaws. They went into action in the summer and fall just following the negotiation of the 1834 treaty. Like their predecessors in the Creek cession, they did not immediately buy full title to the Indian allotments. Operating on a small capital, they made advances to the Chickasaws in money or "store account" in return for bonds obligating the sellers to convey title to their lands. In November, 1834, a Tennessee land agent wrote his employer that on the prairies of eastern Mississippi, "the better part of the good lands" had already been engrossed.[2]

The principal engrossers were organized into two associations, known respectively as "Gordon and Bell" and "The Chickasaw Company." Robert Gordon and John Bell lived in Cotton Gin Port, the principal shipping point on the upper Tombigbee River, adjacent to the Chickasaw cession. Gordon was a merchant and lawyer whose services to the tribe had been rewarded in the treaty of 1834 with a section of land. Bell, son of a former

[2] James Brown to James K. Polk, November 4, 1834, Polk Papers, Library of Congress.

missionary to the Chickasaws, had been associated with early efforts to encourage the tribe to emigrate. Presumably as a reward for services rendered, he was appointed surveyor-general of the Chickasaw cession. This position gave him unique access to information on the location of desirable lands. Bell and his partner hired prominent half-bloods as interpreters, opened a store account for their Indian clients, and proceeded to acquire, at an average price of less than ten dollars a section, claims to more than six hundred 640-acre sections of land.[3] The "claims" consisted in bonds for title to lands which were yet to be located. The Indian seller promised to convey his title, usually at a stipulated price, or at a "fair" price or appraised price, after the allotments had been located and the government had appointed an agent who could certify contracts.

Gordon and Bell acted as land agents rather than as investors. In November of 1834 they enlarged their potential operating capital to $150,000 by going into partnership with a group of Natchez businessmen, most prominent of whom was James Wilkins, president of the Planters' Bank. Ten months later, the partnership sold out their claims to 310,371 acres of land to Henry Anderson and Edward Orne.[4] Both Anderson and Orne were agents of eastern investors. Anderson, formerly of Florence, Alabama, represented the American Land Company, a million-dollar unincorporated joint-stock association which had been organized in New York in the spring of 1835. Orne, a Salem sea captain, represented three joint-stock companies: the Boston and Mississippi Cotton Land Company, the Boston and New York Chickasaw Land Company, and the New York, Mississippi, and Arkansas Land Company. The combined capital of these three companies was reputed to be $850,000.[5] Both Anderson and

[3] Horatio B. Cushman, *History of the Chickasaw, Choctaw, and Natchez Indians*, 514; Chancery Court, Northern District of Mississippi, Final Record, Vol. M, 235–37, Chancery Clerk's Office, Holly Springs, Mississippi.
[4] Articles of Agreement, December 20, 1834, Joseph Vidal Papers, Louisiana State University Archives; Chancery Court, Northern District of Mississippi, Final Record, Vol. M, 194–275, *loc. cit.*
[5] American Land Company, *First Annual Report* . . . ; A. M. Sakolski, *The Great American Land Bubble*; Irene Neu, "A Business Biography of Erastus

Orne made purchases from smaller traders, as well as from Gordon and Bell. They continued to buy allotments and trust lands in the Chickasaw cession until 1838. The American Land Company bought a total of 210,658 acres of Chickasaw allotments; Orne's companies, 334,602.39.[6] The two agents were responsible for the purchase of approximately a quarter of all the allotments.

The Chickasaw Company, the second largest association of the traders buying directly from the Indians, also acted as an agency for eastern investors. David Hubbard, an Alabama congressman, headed this group. John Tindall, president of the branch of the Bank of the State of Alabama at Tuscaloosa, was probably its principal financial backer, and Thomas Coopwood, a professional merchant, its chief contact agent with the tribesmen. The Chickasaw Company sold the greater part of its holdings to Richard Bolton, agent of the New York and Mississippi Land Company, which eventually acquired a total of 206,787 acres in allotments.[7]

Joint-stock associations of eastern investors acquired nearly 35 per cent of the Chickasaw allotments. Most of the remainder went to individual speculators purchasing from 10,000 to 75,000 acres. Although the lands were generally certified as sold to one individual or a partnership of two, a number of the buyers probably represented some sort of joint-venture partnership or managed to sell their interest to such a group after the lands were certified to them. But there is little evidence that individual interests in the various companies were as complex as those in the Creek cession had been. One reason for this is that the traders

---

Corning," (Unpublished Doctoral Dissertation, Cornell, 1950), 183–95; Richard Bolton to Lewis Curtis, October 15, 1835, Papers of the New York and Mississippi Land Company, State Historical Society of Wisconsin; Same to Same, October 30, 1835, *ibid.;* Works Progress Administration, Writer's Project, Assignment No. 15, Mississippi Department of Archives and History; Chancery Court, Northern District of Mississippi, Vol. M, 194–275, *loc. cit.*

[6] Estimated by compiling data from William Carroll, List of Certified Contracts, Special File, Chickasaw, Records of the Bureau of Indian Affairs; Chickasaw Location Book, Records of the Bureau of Land Management; and Edward Orne, Land Book, Mississippi Department of Archives and History.

[7] *Ibid.;* Richard Bolton, "Account of sales . . . ," May, 1845; Bolton to Curtis, July 27, 1835, Papers of the New York and Mississippi Land Company.

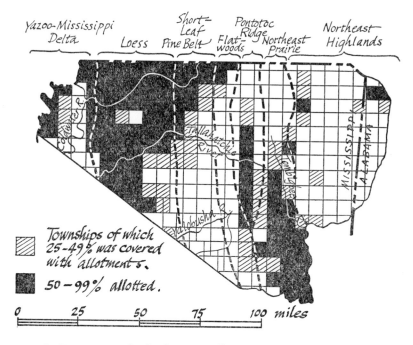

Yazoo-Mississippi Delta — Loess — Short-Leaf Pine Belt — Pontotoc Ridge — Flat-woods — Northeast Prairie — Northeast Highlands

☒ Townships of which 25-49% was covered with allotments.

■ 50-99% allotted.

0   25   50   75   100 miles

MAP 6. Location of Chickasaw Allotments (Mississippi)

did not depend primarily on wealthy individuals in one or two towns to supply their capital. For example, Daniel Saffarans, a Gallatin, Tennessee, merchant, appears to have drawn largely on the Union Bank of Tennessee; David Storke acquired his funds from associates in North Carolina; Thomas Niles sold the greater part of his land, through an associate in Mobile, to a New York company; Patrick H. Prout, of Tuscumbia, Alabama, was a considerable merchant and planter on his own account.[8] Furthermore, the convergence of large quantities of capital on the Chickasaw cession meant that buyers could offer "fair" prices to

[8] De Soto County Deed Records, Vol. D, 131, Chancery Clerk's Office, Hernando, Mississippi; Deed of Theophilus Storke to Charles Fisher, Trustee, October, 1838, Charles Fisher Papers, Southern Historical Collection, University of North Carolina; Chancery Court, Northern District of Mississippi, Final Record, Vol. K, 193–343; Samuel J. Riggs to Riggs, Son and Aertson, February 8, 1835, Letters Received, 1835, Riggs Papers, Library of Congress.

119

the Indians. They had no need to connive at fraud nor to bring partners into their companies to save themselves from exposure or competition.

Although the allotments claimed only a little more than one-third of the area of the Chickasaw cession, the speculators' possession of these claims gave them, as in the case of the Creeks, a virtual pre-emption right to choice lands in the district. Officially, the allotments were to be located by the Chickasaw agent. The treaty stipulated further that the allotments of heads of families must be confined to the section containing the improvements. Actually, however, the purchasers had considerable freedom. Generally they purchased not specific sections of land, but claims which were as yet unlocated. If it could be shown that the Indian's house and field were not on "good average agricultural land" or if, as was often the case, two or more "heads of families" lived on the same section, the allotments might be located apart from the tribesman's improvements. All the allotments for single adults were "floating claims." The Chickasaw agent estimated that without aid he would need twelve years to search out nearly four thousand sections of "good, average agricultural land" for the Indian owners.[9] He therefore welcomed the assistance of traders and land-lookers, and they gave as gladly as he received. The government reserved the bottoms along the Mississippi and Tombigbee rivers to offer at public sale as tribal trust lands. Aside from this reservation, the speculators were able to concentrate their locations in areas where good land predominated: on the black prairie soils of the eastern counties, on the calcareous red loam of the Pontotoc ridge, and westward, on the fertile and friable brown loam of the loess region.

The federal official charged with "certifying" Indian deeds was as co-operative as the locating agent. Deeds transferring title from Indians could be validated only by the President's approval, given by his appointed agent. This agent was required to affirm

[9] Benjamin Reynolds to Lewis Cass, October 24, 1835, 24 Cong., 1 sess., *Sen. Doc. 425*, 353–54.

that the Indian was in fact the owner of the land described in the deed, and that he, the agent, had witnessed the payment which the deed specified. William Carroll, appointed agent for approving or "certifying" the deeds, could naturally not begin his work until the allotments had been located. This meant that generally, the allotment claims had been purchased by Indian traders, resold to investors, and located with the aid of these investors before the deed for the land in question was "certified" —that is, before buyers obtained a secure title. In December, 1835, after most of the reserves had been purchased, resold, and located, Secretary of War Lewis Cass ordered that no contract be approved until March, 1836, and that no deed signed prior to that date might be certified. The object of the requirement was apparently to assure the Chickasaws a fair price for their allotments. But the Chickasaw speculators feared that the order would encourage "understrappers" to buy claims which had already been purchased by others. If this were to happen, the first buyers would lose not only their claims to land, but also the advances they had made to the tribesmen in order to secure the bonds for title. To avoid this catastrophe, they employed the month of March in renegotiating contracts and formed a kind of speculator's claim association, composed mainly of "old buyers," to settle disputes. Agent Carroll co-operated with the association by refusing to settle contested claims and referring disputants to "the committee."[10]

Carroll himself was reputed to have made a tidy fortune in Chickasaw land speculation, and his sympathy with the speculative fraternity was natural.[11] But his co-operation with them need not be attributed to interest or depravity. The land com-

[10] Richard Bolton to Trustees, May 5, 1835, Papers of the New York and Mississippi Land Company; T. P. Moore *et al.* to Lewis Cass, December 28, 1835, Chickasaw File 85; Lewis Cass, "Regulations . . . ," Chickasaw Letter-book, Vol. A, 77–78; Memorial of Malcolm Gilchrist, December 10, 1846; Memorial of Felix Walker, n.d., Chickasaw File 86, Records of the Bureau of Indian Affairs; Chancery Court, Northern District of Mississippi, Final Record, Vol. A, 111, *loc. cit.*

[11] Alfred Balch to James K. Polk, June 15, 1838, Polk Papers, Library of Congress.

panies had lobbied in Washington to obtain a commissioner of known integrity so that his approval might "give tone" to their operations. As has been indicated, these men were more concerned with security of title than with minimizing the price offered for allotments. The prices they paid in pursuance of their renegotiated contracts, while only a fraction of those they currently charged their own customers, generally exceeded the President's stipulated "fair price"—the $1.25 an acre minimum charged for public lands. Carroll's reports of the sales of 3,504.5 sections between April, 1836, and February, 1838, show that the speculators gave an average of $1.70 an acre.[12] Undoubtedly they paid part of the sum in "store accounts" for goods subject to an unusually high markup, but this was never a matter the government considered worthy of its attention. Perhaps most important was Carroll's anxiety that conflicts among speculators be settled privately, so that no such charges and countercharges of fraud as those emerging from the battles over the Creek lands should mar his administration of the Chickasaw business. His main concern, he wrote the President, was that Jackson should be given no trouble in the matter.[13]

The sale of Chickasaw allotments was therefore characterized by co-operation among speculators in adjusting disputes among themselves. The margin between the required minimum price and the average price the speculators gave shows that some price competition prevailed among the buyers of allotments. Four factors probably account for the difference between this and the Creek case: the anxiety of the government to prevent a repetition of the Creek frauds, the more sophisticated business methods of the agents of eastern capitalists, the abundance of their capital, and their primary concern with secure title.

As the upward phase of the business cycle conditioned the purchase of Chickasaw lands, the long downswing following the panics of 1837 and 1839 affected their resale. In some respects the process of liquidation resembled that in the Creek cession.

[12] Compiled from Carroll's List of Certified Contracts, loc. cit.
[13] Carroll to Jackson, August 13, 1836, Jackson Papers, Library of Congress.

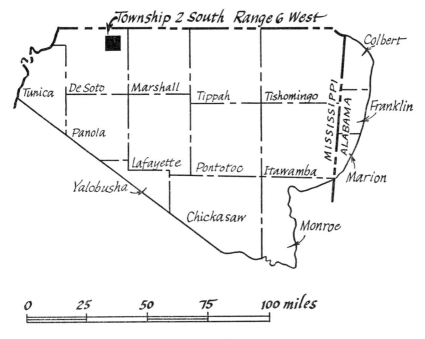

MAP 7. Original Counties of the Chickasaw Cession

Some agents died, and there were delays while interests were partitioned and orders for sale given by probate courts. Agents and principals came into conflict over their respective rights, and partnership accounts were settled by the sale of lands at auction. Individuals went bankrupt and their holdings into the hands of trustees or creditors. But the sales of the joint-stock associations followed a different pattern. These companies did not divide their assets among their members. Their shares represented claims not on land, but on the dividends of the association. The sale of their lands, therefore, was neither hampered nor accelerated by the financial distress of the original shareholders.[14]

[14] Many of the principal shareholders were connected with two ill-fated New York banks; the New York Banking Company and the North American Trust and Banking Company. Joseph D. Beers, trustee of the New York and Mississippi Land Company and principal shareholder of the American Land Company, was president of the North American Trust and Banking Company.

Assessing the profitability of the Mississippi speculation to these original shareholders would be difficult. For many of them, stock in land companies figured only as assets assignable in bankruptcy. In no case is the record sufficient to enable us to discover both the total expenditure and the total returns of any company. Statistics of sale prices compiled for three counties of the Chickasaw cession indicate that the lands almost always sold for more than they cost, and usually returned at least 100 per cent on the original investment.[15] But this return often came over a period of more than twenty years. In the meantime, taxes must be paid, agents must be reimbursed, and their office expenses maintained. The sober merchants and lawyers who directed the companies certainly failed to receive profits either as immediate or as generous as the springtime boom of 1835 had led them to anticipate.

There are several reasons for this shortage of profits. Immediate returns required a constant rise in the price of land. This might come from two sources: lands might be traded among speculators, purchases being made primarily for the speculative gains anticipated from resale, or they might be sold to cultivators. The panic and depression of the late thirties and early forties dampened enthusiasm and limited credit for speculative purchasing; the pace of settlement in the Chickasaw cession was too slow to provide an immediate market for all the land among resident farmers and planters. Even in areas where lands were offered at the $1.25 government minimum price, it was seldom that most of them were included in farms within the first few years after the areas were opened to settlement. In the Chicka-

John Delafield, first president of the New York and Mississippi Land Company, became in 1838 president of the New York Banking Company. Both banks ultimately went into receivership, and hundreds of shares in the Mississippi land companies went into the trust funds formed out of their assets to reimburse their creditors. Chancery Court, Northern District of Mississippi, Vol. B, 62–94; 13 *Smedes and Marshall*, 153–57; Joseph Dorfman, "A Note on the Interpretation of Anglo-American Finance, 1837–41," *Journal of Economic History*, Vol. IX (1950), 140–47.

[15] James W. Silver, "Land Speculation Profits in the Chickasaw Cession," *Journal of Southern History*, Vol. X (1944), 88.

saw cession, where investors held unimproved lands in hopes of receiving $2.50 to $5.00 an acre, it was even more unlikely that settlers would soon purchase all the available area.

Several factors limited the settlers' ability to buy land. Many pioneers needed long-term credit to finance farm-making; such credit was not usually available. The diversion of credit to speculation by the state banks during the boom period was notorious. Land companies customarily offered a credit of "one, two, and three years," to potential buyers. Few companies cared to sue for the recovery of land, even on the expiration of three years, when there was prospect of collecting at a later date. But Chancery Court records show that a buyer's prolonged failure to make payments might overcome their reluctance.[16] Furthermore, the solvency of farmer-debtors depended on the profitable sale of their principal cash crop, cotton. Following the panic of 1837, the price of cotton collapsed. Finally, the cottongrower in quest of a homestead was not limited to the Chickasaw cession. The unoccupied public lands of Alabama, the Choctaw cession, and Arkansas, plus cheap lands, public and private, in the Republic of Texas were open to him. Despite the predictions of the speculators, northern Mississippi was not cotton's last frontier.

And so it came about that the Chickasaw country was settled slowly, and the liquidation of original speculative holdings required more than twenty-five years. But the initial pattern of land disposal did not, as reformers seemed to predict, eternally fix the pattern of land tenure. That design was formed in a complex process which the initial engrossment of land may have affected but did not determine.

This process may be illustrated by an examination of the history of ante-bellum tenure in De Soto County, in the northwestern part of the Chickasaw cession. Approximately 90 per cent of the soil in this county is in the "loess" or "brown loam" cat-

[16] This generalization is based on a study of pre-Civil War Final Records of the Northern District Chancery Courts sitting at Hernando and Holly Springs, Mississippi, and of the scattered volumes of the Final Records of the Federal District Court which met at Pontotoc, Mississippi. These records are in the courthouses at Hernando, Holly Springs, and Pontotoc.

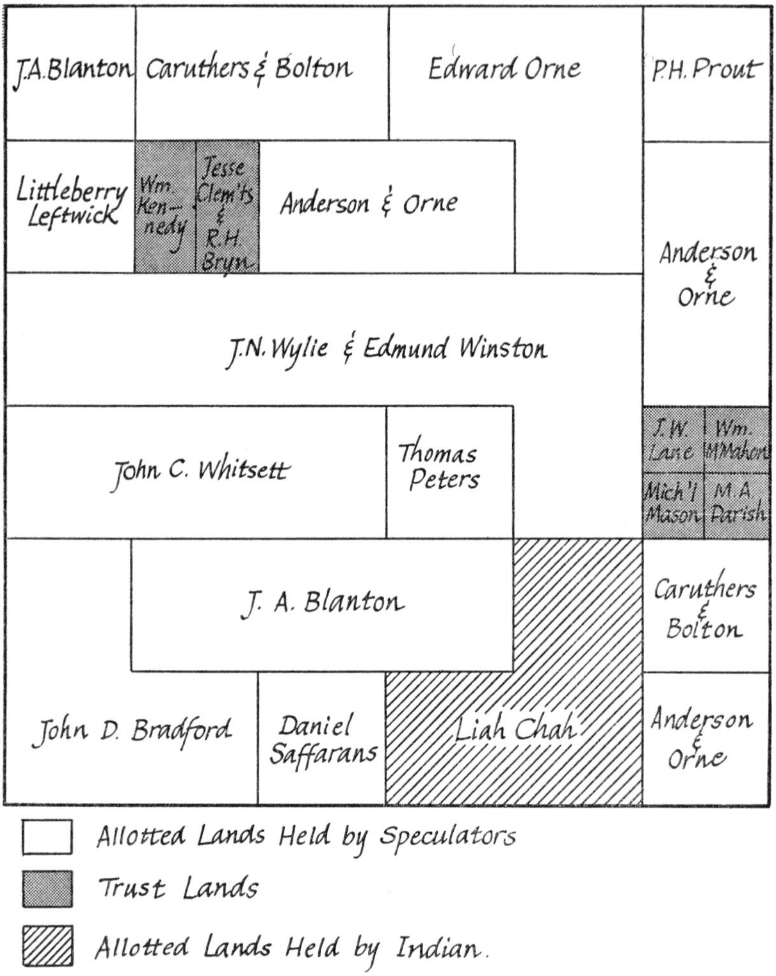

| J.A. Blanton | Caruthers & Bolton | Edward Orne | P.H. Prout |

Littleberry Leftwick | Wm. Kennedy | Jesse Clem'ts & R.H. Bryn | Anderson & Orne

Anderson & Orne

J.N. Wylie & Edmund Winston

John C. Whitsett | Thomas Peters

J.W. Lane | Wm. MMahon
Mich'l Mason | M.A. Parish

J. A. Blanton

Caruthers & Bolton

John D. Bradford | Daniel Saffarans | Liah Chah. | Anderson & Orne

Allotted Lands Held by Speculators

Trust Lands

Allotted Lands Held by Indian.

MAP 8. T2S R6W—Original Entries and Allotment Purchases—1836

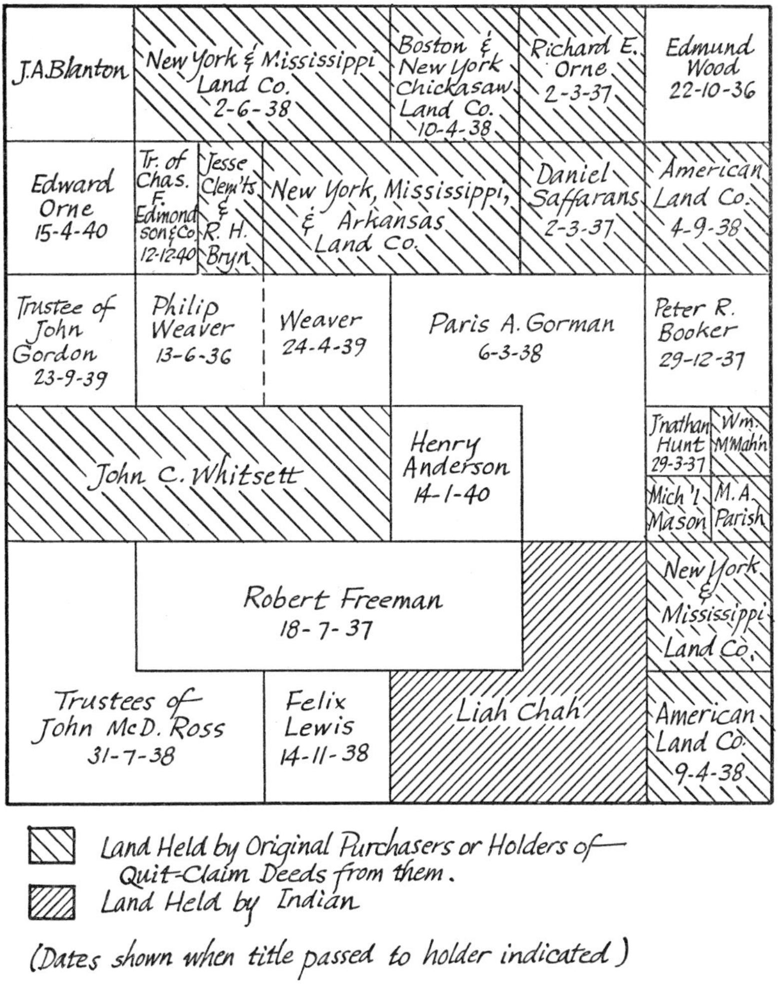

J.A.Blanton	New York & Mississippi Land Co. 2-6-38	Boston & New York Chickasaw Land Co. 10-4-38	Richard E. Orne 2-3-37	Edmund Wood 22-10-36
Edward Orne 15-4-40	Tr. of Chas. F. Edmondson&Co 12-12-40 / Jesse Clem'ts & R.H. Bryn	New York, Mississippi, & Arkansas Land Co.	Daniel Saffarans 2-3-37	American Land Co. 4-9-38
Trustee of John Gordon 23-9-39	Philip Weaver 13-6-36	Weaver 24-4-39	Paris A. Gorman 6-3-38	Peter R. Booker 29-12-37
John C. Whitsett		Henry Anderson 14-1-40		Jnathan Hunt 29-3-37 / Wm. MMahn / Mich'l Mason / M.A. Parish
	Robert Freeman 18-7-37			New York & Mississippi Land Co.
Trustees of John McD. Ross 31-7-38	Felix Lewis 14-11-38	Liah Chah		American Land Co. 9-4-38

Land Held by Original Purchasers or Holders of Quit=Claim Deeds from them.

Land Held by Indian

(Dates shown when title passed to holder indicated)

MAP 9. T2S R6W—Original Entries and Allotment Purchases— December, 1840

127

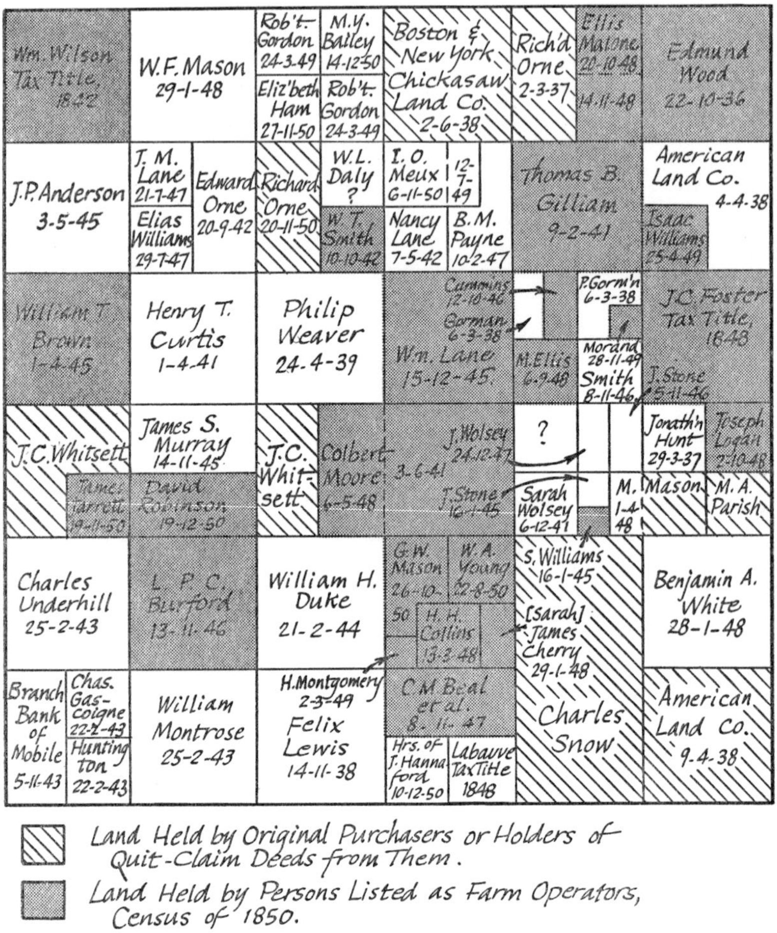

Land Held by Original Purchasers or Holders of
Quit-Claim Deeds from Them.

Land Held by Persons Listed as Farm Operators,
Census of 1850.

MAP 10. T2S R6W—Original Entries and Allotment Purchases—
December, 1850

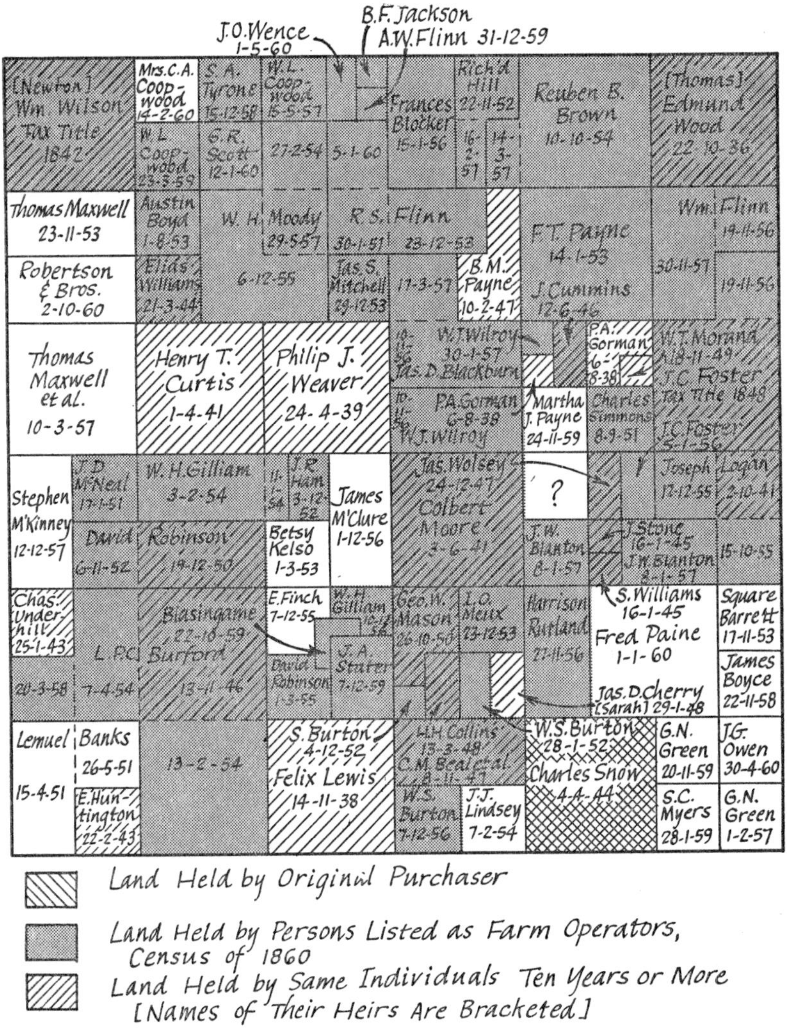

J.O.Wence 1-5-60

B.F.Jackson
A.W.Flinn 31-12-59

[Newton] Wm. Wilson Tax Title 1842

Mrs.C.A. Coopwood 14-2-60
W.L. Coopwood 15-5-59
S.A. Tyrone 15-12-58
W.L. Coopwood 15-5-57

Frances Blocker 15-1-56

Rich'd Hill 22-11-52

Reuben B. Brown 10-10-54

[Thomas] Edmund Wood 22-10-36

W.L. Coopwood 23-3-59
G.R. Scott 12-1-60
27-2-54 | 5-1-60
16- 14- 2- 3- 57 57

Thomas Maxwell 23-11-53

Austin Boyd 1-8-53
W. H. Moody 29-5-57
R.S. Flinn 30-1-51
23-12-53

F.T. Payne 14-1-53

Wm. Flinn 19-11-56

Robertson & Bros. 2-10-60

Elias Williams 21-3-44
6-12-55
Jas.S. Mitchell 29-12-53
17-3-57
B.M. Payne 10-2-47
J.Cummins 12-6-46
30-11-57 | 19-11-56

Thomas Maxwell et al. 10-3-57

Henry T. Curtis 1-4-41

Philip J. Weaver 24-4-39

W.T.Wilroy 30-1-57
Jas. D.Blackburn
P.A.Gorman 6-8-38
W.T.Wilroy
Martha J. Payne 24-11-59
Charles Simmons 8-9-51
P.A. Gorman 6-1-21
J.C. Foster 8-38
W.T.Morand 18-11-49
Tax Title 1848
J.C.Foster 5-1-56

Stephen M'Kinney 12-12-57

J.D. M'Neal 17-1-51
David 6-11-52
W.H.Gilliam 3-2-54
Robinson 19-12-50
J.R. Ham 3-12-54
Betsy Kelso 1-3-53
James M'Clure 1-12-56

Jas.Wolsey 24-12-47
Colbert Moore 3-6-41

?

J.W. Blanton 8-1-57

Joseph Logan 17-12-55 | 2-10-41
J.Stone 16-1-45
J.W.Blanton 2-1-57
15-10-55

Chas. Underhill 25-1-43
20-3-58
L.P.C.Burford 7-4-54
Blasingame 22-10-59
13-11-46
E.Finch 7-12-55
W.H. Gilliam
David Robinson 1-3-55
J.A. Stater 7-12-59
Geo.W. Mason 26-10-50
J.O. Meux 23-12-53
Harrison Rutland 27-11-56
S.Williams 16-1-45
Fred Paine 1-1-60
Jas.D.Cherry [sarah] 29-1-48
Square Barrett 17-11-53
James Boyce 22-11-58

Lemuel Banks 26-5-51
15-4-51
E.Huntington 22-2-43
13-2-54
S.Burton 4-12-52
Felix Lewis 14-11-38
L.H.Collins 13-3-48
C.M.Beal et al. 18-11-57
W.S. Burton 7-12-56
J.J. Lindsey 1-2-54
W.S.Burton 28-1-52
Charles Snow 4-4-44
G.N. Green 20-11-59
S.C. Myers 28-1-59
J.G. Owen 30-4-60
G.N. Green 1-2-57

Land Held by Original Purchaser

Land Held by Persons Listed as Farm Operators, Census of 1860

Land Held by Same Individuals Ten Years or More [Names of Their Heirs Are Bracketed]

MAP 11. T2S R6W—Original Entries and Allotment Purchases—December, 1860

129

egory. This type of soil was particularly attractive to early settlers, for it was both fertile and easy to till. Indian allotments lay thick over the brown loam area of the cession, and speculative holdings were large.

Their liquidation may be illustrated in miniature by the history of a single township within the county—Township Two, Range Six West.[17] We shall consider four maps. The first indicates the pattern of landholding in 1836, when the allotments were sold. The names on the plats are those of the first purchasers from the Indians or the government. The average size of holdings is very large. Only one of the owners, J. W. Blanton, ever appeared on a federal census as a "farm operator" in De Soto county. Since we have no list of farm operators until 1850, this does not prove that all the lands in the township were held for speculation. But that hypothesis is supported by the fact that most of the entrymen shown on the plat were large-scale land dealers. (See list, Table 2.)

In 1840, though there has been some turnover, large speculative holdings still predominate. By 1850 the original speculators' holdings have diminished considerably. The New York and Mississippi Land Company has completely sold out, as have Blanton, Bradford, Leftwick, Prout, Saffarans, and Wilie and

[17] This township may not be "representative" in a statistical sense. Government surveyors classified much of it as "poor and hilly." While their judgments were notoriously not definitive, the fact that the number of farmers increased in this area while the number for the county as a whole diminished (1850-60) probably indicates that it was settled relatively late and tends to corroborate the judgment that this was, for De Soto County, an area of relatively poor land. The purpose of the township study and of the diagrams is simply to illustrate the devolution of speculative holdings in an area where most original entries and purchases of Indian allotments were made by speculators. The information on which this study is based is derived from the De Soto County Abstract Record and Deed Books, Chancery Clerk's Office, Hernando, Mississippi. The dates given on the plats represent the time when title passed to the designated holder of the land, not necessarily the time when he purchased it. Generalizations concerning cultivation and the size of the units the operators held are based on a comparison of the names on the plats with the Seventh and Eighth Censuses, 1850 and 1860, Schedule IV, "Productions of Agriculture," Mississippi Department of Archives and History.

TABLE 2

DISTRIBUTION OF ORIGINAL PURCHASES OF CHICKASAW ALLOTMENTS
(Patented Lands)

Entries over 10,000 acres:

American Land Company	210,658.49
New York and Mississippi Land Company	206,787.42
Edward Orne, mainly for	
Boston and New York Chickasaw Land Company	
Boston and Mississippi Cotton Land Company	
New York, Mississippi, and Arkansas Land Company	334,602.39
Armisted Barton, Tuscaloosa, Alabama	73,417.87
John D. Bradford, Pontotoc, Mississippi	48,470.19
James Brown, Oxford, Mississippi	30,641.31
Goodloe W. Buford	16,787.48
Joseph Caruthers	52,901.92
Wilson T. Caruthers, Holly Springs, Mississippi	75,480.67
Ruffin Coleman, Athens, Alabama	10,047.34
Henry Cook, Pontotoc, Mississippi	22,819.51
William Crain, Marshall County, Mississippi	15,439.66
William H. Duke, Monroe County, Mississippi	15,380.18
David Hubbard, Florence, Alabama	20,038.70
Andrew Kerr, Richmond County, Georgia,	
Tunica County, Mississippi (1838)	14,389.97
Charles W. Martin, Pontotoc, Mississippi	12,353.45
Joseph W. Matthews, Marshall County, Mississippi	11,014.44
Samuel Mc Corkle, Henry County, Tennessee	
Holly Springs, Mississippi	15,964.90
Erasmus P. McDowell, Bolivar, Tennessee	
Pontotoc, Mississippi	21,989.63
Felix Lewis, Columbus, Georgia	11,127.78
Wyatt C. Mitchell	37,339.08
Thomas N. Niles, Mobile, Alabama	
Pontotoc, Mississippi	48,867.42
Thomas Peters, Marshall County, Mississippi	22,622.88
Joel Pinson, Pontotoc, Mississippi	10,869.98
Abner Prewett, Aberdeen, Mississippi	14,119.52

Patrick H. Prout, Tuscumbia, Alabama	15,423.04
Daniel Saffarans, Gallatin, Tennessee	71,120.61
David Storke, Pontotoc, Mississippi	19,099.70
John L. Tindall, Tuscaloosa, Alabama	
Aberdeen, Mississippi	10,046.67
John C. Whitsett, Gainesville, Alabama	55,897.94
John Wightman	11,221.08
John N. Wyllie, Aberdeen, Mississippi	18,738.86
Edmund Winston	15,713.76

1,576,484.33

Size of Entry:	Acreage Entered:
0-499	11,854.02
500-999	89,414.45
1,000-1,999	124,362.33
2,000-4,999	160,167.70
5,000-9,999	176,906.06

562,705.56

Notes on Sources and Method:
   William Carroll's list of Approved Deeds in the Chickasaw Reserve File, National Archives, lists owners to whom deeds were approved. The size of each section was derived from the Chickasaw Location Book. Additional information was derived from Edward Orne's Land Book, Mississippi Department of Archives and History, and the Papers of the New York and Mississippi Land Company, State Historical Society of Wisconsin. Orne's deeds were certified in part to "Anderson and Orne." By comparing the list of lands certified to this partnership with Orne's list, it was possible to separate the two interests. The same procedure was followed in deriving the holdings of the New York and Mississippi Land Company, which were certified under the names of Wilson T. Caruthers and Richard Bolton. The figure for the American Land Company is the sum of lands entered by their agent, Henry Anderson, and those certified to "Trustees, American Land Company," or "C. Butler and others." Since the company may have purchased from other agents, this figure is probably an understatement. Several other "partnership" figures were divided among the individual partners, since it was apparent that most of the "partnerships" were formed only for convenience in certification or to facilitate the settlement of disputes. The total, 2,139,189.89 acres, represents only 92 per cent of the 2,334,759.16 acres of Chickasaw allotments, since Carroll's list is not complete. A small part of the residue was retained by the Indians themselves. Information concerning the residence of the entrymen was derived from Indian Office and General Land Office correspondence, local newspapers, and standard biographical sources. (See Bibliography.)

Winston. The American Land Company and the Boston and New York Chickasaw Land Company retain only a fraction of their original property. Yet this turnover is only partly accounted for by settlement. Less than half those holding title to lands in the township actually cultivate the lands they own. Some of this property may be farmed by tenants or by future owners listed as tenants in the census. By 1860, except for one section held by a man who purchased from the Indian owner in 1844, the original speculators have sold out completely. Secondary speculators—Curtis, Underhill, Weaver, Lewis, and Gorman—still hold a small proportion of the land and do not cultivate it. A few recent purchasers are not recorded in the census as farm operators. The location of much of the "untilled" land, however, corresponds closely with the designation "swamp lands" in the plat of the original township survey.

The liquidation of speculative holdings is only part of the story. Two other developments are of special importance. Only about 35 per cent of the land in the township in 1860 is held by the same persons who owned it ten years previously. Of this, 43 per cent is held by speculators who may have been simply stuck with unsalable property. In other words, 85 per cent of the farm operators in 1860 had gotten title to their land within the previous decade. Furthermore, the disposal of speculative holdings during the fifties has not left a pattern of smaller holdings. Instead, the proportion of holdings under two hundred acres has declined, as has the proportion of holdings larger than five hundred acres. The number of medium-sized holdings has increased, and the percentage decrease of large holdings is slightly smaller than the percentage decrease of smaller holdings. Census records indicate that both in De Soto County as a whole and in neighboring Marshall County, there was a trend toward larger units in the fifties. This trend was less evident in the less fertile counties, such as Tishomingo. (See Table 3.)

The development in our sample township may be indicated graphically:

Size of Holdings

Year	Total No. of Operators	0–99	100–199	200–299	300–399	400–499	500–599	1,000+
1850	24	6	6	1	0	9	9	2
1860	44	4	11	4	6	13	13	2

In 1850 farmers holding two hundred acres or less accounted for 50 per cent of the landholding farm operators in the township. Ten years later they comprised approximately 35 per cent. Several factors account for this. Small farmers becoming wealthier may have bought additional land. In the sample township, this can be demonstrated in the case of only one individual, Joseph Logan. Or perhaps the increasing price of land, both improved and unimproved, may have made it too expensive for small farmers to acquire ownership in the fifties, as well as making it profitable for small owners to sell their farms. The greater efficiency of large-scale operation or readier access to capital may account for the greater prosperity of the planter and may have enabled him to buy out the small farmer. Non-economic factors such as voluntary segregation of small farmers in less fertile areas where the population was mainly white or the planters' desire to rid themselves of uncongenial neighbors may also have played a role in squeezing out the smaller operators.[18]

Rising prices benefited intermediate "speculators"—both cultivators and investors—at least as much as the original speculators in Indian titles. The first buyers of land in Township Two received an average price of $3.52 an acre when they sold their

18 Frederick Law Olmsted, *A Journey in the Back Country*, 121, 258, 308–309, 328–29, 344–45.

19 Figures for Marshall and Tishomingo are derived from Herbert F. Weaver, *Mississippi Farmers, 1850–1860*, 79. Figures for De Soto and Tunica are compiled from the United States Census, 1850 and 1860, Schedule IV, "Productions of Agriculture," *loc. cit.* Weaver's totals for size of holdings do not include tenant farmers but do leave some margin of "unknown" holdings. The marshals responsible for taking the census sometimes listed tenants as holding a given improved acreage and sometimes as holding no land whatever. Since improved acreage is not a reliable index of the total size of the holding—although tenants paid rent only on improved land and therefore might legitimately be listed as holding only improved land—I have included all tenants in separate categories, whether or not their holdings on improved land were listed.

19 of 242

TABLE 3

Size Distribution of Holdings in Sample Counties, 1850–60[19]

County	Number of Operators	0–99 (%)	100–199 (%)	200–299 (%)	300–399 (%)	400–499 (%)	500–599 (%)	1,000–4,999 (%)	Tenants
De Soto									
1850	1,396	19.91	31.02	4.30	9.31	3.15	7.81	1.86	22.64
1860	1,096	8.67	23.63	9.03	9.31	5.38	13.14	6.57	24.27
Marshall									
1850	1,710	30.41	30.70	6.43	10.88	4.33	11.05	3.40	13.51
1860	1,098	13.35	22.54	8.18	9.93	5.93	17.36	8.01	18.83
Tishomingo									
1850	1,452	11.08	46.01	6.27	12.12	4.68	5.99	1.24	24.26
1860	1,610	15.65	38.39	9.94	10.62	6.52	7.14	4.04	35.05
Tunica									
1850	41	19.52	19.51	2.44	14.03	0.00	12.20	31.70	00.00
1860	107	3.73	11.21	5.61	8.41	4.67	24.30	47.66	3.74

property, this average including two sections sold for taxes, on which the owners apparently realized nothing. The average cost of land to its owners in 1860 is quite a different story. Those who purchased in the 1830's paid an average of $1.89 per acre; in the 1840's, $2.25; in the 1850's, $6.92. The great range in prices paid during the fifties suggests that much of the land sold during that decade was improved. Excluding probate sales, where low prices may reflect that the buyers are members of the family of the deceased, prices ranged from $1.78 to $18.75 an acre.

Tunica County, the only portion of the Chickasaw cession lying in the Mississippi Delta, showed an even more clearly marked trend toward large-scale holdings than De Soto. In the Delta, the cost of clearing undergrowth, building levees, and digging drainage canals decreed from the beginning that only wealthy, large-scale operators could make a go of planting. Furthermore, the slow progress of leveeing and drainage meant that the county's period of rapid agricultural development came after the Civil War, not, as in De Soto and Marshall Counties, in the late forties and the fifties.

Tishomingo County, lying principally in the northeast highlands, follows a contrasting pattern of development. Here the total number of farmers increased during the fifties. The proportion—slightly more than 50 per cent—of farmers holding less than two hundred acres remained about the same. The difference between the evolution of tenures in this area of relatively poor land and that in the richer western counties tends to support the hypothesis that small farmers during the fifties continued to take up land in the less fertile regions but were deterred from entering the richer areas by the rising price of land and encouraged, if already established there, to sell out.

Variations in the quality of the lands, and rising land prices in the 1850's, probably affected the pattern of tenure in the Chickasaw cession more directly than did original land speculation. The chief economic incidence of the allotment policy was therefore to place the profits of first-hand speculation, such as they were, in the till of the large-scale operator rather than in the pockets of the farmer-speculator. Unless the government had adopted a policy of land disposal which restricted the right of farmers to sell their lands, the elimination of large-scale buying would probably not have produced a pattern of landholding significantly different from the one which actually prevailed in 1860.

In reaching this general conclusion we have confined our attention to questions of sales and tenure. To examine land company policy and the role of the "speculator" in the community, we shall turn to a study of the New York and Mississippi Land Company.

THE OPENING OF VAST NEW AREAS to cotton cultivation in the thirties offered a variety of opportunities for men to make their fortunes by assisting in the westward migration of capital, the disposal of the public lands, and the building of new towns and farms. The one requisite sought by all enterprising men of the flush frontier was capital; and since Eastern capitalists were meanwhile seeking investment outlets to the west, an alliance was readily confirmed. One easterner whose backing was frequently solicited in this hour of enterprise was the New York merchant, bill broker, and private banker, Joseph D. Beers. By taking parts of the bond issues of Alabama, Louisiana, and Mississippi, Beers made a name for himself in the South as an "available" capitalist. It is not surprising that he became both a trustee of the New York and Mississippi Land Company and a principal stockholder of this and of the American Land Company.

The New York and Mississippi Land Company, Beers' initial venture into Mississippi land speculation, illustrates the courting of supply by demand characteristic of east-west economic relations in the flush times. During the winter of 1834–35, Congressman David Hubbard, of Courtland, Alabama, proposed to Beers that the New Yorker organize a group of eastern capitalists to purchase several hundred sections of land from Hubbard's "Chickasaw Company." Beers quickly complied with the suggestion, and in March, 1835, the New York and Missouri Land Company was formed. The trustees and chief investors included Beers' onetime mercantile partner, Benjamin Curtis; merchants John Bolton, Knowles Taylor, Morris Ketchum and Rufus L. Lord, of New York; Charles Atwater of New Haven; and John Delafield, president of New York's Phoenix Bank. Their articles of agreement called for the issue of 150 shares of stock with a par value of $1,000 a share. Title to land was to be taken in the name of the trustees for the use of the company. Apparently four persons other than the trustees purchased the company's stock.[1]

The company engaged John Bolton as its salaried representative in Mississippi. Accompanying Bolton was his nephew Richard, a young engineer whose knowledge of surveying enabled him to assist in locating allotments. Shortly after arriving in Mississippi, John Bolton agreed to take 100 sections of the Chickasaw Company's lands. He was to buy 120 sections at the price the Chickasaw Company had paid for them, allowing the members of the company 20 sections for their services in contracting for the lands and locating them. Hubbard took pains to make Bolton aware of the extraordinary appreciation in the price of lands in the nearby Tennessee Valley, which were bringing fifteen to thirty dollars an acre only fifteen years following the opening of the area to settlement.[2] Anticipating a similar return on the Chickasaw lands within an even shorter period, Bolton soon recommended that the New York company increase its capital. Eventually the association raised a capital of $512,120, of which it invested $502,754.93 in examining and buying allotments and in purchasing trust lands at the public sales. The

[1] David Hubbard to Messrs. J. D. Beers & Co., March 7, 1835, Papers of the New York and Mississippi Land Company, State Historical Society of Wisconsin. Unless otherwise designated, all citations in this chapter are of manuscripts in this collection. Bolton to Trustees, April 14, 1835; Articles of Agreement, March 2, 1835; Richard Bolton, "Statements of payments made on acct. of stock in the N. Y. and Mississippi Land Company . . . ," February 28, 1837.

[2] Agreement of John Bolton and Trustees, n.d. [1835]; Bolton to Trustees, March 25, 1835; Same to Same, April 20, 1835.

purchases totaled approximately 284,160 acres, of which 206,-787 were included in allotments.[3]

The location of the Indian reserves began shortly after the Boltons reached Mississippi. To facilitate the work of location, Henry M. Lusher, draftsman in the office of the surveyor-general of the district, prepared a map of the cession from the government survey. This map was printed and retailed to prospective settlers and speculators. The Chickasaw agent encouraged the land agents to assist him in the location of the allotments. He set out for the eastern portion of the cession the first Monday in May, 1835, with a retinue of forty land-lookers, each anxious to get his "fair share" of the black prairie land lying between the Pontotoc Ridge and the Tombigbee River. Along the road from Pontotoc, the site of the new land office, to Cotton Gin Port on the Tombigbee, lay the plantation of one of the half-blood chiefs of the Chickasaws. "The corn," John Bolton observed, "was well grown & of a strong healthy dark green appearance very superior to what I have seen on other really rich lands." Bolton was equally impressed by the groves of hickory found at intervals on the prairie. "The best indication of superior soil and trees of such size . . . I never saw before. . . ."[4]

Hubbard's group had spent nearly a year examining lands; they continued their inspection that spring and summer, together with "woodsmen" employed by the New York company. They had already determined that, aside from the eastern prairie, the best lands were in the loess hills west of the meridian. They examined "every eighth of a section" minutely enough to determine its quality, several men walking a parallel course over each section and making notes of their observations. Taking a leaf from Hubbard's experience in the Tennessee Valley, they

[3] Richard Bolton to John Bolton, August 14, 1835; Bolton to Curtis, March 21, 1837; Bolton, "Balance Sheet," March 17, 1837; "Abstract of Land a/c June, 1836–June, 1840"; Bolton's résumé of lands sold and unsold, May, 1845; William Carroll's List of Certified Contracts, Special File, Chickasaw, Records of the Bureau of Indian Affairs; Chickasaw Location Book, Records of the Bureau of Land Management.

[4] Bolton to Trustees, May 28, 1835; Same to Same, April 25, 1835.

tried to select timbered tracts near lands being settled by persons "of superior quality." Already, in the valley planters were at a loss for fencing and building materials, and timbered land was bringing 50 per cent more than cleared and cultivated lands.[5]

While the work of location progressed, the company proceeded to determine its selling policy. The agents made a few sales which netted them approximately 200 per cent on the original cost of their lands. But they at first determined to settle for a 100 per cent profit on sales to actual settlers, expecting that settlement would enhance the value of the remaining lands. The company admitted as shareholders two planters of large means— Benjamin Sherrod, of Alabama, and William Dearing, of Georgia—in hopes that they might direct emigrants to the New York and Mississippi lands. Sherrod advised selling the lands at 100 per cent advance on their original cost, for one third cash, one third in two years, and the final third, in three. Postponing the second payment for two years might enable the purchasers to use the proceeds of their first cotton crop in paying for the land. "Would it not," Sherrod suggested, "be well to make an effort to induce the other land companies to come into the same plan and sell out the entire country?"[6]

Apparently the company rejected this statesmanlike plan and made comparatively few sales to settlers during the year. Instead, they adopted William Dearing's suggestion that they hold a sale at the time of the public sales of Chickasaw trust lands in the autumn of 1836.[7] Here the land fever was at its height, and the company disposed of all its lands west of the principal meridian of the Chickasaw cession to two companies of speculators at $3.50 per acre. Henry Anderson, Edward Orne, Peter W. Lucas, Felix Lewis, Wilkins Hunt, and Samuel McCorkle bought sixty-eight sections. The Pontotoc and Holly Springs Land Company—James Davis, Jesse B. Clements, Ben-

[5] John Bolton to Trustees, March 25, 1835; Richard Bolton to Lewis Curtis, July 27, 1835; Same to Same, April 27, 1835.

[6] Sherrod to John Bolton, December 22, 1835.

[7] Dearing to Hubbard, August 7, 1836.

jamin Clements, William H. Duke, Alexander C. McEwen, William McEwen, William Y. Goodall, and John W. Lane—bought seventy-seven and one-quarter sections.[8]

The trustees were dissatisfied with these contracts, feeling that the prices specified were too low. In defending his negotiations, Hubbard, in November, 1836, explained prophetically that higher returns could be realized only "if cotton keeps up—But suppose it does not and that all property goes down as cotton declines & that your money market continues hard . . . ?"[9]

Among those bankrupted by the panics of the late thirties were many members of the Pontotoc and Holly Springs Land Company. For this reason, they were unable to complete their payments on the seventy-seven and one-quarter sections they had bought in 1836. In February of 1842 they returned to the New York company the thirty-five sections they had been unable to sell, transferred their bills receivable to Bolton, and signed bonds for the payment of the original price of the forty-two and one-half sections they kept and $750 per section as a bonus on the lands they returned.[10] Commenting on this arrangement, Richard Bolton pronounced a post-mortem on their financial status, a fitting obituary of the "flush times":

> The ten members of this Co. are all badly broken except two—Duke & Coopwood—three of them JB and B Clements & J.W. Lane reside out of the state—James Davis a year since ran his negroes into Texas and figured there as an Ajutant [sic] General until in a battle on the frontier he was shamefully beaten by the Mexicans, on which he was cashiered. The other members reside in Marshall county, but embarking in a Real Estate Banking Company failed, & have nothing—Coopwood resides in Aberdeen, has some property, but much pressed by debts & Judgments against him, & if we sued him on the debts to our Co. to any large amount, would

[8] Richard Bolton to Lewis Curtis, October 28, 1836; Same to Same, November 25, 1836; 26 *Smedes and Marshall*, 212 ff.

[9] Hubbard to Curtis, November 24, 1836.

[10] Chancery Court, Northern District of Mississippi, Final Record, Vol I, 107–85, Chancery Clerk's Office, Holly Springs, Mississippi; 26 *Smedes and Marshall*, 212 ff.

have been returned by the sheriff as G.T.T. with his negroes. He has a plantation and some negroes and but for this debt is in easy circumstances.[11]

Even following the panic in 1837, Hubbard continued to hope that the company's lands might be disposed of wholesale. He conducted an extensive advertising campaign in the southeastern states and handed out circulars to appropriate colleagues in Congress "to frank to constituents in the southern atlantic states." He visited Richmond and Tuscaloosa while the Virginia and Alabama legislatures were in session, obtained letters in Georgia and South Carolina, and finally tried to sell the company's holdings to banker Nicholas Biddle.[12] While in Philadelphia dickering with Biddle, he received an offer from a group of southerners to take the remaining 223 sections at $1,600 a section. Recommending this contract to the trustees, Hubbard remarked:

> I do not think the labor of the country has yet overtaken the debt & the very large amount of indebtedness in Alabama and Mississippi must keep [land prices] down for years.
>
> Prosperity may seem again to rush upon us, but I fear not a healthy state.[13]

The trustees failed to take this astute advice, rejecting the bargain because the price did not meet their expectations. Had they accepted it, they might have closed their business profitably before the long depression of the forties set in.

During the forties, the trustees proposed several times to close out their business with a public auction. Richard Bolton, their Mississippi agent, advised against this, and the trustees followed his advice. Bolton remained in Pontotoc, selling the company's holdings, very gradually, to settlers. In the months following the rejection of Hubbard's contract, he was to watch the sudden

[11] Bolton to Curtis, January 14, 1843.
[12] Hubbard to John Bolton, October 13, 1837, December 14, 1837, February 2, 1838; Hubbard to Nicholas Biddle, June 1, 1838, Biddle Papers, Library of Congress.
[13] Hubbard to Curtis, June 1, 1838.

deflation of the "young, rising country" as one scheme of speculation after another had lost its course and run awry.

Men of capital both locally and "at the East" had mortgaged their financial futures on the growth of the new cotton kingdom. Just as she created new counties out of the Indian cessions, Mississippi had proceeded to create the capital with which they were to be developed. The most famous of her instruments were the Union and Planters' banks, whose capital was secured by the sale of state bonds to eastern and foreign investors. Mississippi's repudiation of these bonds forms a notorious chapter in the history of American capital importation.

Eastern and foreign bondholders were not the only losers by bankruptcy of the state's financial institutions. Perhaps the most serious problem created for residents of the state was the radical depreciation of banknotes issued by state-chartered institutions. The Mississippi Legislature linked its program of credit creation with its projected transportation system. The characteristic vehicle of this combination was the "railroad and banking company." Altogether a score of railroads received charters in the thirties. These roads were to connect all the new, rising interior towns with rising towns, new and old, which served as shipping points on the Mississippi and Tombigbee river systems. A number of these companies received banking privileges, and though few of them built railroads, all participated enthusiastically in the business of printing and circulating banknotes.[14]

An interesting example of the species was the Hernando Railroad and Banking Company. The history of this company illustrates something of the role of land-company agents as middlemen for the eastern capitalist as well as the catastrophic consequences of the Mississippi capitalist's financial wizardry. Chartered in May, 1837, the company had an authorized capital of one million dollars. It might receive subscriptions to its capital stock in the form of real estate mortgages and issue bonds

[14] Charles R. Johnson, "Railroad Legislation and Building in Mississippi, 1830–1840," *Journal of Mississippi History*, Vol. IV (1942),195–206; Mississippi *Acts*, 1833–41, *passim*.

for which these mortgages constituted security. The company was to use the proceeds of the sale of its bonds to build a railroad from Jefferson (later Hernando), the county seat of De Soto County, to a village yet unborn on the banks of the Mississippi. Among the commissioners authorized to take subscriptions for the company were several outstanding brethren of the speculative fraternity—Wyatt C. Mitchell, Henry Anderson of the American Land Company, and Samuel McCorkle. Its president was Edward Orne, agent for three Boston and New York joint-stock land companies.

Under Orne's direction, the company cut a wagon road twenty-two miles from Hernando to "Commerce" on the Mississippi. They held a large interest in the new town, and within the six months it took to cut the road had sold a third of the lots in Commerce for $160,000—on credit. The town proprietors built warehouses and commission houses. They planned an inn. They advertised that Commerce was to become the link in a vast chain of railway transportation stretching from the Gulf of Mexico to the Tennessee Valley. By giving northern Mississippi a metropolis within her borders comparable to Vicksburg and Natchez, the town would free neighboring planters from paying tribute to the "foreign" merchants of Memphis. By legislative consent, the Hernando "railroad" became a "turnpike"; together with the bank and the independent marketing center, it was to free the people of Mississippi from their "bondage" to northern capitalists.[15]

The managers of the railroad and banking company adopted a somewhat ironic means of freeing themselves from thralldom to the North. In the fall of 1838, Benjamin Whitney, brother-in-law of Edward Orne and trustee of the Boston and New York Cotton Land Company, deposited the Hernando company's bonds with the New York Banking Company as security for a $100,000 loan. The proceeds of the loan were to be used to buy

[15] *Marshall County Republican* (Holly Springs), January 12, 1838; *The Free Press* (Hernando), October 19, 1839; *Marshall County Republican*, August 25, 1838, January 6, 1839, June 8, 1839, June 15, 1839, July 27, 1839; *Mississippi Acts*, February 9, 1839.

cotton and to redeem the notes issued by the company. The company was to repay the loan by shipments of cotton. Instead, Orne used approximately $40,000 to reimburse himself for notes of the Hernando Bank he had received in payment for lands. The bank's directors, given $60,000 to buy cotton, speculated on their own account but procured no cotton to send to New York.

In June, 1840, the effects of the Hernando Railroad and Banking Company were mortgaged to Orne's Boston and Mississippi Cotton Land Company. A year later the mortgage was transferred to the New York Banking Company, which shortly thereafter went bankrupt. Eight years later the receiver of the defunct New York bank foreclosed on the mortgages pledged for the redemption of the stock of the Hernando company. Meanwhile the town of Commerce languished and died, the railroad remained in limbo, and the governor of Mississippi revoked the charter of the Hernando Railroad and Banking Company.[16]

The result of such overimaginative banking practices as these became evident in 1839 and 1840 when the currency of most of Mississippi's banks became non-current. Like other businesses, the New York and Mississippi Land Company lost heavily from its holdings of depreciated notes. Bolton in making remittances to the trustees in New York had to travel to New Orleans and buy New York funds at a premium—often by way of an intermediate exchange of Mississippi money for New Orleans funds, at a discount. Of $329,129.26 which he took to New Orleans between December, 1836, and May, 1842, the trustees realized only $287,397.51—a loss of 12.7 per cent. This does not include the loss on funds Bolton sold in Mississippi at forty to fifty cents on the dollar to secure himself against total repudiation. In many cases he found it advisable to protect himself from depreciating currency by suspending the collection of debts.[17]

---

[16] Chancery Court, Northern District of Mississippi, Final Record, Vol. B, 62–94; loc. cit.; Deed Record, De Soto County, Vol. F, 26; The Holly Springs Gazette, August 4, 1841; 13 Smedes and Marshall, 153–57; Mississippi Senate Journal, 1841, 15.

[17] "Account Current of Remittances . . . ," filed May 1, 1845; Bolton to Curtis, December 12, 1840, January 5, 1838, February 28, 1840, April 1, 1841.

From Andrew C. McLaughlin, *Lewis Cass*

Secretary of War under Andrew Jackson, Lewis Cass negotiated
the Creek Treaty of 1832.

From Marie M. Owen, *Our State*: *Alabama*

General John Coffee, close friend of President Jackson, was prominent in negotiations with both the Choctaws and the Chickasaws.

In the mid-forties Bolton saw another threat to the company's prospects in the proposed annexation of Texas, which he feared would depress the land market just as it had begun to recover from the effects of panic. But he became convinced that those who were emigrating to Texas were in any case too poor to buy lands in northern Mississippi. By the mid-fifties he found that the bulk of his sales were to long-time residents seeking to enlarge their plantations or find homes for their children.

The rising price of cotton and the projection of a railroad through Pontotoc led to brisk sales, which encouraged the company to reassess their lands. In January, Bolton expounded his price policy to the trustees:

> Prices of land must necessarily be variable—By our examinations we sought to ascertain a correct description of each tract of Land, the character of the soil, the quantity tillable, and its adaptation to agricultural purposes, and whether for corn or cotton.—and also its value for timber land—also its position with respect to roads, water courses, mills, villages, and a market or shipping point— In valuing the lands, the price was fixed with reference to the above considerations—and in some lands represented the present value,— in others the probable value, when the vicinity began to be settled.
>
> The lapse of time often modifies our opinions. Actual cultivation of adjoining and similar lands, shews some to have been underrated, others over rated for productive value. Unexpected changes are made in the routes of old, or location of new roads. Experience shews certain locations to be healthy—others the reverse. And more than all, the progress of settlement, accumulates a larger population, in certain neighborhoods, bringing with it a greater demand for land, and enabling us to sustain prices that were first too high, and advance prices that were originally about the fair value. . . .[18]

Generally, Bolton explained, he departed from set valuations to raise prices when there was an unexpected increase in returns from cotton and concomitant progress of settlement. Furthermore, he was willing to reduce his demands when this was justi-

[18] Same to Same, January 25, 1850.

fied by a large cash payment or the purchase of several tracts by the same man or a group of neighbors. Ordinarily he sold land for one-fourth cash and the rest in three equal yearly instalments with interest. In cases where he expected the buyer to make valuable improvements on the land, he did not even insist on the initial cash payment.

Bolton's letter makes no reference to the price policies of the other land companies. Throughout his correspondence he mentions their practices only to excuse himself for following a different line of action. Since land is not a uniform commodity, study of actual price differences cannot determine the presence or absence of oligopolistic practices. From Bolton's correspondence, however, it appears likely that the various companies formed their price policies according to their individual estimates of what the market would bear, rather than following a price leader. Furthermore, Bolton was apparently unconcerned at competition within the area in which he was selling. When the federal government, acting as trustee for the Chickasaw tribe, sold lands for $.25 to $1.50 an acre, the land company agent welcomed its action as encouraging the settlement of lands contiguous to the company's and thus making them in the long run more desirable. Probably he saw the activities of the other land speculators from a similar point of view. His main concern was competition not from other sellers in his own area, but from other areas, a not unrealistic viewpoint. Had there been no Texas or Arkansas, it is likely that the speculators in Mississippi lands would have profited considerably more than they actually did.

This attitude of Bolton's toward his "competitors" raises certain interesting speculations. Critics of federal land policy were accustomed to refer to settlers' sufferings from "land monopoly." But was not the more relevant collusive practice rather a kind of oligopsony—the banding together of *buyers* to acquire land at noncompetitive prices from the government and, to some extent, from the Indians? Such collusion led federal lands to pass into private ownership more quickly than would otherwise have been the case, for it made speculative purchase more profitable. Once land was privately owned, future purchasers had to pay for it prices determined in the market by supply and demand. But it is unlikely that oligopolistic collusion affected these prices. In the first place, oligopoly would have required more co-operation than contemporary businessmen could long sustain. Furthermore, if one firm in a newly settled area succeeded in underselling another, this sale, because it often led to settlement, increased the value of the lands of the competing firm. Thus price-cutting was no economic tragedy to the company which sustained its own rates, and the chief motive for the formation of oligopoly was absent.

It is true that the settler paid the speculator higher prices than he would have paid the government. But he did this because the speculator acted out of considerations of private profit, charging what the market would bear, whereas the government, acting mainly on political considerations, did not. Finally, the chief limitation on private profit was not competition within a given area, but interarea competition in which the federal and state governments, with their cheap land policies, were the chief competitors of the private speculator.

Like the earlier panic and depression, the Civil War gave an entirely new aspect to the land business. Again the market diminished; offerings at trust and probate sales brought a fraction of their prewar value. In 1866 the New York and Mississippi Company still owned eighteen sections of land and $80,000 worth of notes and bonds. Purchasers were insolvent and desperately opposed to foreclosure. Men were assailed with deadly weapons for trying to collect debts. Lands were unsafe in the hands of Reconstructed sheriffs and brought little or nothing at foreclosure sales in any case. Not until ten years later did Bolton report that applications for the purchase of land were encouraging and the prospect of collections promising. Apparently the company considered it worthwhile to continue his agency, but in 1888 they finally filed a bill asking the chancery court to authorize a public sale of the approximately five thousand acres remaining on their hands.[19]

The company's investment as a whole earned a profit of more than 50 per cent in the years prior to the war. During the twenty-five years between the time of its purchases and the time war broke out, the company's records show that it paid dividends totaling 150 per cent, and at least three other dividends of un-recorded amounts. Since these dividends represent payments out of capital, only the 50 per cent above the amount of capital represents profit. Assuming that the three unrecorded dividends approximately equaled the average, we may call this profit 60 per cent or 2.4 per cent a year. This estimate is somewhat dis-torted since the dividends varied considerably from year to year. Only one very small dividend is recorded following the war, but the records are sparser for that period and it is possible that more dividends eventually were paid.[20]

Richard Bolton remained in Mississippi as agent for the New York land company from 1835 until the time of his death. As a citizen of Pontotoc, he was naturally sensitive to the antagonism against eastern speculators which he frequently remarked among his neighbors. His correspondence therefore provides us with some index to the relations between representatives of "foreign" investors and the local community.

Resentment against eastern speculators in the Chickasaw lands found two practical outlets. The first was a movement to tax land formerly included in Chickasaw allotments five years from the signing of the treaty (1834) rather than from the date the lands were sold. No one questioned that the allotments should enjoy the five-year exemption from taxation generally allowed for public domain lands after their passage into private ownership. But it was maintained that the Chickasaw allotments became private property as soon as the treaty was signed, not

[19] Hubbard to Curtis, May 19, 1866; Bolton to Trustees, March 12, 1866; Bolton to Curtis, February 2, 1876; C. W. Bolton to Benjamin L. Curtis, September 8, 1888.

[20] Compiled from power of attorney, notifications, and receipts in the papers of the New York and Mississippi Land Company.

when the Chickasaws sold them to white men. Governor A. G. McNutt defended the early taxation of allotment lands on the ground that this would encourage the liquidation of speculative holdings:

> A large portion of the finest lands in the Chickasaw Purchase, are held by non-residents, who ask a high price for them, and will not sell until forced by the imposition of taxes. They are generally uncultivated, and if thrown on the market at a fair price; would soon be occupied by an industrious people, able and willing to assist in advancing the wealth, population, and resources of the State.[21]

The result of the movement was a compromise whereby all allotment lands were subject to taxation beginning in 1841, five years after their location was approved.[22]

The second attempt to harry the absentees also involved questions of taxation. Mississippi county taxes were assessed as a percentage of the state tax, which was collected on both real and personal property. Local boards of police, who collected the county taxes, had no opportunity to discriminate against absentee landholders by adjusting the assessment of their property, since each landholder, or his agent, evaluated his own property for tax purposes. But in 1847 the boards of police of Tunica and Panola counties attempted to shift a greater part of the tax burden on absentee investors by levying a higher proportion of the county tax on real than on personal property. This was hardly a crusade of the poor yeoman against the rich speculator, since the principal relief went to large slaveholders whose human chattels were assessed as personal property. But it was resisted chiefly by the eastern land companies, who banded together to obtain an injunction against the collection of these taxes. The courts upheld the local boards of police.[23]

[21] Mississippi *Senate Journal*, 1842, 13.

[22] Bolton to Curtis, September 2, 1839, February 8, 1842; Mississippi, *Acts*, February 16, 1838, February 20, 1840, February 4, 1841.

[23] Bolton to Curtis, February 8, 1842, February 2, 1847, July 1, 1848; Chancery Court, Northern District of Mississippi, Final Record, Vol. E, 277 ff., 281–86, *loc. cit.*

The holding of lands by speculators clearly made it more difficult for settlers to obtain title. Bolton himself testifies to this
fact. The usual prices speculators charged were higher than
those charged by the government, except for rare occasions of
distress or tax sales. An advertisement like the following suggests that some farmers relieved themselves of the burden of
purchase by trespassing:

LET IT ALONE

John R. Carrol, agent for owner, forewarns all persons that he
will prosecute all trespassers who cut or haul timber off SW 8 in
the vicinity of Holly Springs.[24]

The lack of any reference to this problem in Bolton's correspondence and the dearth of ejectment suits in the local chancery proceedings make it seem highly improbable that "squatting" on
private lands ever became a burning issue. Bolton makes a number of references to renting lands in the early forties, though
his accounts show very few receipts from rents. Probably he
allowed squatters to remain on the lands in return for making
improvements.[25]

There are a number of explanations for the absence of serious
or sustained conflict. None of the absentee companies apparently
contemplated holding their lands as permanent investments,
leasing them to settlers and fostering landlord-tenant controversies comparable to the New York antirent wars. Share tenancy
and cash renting were familiar to Mississippians, and census
records for 1850 and 1860 show that non-landholders constituted
in some counties as much as 35 per cent of the agricultural population. But most of the non-landholders were probably persons
in process of paying for lands they had bought. A study of Mississippi tenures in 1850 and 1860 shows almost uniformly that

[24] *Holly Springs Gazette*, December 22, 1843.
[25] An instance of such an agreement, made by Edward Orne, is explained in
some detail in *Orne* v. *Sullivan*, 3 Howard 161. The Deed Books of Marshall
and De Soto counties reveal only one other such agreement, although there may
have been many which were not recorded.

older-settled counties with more stable agricultural population had the smallest percentage of landless farmers.[26] In the ante bellum decades there seemed no danger that tenancy would become a permanent status for a large proportion of the population, and there is no evidence that the absentee investors had anything of the sort in mind. Furthermore, the absentee land-holders had not used illegal or improper methods to obtain their holdings. No pre-emption rights or other potentially conflicting claims were allowed in the Chickasaw cession. For these reasons, no group had the legal leverage to sustain a claim adverse to those of the speculators.

Criticism of land speculation there was, but most often it was focused on the banks whose loans were alleged to have facilitated speculative investment. Given the preponderance of land dealers on the boards of directors of these banks, the charge is not unreasonable. But in any case, it would not have been wise for local critics to name names in their sallies at the ferocious land shark, for large- and small-scale "speculators" were to be found among their near and prominent neighbors: J. N. Wilie, proprietor of the general store in Aberdeen; Joseph W. Matthews, Marshall County's state senator and onetime governor of Mississippi; great planters like Robert Gordon and Samuel McCorkle; members of the boards of trustees of the female academies and the county boards of police; sheriffs, judges, leading Whigs and leading Democrats—all were tainted with "speculation."[27]

Agents of eastern land companies also took up membership in the local elite of planters, promoters, and potentates. Hugh Craft, agent for a number of absentee investors who held lands in northern Mississippi, was remembered as a citizen especially

---

[26] Weaver, *Mississippi Farmers*, 64–66.

[27] *Southern Tribune* (Pontotoc), February 2, 1843; *Holly Springs Gazette*, April 19, 1845, June 8, 1844; obituary of W. T. Carruthers in *The Guard* (Holly Springs), February 2, 1845; William H. Duke *et al.* to his Excellency James K. Polk, September 23, 1840, Polk Papers, Library of Congress; Seventh and Eighth Censuses, Schedule IV, "Productions of Agriculture"; Robert Gordon Diary, Mississippi Department of Archives and History.

active in educational matters. "Their home," comments a local historian, "was noted for its hospitality and for the abundance of books, flowers, and music." Walter Goodman, who succeeded Henry Anderson as agent for the American Land Company, was a leading promoter in the fifties of the popular Mississippi Central Railroad. Richard Bolton, the New York and Mississippi Company agent, became a large planter and consciously attempted to integrate himself into the community: he sided with the dominant Democratic party, and was rewarded with the offer of a nomination to the state legislature on the Democratic ticket; he acted as trustee for the Pontotoc Female Academy; and he conscientiously subscribed to such local projects as the telegraph line connecting Pontotoc with the East.[28]

Although he was often uneasy over antispeculator sentiment, Bolton was aware of the consequences of the speculators' position in the community. In February, 1847, he read an article in one of the Hernando papers, condemning the land companies as "pirates" and referring ominously to the antirent disturbance in New York. "The Editor," he remarked smugly, "is a thorough Agrarian, & has no influence—Rest satisfied that no agitation of that kind, can prevail or create disturbance in North Mississippi. There are too many home interests here in lands, and the people are well satisfied with very few exceptions with the liberal course of the Land Companies."[29]

[28] Mrs. W. A. Anderson, "A Chapter in the Yellow Fever Epidemic of 1878," Mississippi Historical Society *Publications*, Vol. X (1909), 223; William A. Hamilton, "History of Holly Springs, Mississippi, to 1878," (Unpublished Master's Thesis, 1931, on file at Mississippi Department of Archives and History); Eighth Census, Schedule IV, "Productions of Agriculture," Pontotoc County; Bolton to Curtis, September 23, 1843, June 23, 1846.

[29] Bolton to Curtis, February 6, 1847.

·8·

PUBLIC LAND SALES
AND THE CESSION IN TRUST

THE TRADING IN INDIAN ALLOTMENTS represents only a fraction of the land speculations which flourished in Mississippi during the flush times. Speculation in allotments should be seen against a perspective of rapid offering and purchase of the remaining lands ceded by the tribesmen. The Chickasaw and Choctaw cessions of 1830–34 contained nearly two-thirds of the area of Mississippi. During the years 1833–39, the federal government offered 10,827,060.5 acres in the state for the first time. Almost half of the 9,739,942.79 acres it sold during the same period were newly offered lands.[1] The Choctaw territory remaining after the location of allotments was offered as federal public land; the Chickasaw lands were sold by the government "in trust" for the Indians. In both cases the government offered the lands at public auction, then disposed of the lands remaining unsold after the auction through private sales.

The first public sale of Choctaw cession lands took place in Chocchuma, Clinton, and Augusta, in October and November, 1833. The Chocchuma sale of October, 1833, received extraordinary public attention. For political reasons, it was extensively

[1] Compare 30 Cong., 2 sess., *House Exec. Doc. 12, Appendix,* 226–29 and Table 6.

155

investigated by the Senate Committee on Public Lands, which published the documents submitted in the course of its investigation. The alleged behavior of the speculators at the Chocchuma sale, as revealed by the documents published in the *American State Papers,* has been cited as the "pattern" of land speculation in the "Old Southwest."[2] The sale is interesting, therefore, as a study in both speculation and the historiography of speculation.

The close Congressional attention given the Chocchuma sale resulted from a conflict between President Jackson and Senator George Poindexter, of Mississippi, over the appointment of a register for the Chocchuma land office. On December 18, 1830, Rev. James Gwin, of Nashville, chaplain to Jackson's troops during the Battle of New Orleans, petitioned his old companion-in-arms to find a federal office in the newly acquired Indian cession for his son Samuel. The President first nominated Samuel as register of the land office at Mt. Salus, Mississippi. Poindexter successfully opposed this nomination on the ground that Samuel was not a citizen of Mississippi. The "case of Samuel Gwin" then became a pawn in the struggle between senatorial patrons and the President over "Presidential" appointments. The immediate outcome of the controversy was Gwin's appointment as register at Chocchuma. Jackson forced this appointment through the Senate by threatening not to fill any more land office vacancies in Mississippi until he won his way. This was in March, 1833. A year later, following the first public sale of lands in the Chocchuma district, Poindexter offered before the Senate a series of resolutions calling for investigation of the sales of Choctaw lands. The wording of his proposal implied that the sales had been held on unusually short notice and that governmental officials had participated in fraudulent combinations to reduce the price of land at the sale and to put "actual settlers" at the mercy of conniving speculators.[3]

[2] Gordon T. Chappell, "Patterns of Land Speculation in the Old Southwest," *Journal of Southern History,* Vol. XV (1949), 463-77.

[3] Gwin to Jackson, October 14, 1831, Claiborne Papers, Vol. A, Mississippi Department of Archives and History; *Niles' Weekly Register* (Baltimore), Vol. XLII, 445, August 18, 1832; *ibid.,* 411, August 4, 1832; Jackson to Robert J.

Senate appointees W. S. Jones and Isaac Caldwell collected affidavits accusing Gwin of having an interest in a land company formed to monopolize purchases in the public sale at Chocchuma in October, 1833. The affidavits asserted that the company forbade settlers to bid against it on pain of having their land bid up to a price beyond their means.[4]

The investigators' evidence implicated Robert J. Walker, a supporter of Jackson, in the "fraudulent" speculations. Walker, running for the Senate in opposition to Poindexter, joined Samuel Gwin in collecting evidence to refute the charges. He forwarded to Washington more than forty depositions which denied that Samuel Gwin had been interested in the transactions of the land company, or that settlers had been forbidden to bid against it, or that the company had broken the law in any way.[5]

Three issues arise repeatedly in the conflicting testimony. Did the speculators at the Chocchuma sale succeed in eliminating competition from the public auction of government lands? Did they deprive the settlers of their improvements or force them to pay exorbitant prices for them? Did Gwin as register of the land office aid the speculators in breaking the law in return for a share in their ill-gotten gains?

The speculators at Chocchuma did combine for the purpose of eliminating competition. Prior to the sale, investors from Alabama and Mississippi river towns had sent surveyors into the Choctaw territory to take note of desirable tracts of land. On October 22, the second day of the public sales, a "company" of Mississippians came into conflict with a "company" of Alabamians in bidding for Yazoo River lands. That night representatives of the two groups held a meeting in a tavern not far from the land office. Robert J. Walker as representative of the Mississippians and Robert Jamison, Jr., representing the Ala-

Chester, March 3, 1833, Tennessee Historical Society Collection, Tennessee Historical Society; *American State Papers: Public Lands,* VII, 448.

[4] *Ibid.,* 377–507.

[5] William M. Gwin to Jackson, August 9, 1834, Jackson Papers, Library of Congress. The "defense of Samuel Gwin" is printed in *American State Papers: Public Lands,* VIII, 711–88.

bamians, consulted with three representatives of the "settlers" of the Choctaw cession and drew up the Articles of Agreement of the Chocchuma Land Company. The agreement formed a company with shares ranging from one hundred to one thousand dollars. Walker, Jamison, Thomas G. Ellis, and Malcolm Gilchrist were to bid for the company. Each settler was to submit to the company a numerical description of his lands. The company agreed to bid for the settlers' lands and to resell to the settler, at cost, 80 or 160 acres covering the improvements. In addition, the company acted as a claim association, adjudicating contests among settlers with overlapping claims. Company bidders, pooling information on the quality of the lands, agreed to buy those deemed "desirable." Yet no one was to be prohibited from bidding against them.[6]

The Chocchuma Land Company bought most of its lands at $1.25 an acre, but it did not succeed entirely in eliminating competition from the government sale.[7] Immediately following the government sale, the company held its own auction, at which it realized a profit of 30 per cent. Since all the lands not sold at this auction were handed over to an individual speculator by private arrangement, it is clear that the only functions of the Chocchuma company were to mediate between settlers and speculators, to allow the speculators to pool the information obtained by their land-lookers, and to secure the profits of competition to private investors rather than to the government.

What of relations between the speculators and the "settlers"? The most accurate analysis was that given by deponent Patrick Sharkey: "I do not think they [the sales] were managed in the best manner for the good of the government. I think they were managed for the interest of such of the settlers as were interested in said company; and I think most of the settlers were interested in said company."[8]

[6] Testimony of John A. Lane, *ibid.*, VII, 454–55; Testimony of Samuel Foster, *ibid.*, 493; Testimony of Abel Beaty, *ibid.*, 495; Testimony of John Smith, *ibid.*, 502; Articles of Agreement, *ibid.*, VIII, 743; *ibid.*, 502.

[7] A list of buyers with the prices they paid for each tract is printed in *ibid.*, VII, 414–47.

[8] *Ibid.*, 469.

Whatever action the speculators might have taken, the settlers operated under a disadvantage because of the timing of the sale. The President had urged the General Land Office to prepare the Choctaw lands for sale as soon as possible.[9] They were therefore proclaimed less than three years after the Choctaws had ceded them. Since the lands had belonged to the Indians when the pre-emption law of 1830 was passed, the settlers could not pre-empt their farms at the minimum price. Furthermore, October was a month when money was scarce in the South, and the capitalist had better access to outside credit than did the settler. Some of the land-lookers employed by the speculators claimed that they were instructed to buy the improvements of farmers who were not planning to purchase their lands from the government. They themselves promised not to bid against settlers who intended to become owners, but others, they alleged, had "taken the numbers" of improved lands in order to overbid the settlers on them and resell the tracts to the settlers on credit at a higher price.[10] The Chocchuma Land Company did bid against a settler who refused to join their organization, but company bidders turned over a large quantity of land to small buyers who presumably had joined them. Actually, it was advantageous for both speculators and settlers to keep down competition and minimize the prices paid to the government. The land company was the instrument through which they might co-operate to that end. Many settlers held stock in the company and used it as an agent in buying from the government, for by no means all the "actual settlers" in this plantation country were impoverished squatters.

The Chocchuma sale therefore demonstrates that land sales did not have to become a focus of contention between farmers and investors. Low prices to original buyers and rapid settlement of the country were advantageous to both. Co-operation

---

[9] Register of Letters Received, General Land Office, 1831–33, page for July, 1833, Records of the Bureau of Land Management.

[10] Testimony of Samuel McCall, *American State Papers: Public Lands*, VIII, 748; Testimony of George Dougherty, *ibid.*, 766.

against the revenue interest of the government, rather than conflict against each other, was the logical procedure.

It is difficult to determine to what degree Gwin as a federal official may have co-operated in helping the company put down competition. He nowhere denied that he received fees for recording the transfers of land office receipts from the Chocchuma Land Company bidders to those who bought lands at company sales. There were enough of these transfers to earn the register several hundred dollars without his taking the slightest direct interest in the affairs of the company. On the other hand, the only way to frustrate the company's design was to stop the sales, and Gwin was advised that he had no legal ground for doing this. We have seen that Gwin tried to "expose" the machinations of the speculators in Choctaw allotments, and it is likely that he made enemies by this and other attempts to frustrate the enterprising architects of fraud. Among those who accused him of improper complicity with the speculators was one Joseph B. Marsh, whose illegal pre-emption claim he had rejected. In a testimonial to Gwin, H. S. Foote characterized Marsh as follows: "His countenance is generally admitted to be the most hideous ever presented to view in this region, and is doubtless correspondent to his character, as described."[11] One might not cast aspersions on the character of a public officer with impunity, especially if that officer was as contentious and impulsive a man as Samuel Gwin. He himself was severely wounded in a duel with investigator Isaac Caldwell of "Poin's inquisitorial committee."

The only constructive measure to emerge from Poindexter's investigation was a bill requiring three months' interval between the proclamation and sale of public lands. It is interesting to note that while the offering of lands at short notice was the feature of the Chocchuma sales most obviously disadvantageous to the settlers, it was also the feature which received the least attention. Poindexter's main object was to discredit the administration by showing that its chosen men used illegitimate means

[11] Testimony of H. S. Foote, *ibid.*, 761.

to favor the speculator at the expense of the pioneer, not to eval-
uate or remedy basic problems of land policy.

The documents arising out of the investigation do, however,
indicate important features of the public land sales of the thirties: the importance of investment buying and the tendency of
co-operation among land buyers, both settlers and speculators,
for the purpose of minimizing competition. But how accurately
do the events at this isolated sale reflect the role of speculation
in the disposal of public lands? How important was investment
buying as a proportion of the total sales of government lands?
Was it confined mainly to public auctions and "boom" years, or
was it a relatively constant feature? Some answers to these questions will be suggested as we examine the sales of the Chickasaw trust lands.

Strictly speaking, the unallotted Chickasaw lands were not
public domain. They were segregated into a separate land district and sold by the government in trust for the tribe. Revenues
from the sales were used to pay the expenses incident to emigration and resettlement, and the surplus after these expenses were
paid was invested by the government for the benefit of the tribe.
One object of this policy was to make the purchase of Indian
lands self-liquidating.[12] Jackson, a devotee of economy in government, had suggested giving the Chickasaws the net proceeds
of the sale of their lands as early as 1826.[13] In his instructions of
October, 1831, the President reiterated the stipulation that the
negotiators should adjust the terms of purchase so that the
amount to be paid the Indians might be raised out of the sale of
their lands, "bearing in mind, that I keep in view steadily, the
full discharge of the public debt on the 3d of March, 1833, and

12 Precedents for this policy had been established in the reservation of small
areas to be sold for the benefit of orphans or of tribal schools, and, in the thirties,
the sale "in trust" of the highly improved tribal reservations of certain Ohio,
Indiana, and Michigan tribes. 7 *Statutes at Large*, 197, 212, 242, 327, 337, 349–
50, 352–53, 357, 361–62, 364, 366–67, 453, 502–504. See also John H. Eaton to
H. M. Gardiner, March 29, 1831, 22 Cong., 1 sess., *House Doc. 171*, 52–54.

13 Jackson to Coffee, September 2, 1826, in *Correspondence of Jackson*, III,
312.

that I wish no debt created that will interfere with the revenue that is to meet that object."[14]

Negotiator John Coffee wrote into the treaty of 1834 another policy favored by some Jacksonian legislators—graduating the price of land in proportion to the length of time it had been on the market. Thus, while the Chickasaw lands were offered in the usual manner at public and private sales and at the usual $1.25 an acre minimum price, their price at the end of the first year they had been on the market was to be reduced to $1.00 an acre; the second, to 75 cents; the third, to 50 cents; the fourth, to 25 cents; and the fifth, to 12.5 cents. The application of the graduation policy to Chickasaw lands was ostensibly justified by the need for quick cash to finance the removal of the Indians.[15]

Once the Chickasaws ceded their land, President Jackson pressured the land office to prepare them as quickly as possible for sale. The General Land Office directed the surveyor-general of the cession to survey first the lands most in demand "by those who want to purchase."[16] On June 24, 1835, Jackson proclaimed the first sale of the Chickasaw lands for the first Monday in January, 1836. The government publicized the sale as widely as possible among prospective local buyers and absentee investors. Five hundred handbills of the proclamation were struck off for distribution to individuals in the neighborhood of the lands. The sale was advertised in the newspapers of all the southern states, as well as newspapers in the northern cities.

The sale, held at Pontotoc near the center of the Chickasaw district, attracted a swarm of investors. One of them estimated that there was perhaps a million dollars in town, in the hands of individuals and companies from New York, Georgia, Virginia, Mississippi and adjoining states.[17] From the movement of land

[14] Same to Same, October 23, 1831, *ibid.*, IV, 363.
[15] 27 Cong., 1 sess., *House Doc. 213; 7 Statutes at Large*, 383–85, 454.
[16] Elijah Hayward to John Bell, March 24, 1834, Chickasaw Letterbook, Vol. I, 55, Records of the Bureau of Land Management.
[17] Bolton to Lewis Curtis, January 8, 1836, Papers of the New York and Mississippi Land Company, State Historical Society of Wisconsin.

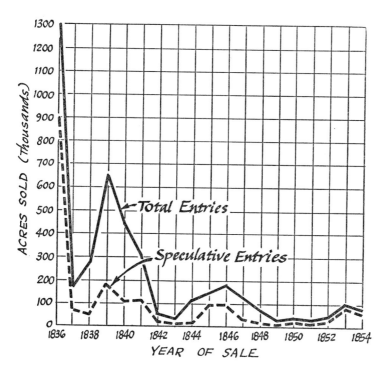

GRAPH 1. Quantities of Land Entered Yearly, Pontotoc Land District

prices at the sale, it appears that these investors were able to combine occasionally and sporadically, but that the competitive urge frequently broke through their tenuous bonds of co-opera-tion.[18] During the first few days of January, a few investors dominated the market and most of the lands went at $1.25 an acre. The lands offered during this period were among the less valuable in the district. As investors came into competition for the black-earthed prairie regions of the eastern ranges, prices rose to two to three dollars an acre. By January 11, prices sta-bilized, and seven bidders, perhaps representing a coalition,

[18] This and other descriptions of the sale are, unless otherwise documented, based on the Abstract of Cash Entries, Pontotoc Land Office, Records of the Bureau of Land Management.

163

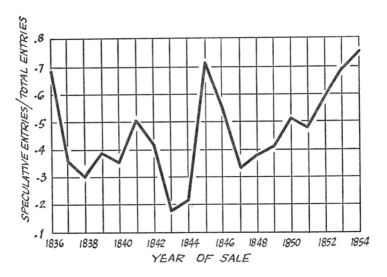

GRAPH 2. Ratio of Speculative Entries to Total Entries

dominated the buying. By January 16, prices began to rise again, with a number of large investors and small buyers entering the bidding. The 266,441.91 acres sold during January brought an average price of $1.88 an acre. Following the public auction, the unsold lands were offered at private sale. For two and one-half weeks, competitive bidding continued at the private sales. By February 15, prices stood at $1.25; large investors continued to purchase at private sale at the minimum price during the spring and summer.

The active demand for Chickasaw lands spurred the administration to forward sales as quickly as possible. The second auction of Chickasaw lands began September 5, 1836. This sale was advertised in the newspapers throughout the South and in Boston and New York. Despite its anxiety to market the Chickasaw lands while the demand continued, the administration was at the same time pursuing a general policy of putting a damper on speculation in lands. On July 11, 1836, the Treasury Department had issued the Specie Circular, prohibiting the acceptance of any currency other than gold or silver in payment

TABLE 4

ANALYSIS OF SPECULATIVE ENTRIES IN EXCESS OF 10,000 ACRES:
PONTOTOC LAND DISTRICT, 1836–54

	Total
Amos Alexander, Adams Co., Miss.	13,245
Richard W. Anderson, Madison Co., Ala.	18,236
Armisted Barton, Franklin Co., Ala.	16,791
James A. Blanton, Pontotoc	14,922
Benjamin M. Bradford, Pontotoc	32,423
John D. Bradford, Pontotoc	18,948
Samuel Bullen, Jackson Co., Miss.	25,725
James Brown, Lafayette Co., Miss.	42,096
Ibid., with Austin Miller, Hardemann Co., Miss.	23,292
John L. Brown, Davidson Co., Tenn.; De Soto Co., Miss.	13,156
Martin N. Burch, Fayette Co., Ga.	16,226
Boling C. Burnett, Monroe Co., Miss.	12,184
William Carroll, Davidson Co., Tenn.	10,605
Willis W. Cherry, Monroe Co., Miss.	14,222
Thomas Coopwood, Lawrence Co., Ala.	11,701
William Coopwood, Lawrence Co., Ala.	12,068
George G. Cossit, Fayette Co., Tenn.	15,054
John Davis, Pontotoc	13,542
John Donelson, Franklin Co., Ala.	22,064
James W. Drake, Pontotoc	20,946
Eli M. Driver, Madison Co., Ala.; Pontotoc; Yalobusha Co., Miss.	96,269
William H. Duke, Pontotoc	17,769
Edward Featherston, Columbus, Ga.	37,971
George Fisher, Yazoo Co., Miss.	10,515
James Fort, Marshall Co., Miss.	26,601
Ebenezer Gaston, Wilcox Co., Ala.	16,798
Malcolm Gilchrist, Lauderdale Co., Ala.	30,880
David B. Grant, Muskogee Co., Ga.	11,542
Ralph Graves, Lownds Co., Miss.	10,782
Daniel Green, Sumpter Co., Ala.	38,376
James Greer, Henry Co., Tenn.	30,931
M. A. Gwin, Warren Co., Miss.	40,900

Jesse Herd, Madison Co., Ala.	11,150
Daniel Hook, Richmond Co., Ga.	11,907
Thomas B. Hoover, Madison Co., Miss.	20,069
Thomas Hoxey, Columbus, Ga.	10,732
David Hubbard, Courtland, Ala.	29,897
Jonathan Hunt, Mobile, Ala.	23,713
John P. Jones, Lafayette Co., Miss.	33,119
Weldon Jones, Marshall Co., Miss.	19,650
J. W. Lane, Morgan Co., Ala.	20,262
Felix Lewis, Columbus, Ga.	24,668
Samuel McCorkle, Henry Co., Tenn.; Marshall Co., Miss.	21,307
Charles McDonald, Giles Co., Tenn.	13,079
Thomas McGee, Lownds Co., Miss.	12,584
John A. McNeill, Pontotoc	16,203
Kenneth McRae, Pickins Co., Ala.	13,163
Charles W. Martin, Monroe Co., Miss.	17,336
Joseph D. Matthews, Marshall Co., Miss.	44,795
John H. Miller, Jr., Pontotoc	14,212
Charles C. Mills, Baldwin Co., Ga.	27,805
Philip O'Reiley, Franklin Co., Ala.	12,740
Richard E. Orne, Suffolk Co., Miss. and Pontotoc	19,076
Daniel Saffarans, Gallatin Co., Tenn.	10,720
William H. Saunders, Monroe Co., Miss.	52,589
Wolf Steppacher & Henry Bissinger	17,678
Swepson Taylor, Harris Co., Ga.	21,709
John N. Willie, Pontotoc	22,388
James I. Wilson, Pontotoc	13,660
James Word, Tishomingo Co., Miss.	10,245
Edward Orne, New York & Mississippi Land Co.	77,373

ANALYSIS OF TOTAL ENTRIES IN EXCESS OF 2,000 ACRES

1836	1837	1838	1839	1840	1841	1842
894,491	71,754	55,347	185,395	110,768	125,024	25,027
1843	1844	1845	1846	1847	1848	1849
6,665	26,546	104,044	100,862	41,812	28,565	8,872
	1850	1851	1852	1853	1854	
	23,547	18,941	31,163	71,733	60,334	

Total: 1,990,592

for public lands. This attempt at forcing a contraction of the currency did not inhibit the speculators in Chickasaw lands. They hired dummy entrymen among the "actual settlers," who by the terms of the circular could continue buying lands with state bank notes. They also borrowed specie or specie certificates from the "pet banks" at Pontotoc and Decatur, Alabama. As long as the receiver at the Pontotoc Land Office continued to deposit the proceeds of the sales into these banks and the government did not call for the transfer of his deposits, cash in the bank vaults operated as a kind of revolving fund for the speculators. Thus there were ample funds for speculation, and the sales in the fall of 1836 were characterized by the same sort of oscillation between competition and co-operation as had prevailed at the earlier auction.[19]

At the request of the commissioner of Indian Affairs, the General Land Office issued a further proclamation for May, 1837. Despite the money panic prevalent during this month, there was extensive competition among speculators for the newly-offered lands. Throughout 1837, however, the quantity of land sold dropped rapidly, and the proportion sold for speculation fell even further. Sales to large investors declined until the graduation of the price of part of the land to twenty-five cents an acre in January, 1839, produced a new flurry. The panic and the general suspension of specie payments by the banks in 1840 led to still further drops both in total purchases and in the proportion of purchases made by speculators. The market began to recover with the last auction of Chickasaw lands in 1844, speculative purchasing taking a spurt in 1845 as lands in the Mississippi bottom, heretofore covered by improperly located allotments, were reopened to entry. After this flurry the level of speculative buying fell back to the point it had reached in the

---

[19] Bolton to Curtis, August 13, 1836, Papers of the New York and Mississippi Land Company, *loc. cit.* The effect of such practices was admitted by President Van Buren in his message to the special session of Congress, September 4, 1837. James D. Richardson (ed.), *A Compilation of the Messages and Papers of the Presidents*, IV, 1551. A detailed explanation of the practices of the Agricultural Bank at Pontotoc may be found in the Mississippi *House Journal*, 1840, 106 ff.

early forties. It rose again in the fifties, probably on account of the projection of railroads through the cession and because land then in the market was worthless to anyone except planters and merchants who could unload it at an inflated valuation on unsuspecting northern creditors.

By this time the expenses of the Pontotoc Land Office exceeded its revenues. For this reason a final sale was held in May, 1854, the remaining land being sold for what it would bring: prices ranged from two to ten cents an acre. Here again "companies formed suddenly & buying to sell again among themselves" purchased about 60,000 acres. Leading citizens of the city of Pontotoc combined at this final sale to speculate at the government's expense. The two-section land office reserve bordering the city was divided into city lots and auctioned at the $1.25 an acre governmental minimum. After agreement among the citizens of the town and the speculators at the sale, a committee of three bid off the lots at the minimum price, resold them, and contributed the net profit, $4,175, to the building of a "male academy" for the town.[20]

Partly as a consequence of the land boom of the late 1830's and partly on account of the graduation of land prices, the Chickasaw district sold more rapidly than was usual for public domain lands, though it produced a smaller gross return. The four and one-third million acres of the cession brought in approximately three and one-third million dollars.[21]

The course of speculation in the Pontotoc districts supports the hypothesis that speculative purchase of governmental lands was a constant factor so long as the lands remained on the market, rather than an ephemeral phenomenon confined to "boom" years or public auctions. Speculative buying, though its propor-

[20] John Wilson to Robert McClelland, September 20, 1854, Chickasaw Letterbook, Vol IV, 40–41, *loc. cit.* Bolton to Curtis, October 12, 1854, Papers of the New York and Mississippi Land Company, *loc. cit.* Compare this with Abstract of Cash Entries, Pontotoc Land Office, May, 1854, *loc. cit.*

[21] Figures for the period to June 30, 1845, in 29 Cong., 1 sess., *Sen. Doc. 16,* 11; the remainder in annual reports on the Chickasaw Fund printed for each session in the *House Executive Documents.*

tion was greatest at the opening of the district, accounted for more than 15 per cent of the total sales in every year from 1836 to 1854.[22] Persons buying more than two thousand acres purchased nearly half the land offered.

Nonetheless, the term "monopolists" could hardly have applied to those who speculated in the Chickasaw lands, even supposing that theirs was a uniform commodity. In the Pontotoc district alone, the company of "speculators" included 192 names. Many of these investors, especially those buying 10,000 acres or more, are persons whose names may be found on the entry books of other land offices in the Old Southwest, as well as on the list of speculators in Chickasaw, Choctaw, and Creek allotments. Richard W. Anderson, of Madison County, Alabama; Armisted Barton, of Franklin County, Alabama; James A. Blanton and Benjamin Bradford of Pontotoc; James Brown of Lafayette County, Mississippi; Willis W. Cherry, of Monroe County, Mississippi; Thomas and William Coopwood of Laurence County, Alabama; John Donelson of Franklin County, Alabama; Eli Moore Driver, of Madison County, Alabama, and Pontotoc and Yalobusha counties, Mississippi; William H. Duke, of Pontotoc; Edward Featherston, of Columbus, Georgia; Malcolm Gilchrist, of Lauderdale County, Alabama; Daniel Greene, of Sumpter County, Alabama; Felix Lewis, of Columbus, Georgia; and Daniel Saffarans of Gallatin, Tennessee, are all speculators who figured prominently not only in the Pontotoc district, but also at the Chocchuma sale, and in the buying of Indian allotments.

In view of the uncomplimentary references to the rapacity of the so-called "monopolists" in the political dialog of the time, it is interesting to note evidence that speculation itself was hardly sufficient to make a man unpopular in the community where he practiced it. Joseph D. Matthews, of Marshall County, Mississippi, was the fourth largest buyer of trust lands in the Chickasaw cession. He purchased a total of 44,795 acres. Over

[22] Statistical generalizations derived from compiling figures in Abstract of Cash Entries, Pontotoc Land Office, *loc. cit.*

half this total he bought in 1836, but his acquisitions extend through 1854 and cover twelve of the nineteen years during which the land office was open. Yet Matthews' home community, in the center of the Pontotoc Land District, sent him to the state legislature, and in 1848 he was elected governor of Mississippi.[23]

Although the proportion of speculative buying was smaller in connection with the public sales than in the case of the Indian allotments, a study of public land sales in Mississippi during the 1830's shows that a significant number of buyers were men whose interests were investment in land, rather than its cultivation. Many of this group put in an appearance at sale after sale in the Old Southwest. They worked out a system whereby they sometimes succeeded in reducing the amount of competition at public auctions and in appropriating the revenue derived from competitive bidding to themselves. The speculative fraternity, however, included not only these habitués, but also hundreds of others, settlers and investors alike, whose presence at the public sales precluded a consistent "monopoly" of the bidding. Furthermore, the organization of even major speculators was short-lived, having as objectives simply the pooling of information on the quality of lands and the reducing of original costs of their investments. Thus while the speculators, as a group, were ever-present competitors of the settler in the purchase of government lands, they showed themselves willing to combine with the settlers against the "revenue interest" of the government; and while quantitatively the total of purchases for investment was significant, the number of investors alone appears to preclude the possibility that they might adopt the uniform sales policy characteristic of genuine monopoly. The conflict of interest between settler and speculator was sufficient to make "speculation" a political shibboleth, but participation in speculation was not in itself enough to bar a man from a career in politics: witness Joseph D. Matthews, David Hubbard (a congressman from Alabama), and Robert J. Walker. In certain re-

[23] Mississippi *House Journal*, 1840, 4; *ibid.*, 1842, 4; *National Cyclopedia of American Biography*, XIII, 489.

spects, the usefulness of the speculation issue in creating political "devils" tended to obscure rather than illuminate the basic problems of land policy, personalizing the issues and distorting the fact that, under the going system, one of the speculator's chief assets was the area of common interest between himself and the settler.

·9·

THE ALLOTMENT POLICY
AND THE PUBLIC LAND SYSTEM

THE INDIAN LAND POLICIES OF THE JACKSON ADMINISTRATION should be examined not only as a part of the pattern of land speculation, but also as an element of the general land system. The relevant question here is the accommodation of land laws and administration to the accomplishment of real or alleged goals of land policy. The allotment and trust systems operated in opposition to certain policies designed to benefit settlers on the public domain. Yet their effect as a whole was consonant with the dominant laissez faire tendency of public land administration, and exhibits the generally equivocal advantages of this tendency.

Jackson expressed his views of land policy in two annual messages to Congress. His words echo the familiar Jeffersonian shibboleths, and his attitude is one which might be expected of a champion of the small entrepreneur. In December, 1832, he proclaimed, "The wealth and strength of a country are its population, and the best part of that population are cultivators of the soil. Independent farmers are everywhere the basis of society, and the true friends of liberty."[1] The "true policy" therefore was the sale of the land to the settler "in limited parcels,

[1] Richardson (ed.), *Messages and Papers of the Presidents*, III, 1164.

at a price barely sufficient to reimburse to the United States the expense of the present system, and the cost arising under our Indian compacts." In his annual message of December, 1836, the President justified the Specie Circular on the ground that it would check speculation in the public lands. Furthermore, he added, "Much good, in my judgment, would be produced by prohibiting sales of the public lands except to actual settlers at a reasonable reduction of price, and to limit the quantity which shall be sold to them."[2]

Jackson's views agreed with those of the southwestern state legislatures and of such inveterate champions of a "liberal" land policy as Thomas Hart Benton. Taking the prescriptions of the liberals systematically, the land system would work like this: The purchase of public lands would be limited, temporarily or permanently, to actual settlers, who would be allowed to pre-empt the 160 acres including their improvements at prices graduated according to the length of time the lands had been on the market. This would encourage concentrated settlement of the public domain, since poorer settlers might take up refuse lands at reduced prices and speculators could not engross large tracts and withhold them from sale and settlement. The denser settlement would give local governments a larger tax base in improved lands, thus enabling them to support schools and internal improvements. Although excluding speculators from the market might reduce federal revenues, the more rapid sale of second- and third-class lands would enlarge them. Furthermore, income from the public domain would continue longer if lands were sold gradually. The increasing population and production of the western states would indirectly augment government revenues by enhancing the wealth of the entire nation.[3]

[2] *Ibid.*, IV, 1469.

[3] Compare petitions of the legislature of Alabama, January 6, 1831, February 13, 1833, *American State Papers: Public Lands,* VI, 260–61, 609; Resolution of the legislature of Mississippi, January 22, 1846, Records of the United States Senate, National Archives; Report of the Committee on Public Lands, February 5, 1828, 20 Cong., 1 sess., *House Report 125;* Report of the Committee on Public Lands, December 10, 1834, 23 Cong., 2 sess., *House Report 1.*

None of these liberal proposals were written in full into the land laws of the period. In the winter of 1837, the Senate passed a bill for limiting entries to actual settlers under the pre-emption laws and abandoning the auction system, but this was tabled in the House.[4] The principal legislation favoring the "actual settler" was that giving him the right to pre-empt the 160 acres surrounding his improvements. In 1830, 1834, and 1838, Congress provided that anyone living on the public domain who had cultivated his lands during a given number of months preceding the law's passage might purchase up to 160 acres at the minimum price of $1.25 an acre. These laws were retrospective: that is, they applied only to settlements established before their passage, and the pre-emptor had to pay for his land before it was offered at public auction.[5]

Except for occasional debates over the graduation of land prices; pre-emption, public sales, and their various abuses dominated the discussion of national land policy. The arguments revolved about the rights of pioneer settlers, whose hardships and whose contributions to the winning of the west were real, dramatic, and well-suited to declamation. In fact, however, the predominant mode of obtaining federal lands was purchase at private sale. In Alabama, for example, between the first offering of lands in 1809, and 1860, there were only ten years when newly offered lands constituted more than half the quantity sold. For the whole period, the ratio was only 0.15. In Mississippi, 1807–60, there were only six years when more than half the lands sold were newly offered; the ratio for the period as a whole was between 0.19 and 0.22.[6] Since townships were offered at auction during periods of only two weeks, only a part of the above ratios represent lands sold *at auction*. Probably more than 90 per cent of the land sold under regular public land laws during the pre-

[4] Report from the Senate Committee on Public Lands, June 15, 1836, 24 Cong., 1 sess., *Sen. Doc. 402*; 13 *Register of Debates in Congress*, 204–777; 2901–902.

[5] 4 *Statutes at Large*, 420, 603, 663–64; 5 *ibid.*, 252.

[6] The Mississippi figures cannot be determined precisely, since no estimate of percentage of sales of newly offered land can be made for the Chickasaw cession after 1837.

TABLE 5

LAND OFFERING AND LAND SALES IN ALABAMA, 1809–60

Year	Amount Offered	Amount Sold	Amount of Newly Offered Land Sold	Ratio of Sales of Newly Offered Land and Total Sales
1809	315,906.34	61,067.77	61,067.77	1.00
1810		32,030.01		.00
1811	878,424.35	51,205.12	14,867.98	.29
1812		24,338.26		.00
1813		19,720.48		.00
1814		25,439.59		.00
1815	507,114.06	52,210.81	30,529.86	.58
1816		38,577.51		.00
1817	895,548.53	122,495.49	99,781.70	.82
1818	2,943,932.78	531,691.12	500,710.79	.94
1819	3,059,157.81	420,310.75	308,753.29	.73
1820	1,499,071.98	190,339.61	110,184.59	.58
1821	2,736,944.55	214,311.40	131,897.64	.62
1822		141,014.60		.00
1823	2,117,935.75	153,429.27	105,223.70	.69
1824	670,388.33	124,588.78	319.93	.003
1825	665,351.97	195,783.75	49,912.75	.25
1826	360,723.32	143,362.65	59,690.80	.42
1827	315,511.96	95,138.41	22,015.42	.23
1828	775,914.55	163,194.78	75,341.44	.42
1829	388,657.81	120,542.13	19,250.34	.16
1830	1,352,349.06	369,379.06	210,064.80	.57
1831	2,496.995.38	723,574.36	131,047.78	.18
1832		405,497.60		.00
1833		443,299.72		.00
1834	3,507,072.69†	1,043,021.54	530,699.97	.51
1835		1,542,005.23		.00
1836		1,488,549.18		.00
1837	22,287.72	371,459.25		.00
1838	501,304.93	157,464.41	23,288.05	.15
1839		124,185.28		.00
1840	34,260.00	57,626.15	4,116.78	.07

Year	Amount Offered	Amount Sold	Amount of Newly Offered Land Sold	Ratio of Sales of Newly Offered Land and Total Sales
1841		50,030.45	6,524.58	.13
1842		110,265.12	73,948.04*	.67*
1843	1,557,359.29	189,402.13	135,687.15	.72
1844		83,093.77		.00
1845		77,635.37		.00
1846		78,506.15		.00
1847		146,859.45		.00
1848		94,478.78		.00
1849		144,807.39		.00
1850		303,203.03		.00
1851		286,862.08		.00
1852		117,087.32		.00
1853		274,668.67		.00
1854		1,763,665.79		.00
1855		1,526,069.79		.00
1856		755,081.05		.00
1857		258,423.30		.00
1858		291,425.88		.00
1859		637,098.15		.00
1860		766,247.64		.00
Totals:		17,611,765.38	2,704,925.15	.15 (for whole period)

* Land offered in January, 1843, apparently sold under Pre-emption Act of 1841 in 1842.
† Estimated: Quantity of unallotted Creek lands offered assumed as 2 million

---

homestead period in Alabama and Mississippi went at private sales for not more than $1.25 an acre. In the nation as a whole, of the 63,056,785 acres of the public domain sold in all states and territories between 1828 and 1840, more than half, or 35,-247,516 acres, were lands offered *prior to 1828.*[7]

The reason why the largest proportion of the lands sold were

[7] 26 Cong., 2 sess., *Sen. Doc. 92,* 22.

TABLE 6

Land Offering and Land Sales in Mississippi, 1807–60

Year	Amount Offered	Amount Sold	Amount of Newly Offered Land Sold	Ratio of Sales of Newly Offered Land and Total Sales
1807		16,096.97*		
1808		824.49*		
1809	813,610.58	47,155.35*	11,737.14	.25
1810		5,642.12		.00
1811	4,283,875.18	56,250.78	48,410.53	.87
1812		25,409.78		.00
1813		7,289.64		.00
1814		2,485.59		.00
1815	734,828.46	143,218.01	74,509.11	.52
1816		229,749.26		.00
1817		145,376.09		.00
1818		144,888.74		.00
1819		43,829.89		.00
1820	68,121.90	15,922.15	8,390.86	.53
1821	175,824.71	41,068.64	22,806.10	.54
1822		25,899.55		
1823	1,024,173.55	33,282.11	27,151.47	.82
1824	907,636.67	76,297.03	31,761.03	.43
1825	481,245.90	81,522.51	1,846.79	.02
1826	770,187.44	77,886.81	25,412.40	.33
1827	412,219.54	58,921.17	5,681.07	.10
1828	189,484.48	70,323.88	2,118.68	.03
1829	867,502.31	98,931.65	28,537.63	.29
1830	196,324.50	105,807.19	5,425.71	.05
1831	779,680.37	150,536.40	30,491.61	.20
1832		236,894.39		.00
1833	2,855,832.63	1,126,232.13	467,189.28	.41
1834	2,931,789.94	1,063,490.64	494,182.53	.47
1835	1,098,073.93	2,874,559.10	388,657.85	.14
1836	3,123,306.00	3,267,299.33	1,304,161.42	.40
1837	545,380.00	430,096.21	167,991.53	
1838	116,608.00	327,807.14	116,608.00	

Year	Amount Offered	Amount Sold	Amount of Newly Offered Land Sold	Ratio of Sales of Newly Offered Land and Total Sales
1839	156,070.00	650,458.24	156,070.00	
1840		471,548.65		
1841		348,717.92		
1842		325,790.34		
1843	1,070,163.96	73,392.50	10,131.78	.14
1844	383,343.00	153,364.43	124,269.18	
1845		188,100.87		
1846	1,869,746.00	306,816.06	49,337.44	.16
1847		227,156.93		
1848		103,899.71		
1849		71,183.14		
1850		89,257.39		
1851		105,473.43		
1852		87,429.25		
1853		280,848.40		
1854		886,153.66		
1855		337,116.52		
1856		126,327.91		
1857		169,434.31		
1858		132,331.93		
1859		271,857.48		
1860		185,769.89		
Totals		16,427,053.45	3,037,220.43– 3,602,159.15	.18–.22

* Land in section offered 1815, sold under pre-emption prior to offering.

Note: These charts are compiled on the basis of 30 Cong., 2 Sess., *House Ex. Doc. 12*, Appendix. This document does not include figures for the Chickasaw cession, which are derived from special annual reports of Chickasaw sales made by the Secretary of the Treasury and printed in the Congressional documents. The entire Chickasaw cession is counted as a part of Mississippi, since the figures available do not distinguish between the cession in Mississippi and the 434,000 acres in Alabama. Figures for the period of credit sales, ending in 1820, are apparently net figures, forfeitures being subtracted from the total sales reported during those years.

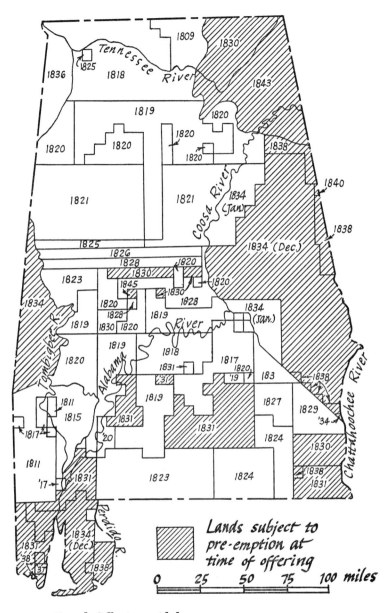

MAP 12. Land Offering: Alabama

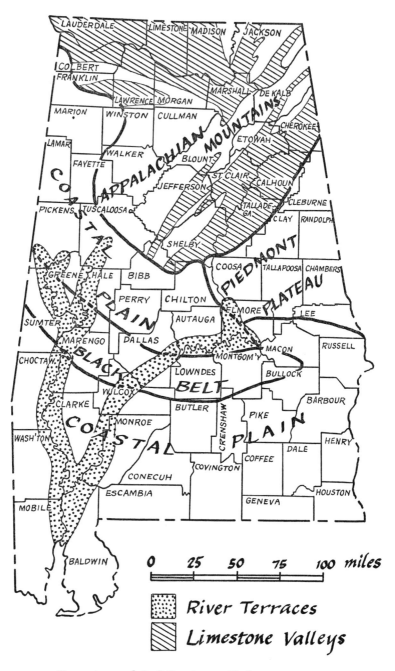

MAP 13. Counties and Soil Regions: Alabama

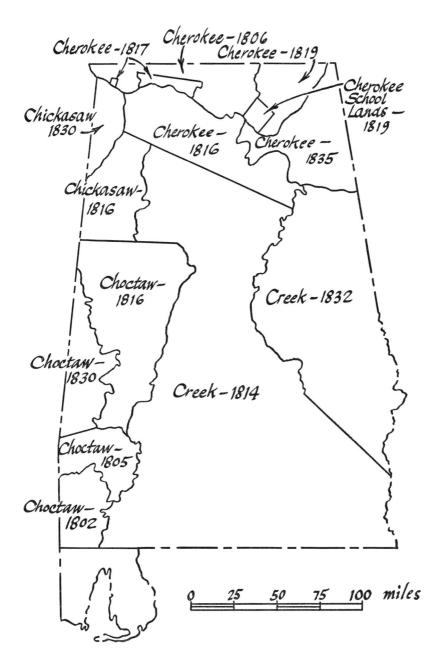

MAP 14. Indian Land Cessions: Alabama

those which had been on the market for some time was that the federal government made a consistent practice of offering more land for sale each year than could possibly be purchased. The Indian allotment policy, which gave the land speculator rather than the early settler the effective right of pre-emption to lands in the Chickasaw, Choctaw, and Creek cessions, and the Chickasaw cession in trust, which debarred settler pre-emptions altogether, apparently contradicted the stated land policy of the Jacksonians. Yet, since their aim was to secure lands for public offering as rapidly as possible, they were consistent with the standard administrative practice of the land office at the time. Rapid offering of the public lands was sometimes inconsistent with the "settler interest." It threw large areas into market before many settlers had realized enough from their crops to purchase their claims. In combination with the policy of unrestricted entry, it promoted speculative buying in advance of settlement, which operated to the disadvantage of farmers who emigrated to the offered areas after the sales.[8]

Although the policy of rapid offering seemed to defeat some of the basic goals of the "Jacksonians," President Jackson during the thirties put pressure on the General Land Office to accelerate the offering of land.[9] Furthermore, the pre-emption laws themselves provided that granting special rights to settlers was not to be construed so as to delay sales while the settlers established their claims.[10] In 1835, the commissioner of the General Land Office cited this provision in refusing to comply with an Illinois petition for postponing a sale, and the President acquiesced in this decision.[11] Why did Jackson call for legislation to protect

[8] Compare Paul W. Gates, "Land Policy and Tenancy in the Prairie States," *Journal of Economic History*, Vol. I (1941), 66 ff.

[9] Compare General Land Office, Register of Letters Received, 1831–33, 43; *ibid.*, August 1, 1835, May 23, 1835, March 18, 1836; Elijah Hayward to the President, November 11, 1833, June 23, 1834, General Land Office, Miscellaneous Letters Sent, Vol. LXIX, 156 and Vol. LXX, 12, Records of the Bureau of Land Management.

[10] 4 *Statutes at Large*, 420–21; 5 *ibid.*, 453–58.

[11] Elijah Hayward to the President, May 2, 1835, General Land Office, Miscellaneous Letters Sent, Vol. LXXI, 16, Records of the Bureau of Land Management.

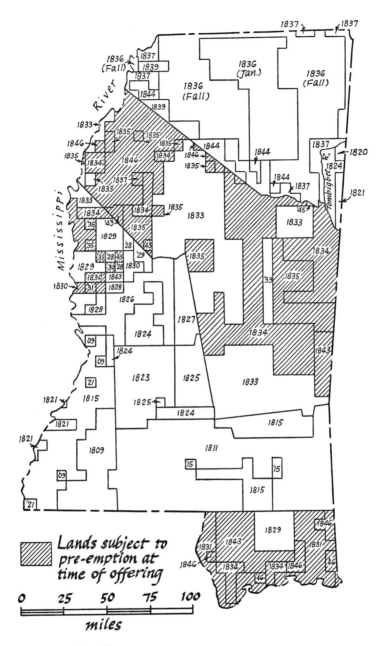

MAP 15. Land Offering: Mississippi

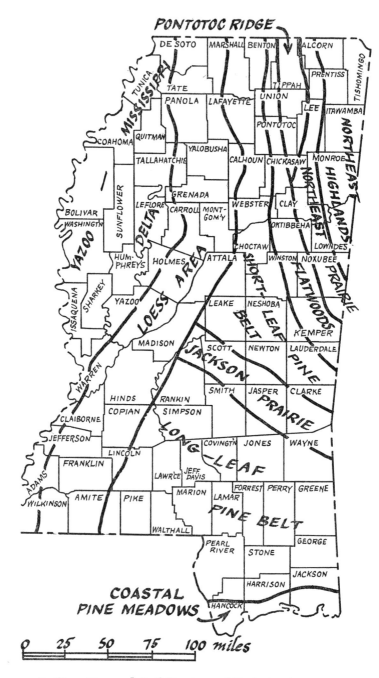

MAP 16. Counties and Soil Regions: Mississippi

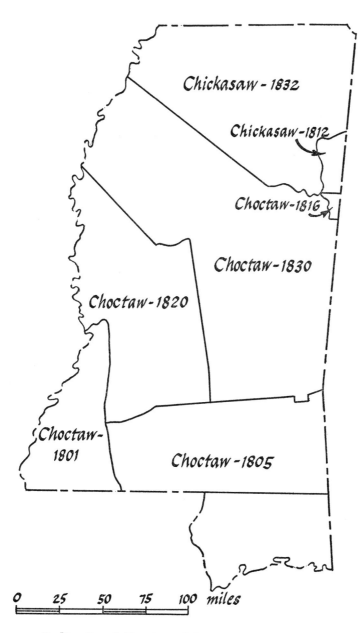

Chickasaw - 1832

Chickasaw - 1812

Choctaw - 1816

Choctaw - 1830

Choctaw - 1820

Choctaw - 1801

Choctaw - 1805

0   25   50   75   100 miles

MAP 17. Indian Land Cessions: Mississippi

the settler and to limit speculation, and yet invoke administrative policies—such as the use of Indian allotments and the rapid offering of lands for sale—which seemed to facilitate speculation, perhaps at the expense of the "actual settler"?

The Whig journalists offered a ready solution to this paradox. Jackson's messages in defense of the settler were sheer cynical demagoguery. One writer asserted that the whole aim of the Jackson policy was to offer lands at the instance of speculating Democrats, who combined with land officers to make princely fortunes at the expense of the honest settler.[12] Senator Poindexter's investigation of the Chocchuma sale was intended to document such assertions. In the Whig view, Jackson's advocacy of settlers' rights was undertaken solely in order to attract settlers' votes.

Probably this explanation fitted some of the "Jacksonians." Witness the following letter, written by Democratic Congressman David Hubbard of Alabama, himself an active and enterprising speculator. Advising President Van Buren, Hubbard asserted that the poor settlers in the public domain states "turn the scale of opinion in all elections." Since they are generally too poor to buy their lands in competition with speculators, there is no question on which they unite so readily as on the demand for pre-emption rights. There follows a stirring condemnation of "this odious scheme of fraud and speculation practiced at public sales by monopolizing combinations . . . ," of which Hubbard himself had been a prominent figure. But, he says, a man in whose administration a permanent pre-emption law is passed, "will secure for himself a name in the West which will never be forgotten." In conclusion,

> . . . the country people in the new states waking or sleeping eating or working never think of anything but "Land"—Tennessee has a good quantity of public land within its limits of so poor a quality that land warrant holders would not take it up with warrants which

[12] *Daily National Intelligencer* (Washington), October 6, 1834, quoting the *New Jersey Journal.*

cost but twelve and one half cents pr. acre which poor lands had many squatters settled upon them and yet Sir although the lands were so very poor, David Crocket (without talent) was enabled to maintain his popularity for years against Genl. Jackson and every other member of Congress from Tennessee solely on the ground of his wanting rights of pre-emption to that portion of his constituents who were termed squatters. . . . what must be the influence of such a question in eight or ten new states where poor lands are scattered in every district?[13]

Although Jackson may not have been cynically indifferent to the fate of the squatter, he apparently did not regard the problem of speculation as a pressing one until the "boom" of 1836, combining as it did the banking question with the land question and thus bringing the latter forcibly to his attention. In December of 1832, Jackson may have believed it desirable to allow settlers to take up lands at low prices; yet he favored rapid offering of lands as long as the money spent by the government to secure them from the Indians and prepare them for market had not yet been returned. Only when rapid offering, combined with other federal policies such as the placing of government deposits in state banks and the distribution of the surplus revenue, led to wildcat speculation and wild inflation did Jackson propose effective measures to inhibit speculation.

Up to the time of his annual message in December, 1836, there is nothing in Jackson's behavior or his writings to suggest that he considered land speculation, as such, discreditable. He had invested in lands himself, and as late as November, 1833, he advised his protégé, Andrew Jackson Hutchings, to invest his money in "good land well situated, that will improve in value. Your investment is then safe and while you are sleeping your land will be increasing in value."[14]

Nor is it certain that Jackson regarded the rapid offering of public lands as detrimental to the interests of western communi-

[13] Hubbard to Van Buren, November 20, 1837, Van Buren Manuscripts, Library of Congress.
[14] November 3, 1833, in *The Correspondence of Jackson*, V, 224.

ties as a whole. Some insight into his views on this issue may be derived from his comments to General John Coffee in December, 1816, regarding the offering of public lands in the Tennessee Valley of Alabama. "Mr. Crawford [secretary of the treasury] is opposed to bringing this land into markett speedily—he says it would glutt the markett, & the U. States would lose by it—Mr. C. has a better reason than this, he does not like us, wishes at the hazard of the safety of the Union, to Cramp our growing greatness, & wishes to prevent the population of Georgia to be drained by the emigration to this new country."[15]

In this statement, Jackson seems to equate permanent settlement with the offering of the public lands. Perhaps this is because his view of the western community embraces not only impoverished farmers, but also substantial planters, townsite promoters, and others whose "settlement" required a large cash investment and therefore a secure title to their property. Even a squatter who wanted to sell his improvements or a permanent settler who wanted to buy them might have the same desire for security. The existence of petitions for the postponement of sales need not imply that the majority of "actual settlers" preferred a long period of grace before sales to a secure title.

The President's administrative practice was clearly inconsistent with his stated policies only if one assumes that the "interest" of speculator and settler were invariably opposed and that it was desirable to use restrictive legislation to promote the interest of the settler over that of the speculator. Most features of the liberal land program, which would have reduced the price of public lands and made larger quantities available, were potentially as profitable to the speculator as to the settler. The only exception is the restriction of entries to cultivators, which was discussed only during the land boom of 1836–37. Effective restriction of land accumulation would have required that the government limit not only the speculator's right to buy government land, but also the settler's right to sell the land he had bought. It seems improbable that Jackson would have found

[15] November 25, 1816, Robert Dyas Collection of John Coffee Papers, Tennessee Historical Society.

such a restriction congenial to his philosophy of government.

Jackson did not believe in shaping government policy to forward the interest of private "monopolies." But his conception of the role of government did not include the idea that close regulation of the economy or any part of it for the interest of the farmer, the poor, or any other unprivileged group was desirable. A land system which effectively excluded from ownership all but actual cultivators of the soil would have required a check on acquisitive enterprise quite out of keeping with the spirit of "Jacksonian democracy." As Richard Hofstadter has written about Jackson's views on banking, "The popular hatred of privilege and the dominant laissez-faire ideology made an unhappy combination."[16]

The argument against limiting entries on public lands to actual settlers was neatly summarized by Senator Collamer, of Vermont, reporting from the Committee on Public Lands on June 23, 1848.[17] Collamer emphasized that the only certain way of preventing speculation in lands was to prohibit settlers from selling their farms for a long period after they had bought them. He condemned such a policy as a relic of feudalism, an improper practice for a free government. Although he was rationalizing the eastern conservative position, his assertions reflect the assumptions of contemporary western reformers. Westerners advocated both pre-emption and graduation as means for facilitating the passage of land from public to private ownership. As one Alabama petition put it, "Lands are not a suitable property to be owned by the United States; they are better adapted to the people."[18] Since the small farmer as well as the large investor speculated in lands, restrictions on alienation would probably have been as unacceptable to most pre-emptors as they were to a conservative such as Collamer.

Collamer's report included a description of contemporary practice in federal land administration—alternatives to limiting en-

[16] Richard Hofstadter, *The American Political Tradition and the Men Who Made It*, 64.

[17] 30 Cong., 1 sess., *House Report 732*.

[18] January 6, 1836, Records of the United States Senate.

tries and alienation. Rapid survey and offering of lands plus the granting of pre-emption rights gave settlers a continuous opportunity to select and exploit the best of the new lands. Furthermore, the continual offering of lands placed the government in competition with speculative landholders, thus depressing the price of all lands and benefiting the settler who wanted to buy a farm.

The General Land Office policy was consistent with the principles of a free contractual system. Save for the settler's right of pre-emption, it opened natural resources to all comers on the same basis, and it gave private owners secure title and freedom to use their property as they pleased. If such a policy often led to consequences incompatible with Jeffersonian ideals of a democratic land system, it had the advantage of allowing private freedom often as useful to the small operator as to the large investor—the opportunity to obtain capital by selling a pre-emption claim, to change residence at will, or to profit from the appreciation in value of cultivated lands by the sale of his farm to a late-comer.

In this context, the consequences of any given land policy were indeterminate. A scheme ostensibly designed to meet the needs of the settler or the Indian might be perverted to the uses of speculation. Speculative demand for the offering or withholding of a district from sale (as in the Choctaw cession) might ultimately benefit the settler at the speculator's expense. In the case of the allotment policy, both Indian and settler were disadvantaged in order that the areas under Indian title might be converted into public domain and brought into market; but had the Indians continued to hold their former share of Alabama and Mississippi, the settler would have been still further deprived.

As in other spheres of the political economy during the "Age of Jackson," freedom in the acquisition and use of property gave scope to the implementation of a variety of purposes, not simply those professed by politicians. It also gave a strong competitive advantage to the rich, the clever, and the well-connected.

THE JACKSONIAN REMOVAL POLICY
IN RETROSPECT

To EXPLOIT THE RESOURCES of a virgin continent as God intended them to be exploited and to acquire a competence for oneself by doing so—such were the true motives conveniently wed in the westward expansion of the American people. One of the chief enterprises of the Jacksonian generation was the establishment of homes, villages, and prosperous farms, "full of the blessings of liberty, civilization, and religion," in the wastelands hitherto roamed by the spendthrift savage.[1] Yet the savage proved an impediment to this enterprise in both the moral and the practical sense. Before the time had come when he must be removed, the savage began to imitate the ways of civilization. The time came, and the problem of his removal had been transformed. For if it had been right to supplant the savage hunter with the civilized farmer, was it now right to remove the Indian farmer so that the white farmer could enjoy his country? And, considering the political acumen of the half-blood tribal leaders and their humanitarian champions in Congress, *could* the Indian be removed?

The answer, of course, was yes. To treat an Indian fairly, after

[1] Jackson's First Annual Message, in Richardson (ed.), *Messages and Papers of the Presidents*, III, 1084. Compare Roy H. Pearce, *The Savages of America: The American Indian and the Idea of Civilization.*

all, was to treat him like a white man. One must respect his property, defined in the Lockian sense as that with which he has mixed his labor—his improved land. One must respect his right to make a free contract in transferring title to his property. And one must, of course, expect the beneficiary of such respect to make responsible use of what he owns—to take care of himself. In dealing with some of the most "civilized" of the Indian tribes—the Chickasaws, Choctaws, and Creeks of Alabama and Mississippi—Jacksonian negotiators found it possible to treat them fairly, and deprive them of their lands.

With ruthless and willfully blind consistency, the Jacksonians proceeded to treat the tribesmen like white men. They extended state laws over the Indian tribes, destroying the "tyrannical" tribal governments in the process. Having fractured tribal solidarity, they proceeded to fragment the tribal domain. They allotted tribal lands to individual Indians, attempting to give each secure title to the lands he had cultivated. They offered Indians who could not live under those conditions of freedom and responsibility the alternative of emigrating to Indian Territory. They assumed, of course, that the incompetent would be in the majority.

This policy had certain obvious advantages. It was moral. It protected the Indian's right to private property and freedom of contract. It was practical, for it also opened lands to settlement and offered opportunities for speculation in Indian allotments. In violation, of the spirit, and finally the letter of the treaties, the government encouraged settlement on the ceded lands. In conformity with the treaties' true spirit, it also encouraged speculations in Indian allotments. The result was a series of bitter conflicts between Indians and settlers, Indians and speculators, and speculators and speculators. There were frauds, judicially and impartially investigated and found irremediable. There was a delay in emigration, while testimony was taken and Indians waited in vain hope of salvation by or from the speculative fraternity. There was even a fairly administered treaty, and some of the Chickasaws left Mississippi with money in the bank. The speculators won every time, at least until they tried to sell their lands at a profit. Generally they sold them at an advance, but their profits were less than they had expected.

The government finally decided that the allotment policy, whatever its advantages, was too much trouble. The spectacular frauds led to administrative complications and bad publicity. The administration therefore refused allotments to the Cherokees, and the policy was not revived on any considerable scale until 1854, when it was applied with similar consequences, to the Indians of Kansas.[2]

As a land policy, as well as an Indian policy, the allotment system was less than perfect. Like other features of the contemporary land system, it was rationalized as benefiting the underprivileged, and worked so as to give special advantage to the wealthy. The allotment policy and the land system alike reflected the ambiguous values of Jacksonian democracy. They opened the way for the rapid exploitation of the earth's resources. Legally, at any rate, they offered these resources to all on an equal basis. They respected the conditions of free contract, the individual's right to his property and his right to do what he chose with it. The unlettered savage, the unenterprising poor, and, one suspects, the scrupulously honest alike were at a disadvantage under such a system. But none of these were model Jacksonians. The model Jacksonian who emerges from this account is active, enterprising, and shrewd. As a politician, he eschews monopoly; as a businessman, he seeks it but is too individualistic to carry it off. From his government, he wants freedom, frugality, and equality of opportunism. In the realm of conscience, he seeks the optimum combination of interest and scrupulosity. If the compound was unique to his generation, the search is not.

[2] For the Cherokees, see Hon. R. Chapman to Lewis Cass, January 25, 1835, Cherokee File 7, Records of the Bureau of Indian Affairs; Lewis Cass to Commissioners Carroll and Schermerhorn, April 2, 1835, Office of Indian Affairs, Letters Sent, Vol. XV, 261, *ibid.;* "A Journal of the Proceedings at the Council Held at New Echota . . . ," Cherokee File 7, *ibid.;* 7 *Statutes at Large,* 484–85; 488–89. For the Kansas treaties, see Paul W. Gates, *Fifty Million Acres: Conflicts over Kansas Land Policy, 1854–1890,* 11–48.

BIBLIOGRAPHY

1. Government Manuscripts

a. Federal
  (1) Bureau of Land Management, Department of the Interior
      Alabama Patents (Creek Allotments).
      Chickasaw Patents.
      Choctaw Scrip Patents.
  (2) Records of the Bureau of Indian Affairs, National Archives
      Office of Indian Affairs
      Cherokee Reservation Book.
      Letters Received, Old Files, 1825–50
        Cherokee, Cherokee Emigration, Cherokee Reserve.
        Chickasaw, Chickasaw Emigration, Chickasaw Reserve.
        Choctaw, Choctaw Emigration, Choctaw Reserve.
        Miscellaneous.
      Letters Received, Choctaw, 350 (1915).
      Letters Sent, 1814–54.
      Letters Sent, Chickasaw, 1832–54.
      Ratified Treaty File.
      Special Reserve Files, A and C, with Reserve Books A and C.
  (3) Records of the Bureau of Land Management, National Archives, General Land Office
      Abstract of Cash Entries, Grenada Land Office, 1846–47.

194

Abstract of Cash Entries, Pontotoc Land Office, 1836–54.
Chickasaw Location Book.
Circulars to Registers and Receivers, 1830–50.
Letters Sent, Miscellaneous, 1830–50.
Letters Sent to Registers and Receivers, 1830–50.
Miscellaneous Letters Received by the Secretary of the
  Treasury, 1825–45.
Records of Proclamations, 1809–47.
Register of Letters Received, 1830–50.

b. State
  (1) Alabama Department of Archives and History
      Correspondence of Governors Clement C. Clay and
        John Gayle.
  (2) Georgia Department of Archives and History
      Correspondence on Creek and Cherokee Removal.
      Creek Letters.
      Governor's Letterbooks, 1825–40.
  (3) Mississippi Department of Archives and History
      Seventh Census, 1850, Schedule IV, "Productions of
        Agriculture."
      Eighth Census, 1860, Schedule IV, "Productions of
        Agriculture."
      Governors' Correspondence, 1825–60.

c. County
  (1) Alabama: In the courthouses of Macon, Montgomery, Russell,
      and Talladega counties
      Chancery Court Final Records.
      Deed Records.
      Minutes of the Orphan's (Probate) Court.
      Records of Annual and Final Returns of Administrators.
      Will Books.
  (2) Georgia: In the courthouse of Muscogee County
      Records of Annual and Final Returns of Administrators.
      Will Books.
  (3) Mississippi: In the courthouses of Marshall, Tunica, and
      De Soto counties
      Chancery Court Final Records.
      Deed Records.

Land Index.

(4) ——: In the courthouse of Pontotoc County
Final Records of the Federal District Court for the Northern
District of Mississippi.

2. Personal and Business Manuscripts

American Board of Commissioners for Foreign Missions Archives,
Houghton Library, Harvard University.
Nicholas Biddle Papers, Library of Congress.
Charles Butler Papers, Library of Congress.
G. W. Campbell Papers, Library of Congress.
J. F. H. Claiborne Papers, Library of Congress.
J. F. H. Claiborne Papers, Mississippi Department of Archives and
History.
Clement C. Clay Papers, Duke University Library.
John Coffee Papers, Alabama Department of Archives and History.
John Coffee Papers, Robert Dyas Collection, Tennessee Historical
Society.
Jeremiah Evarts Papers, Library of Congress.
Charles Fisher Papers, Southern Historical Collection, University
of North Carolina.
H. S. Halburt, Notes, Alabama Department of Archives and
History.
Andrew Jackson Papers, Library of Congress.
Papers of the New York and Mississippi Land Company, State
Historical Society of Wisconsin.
Edward Orne's Land Book, Mississippi Department of Archives
and History.
John Overton Papers, John Claybrooke Collection, Tennessee His-
torical Society.
Joel R. Poinsett Papers, Historical Society of Pennsylvania.
James K. Polk Papers, Library of Congress.
Riggs Papers, Choctaw Agency File; Letters Received, 1843–50,
William S. Paradise Letterbooks, Account Books; Elisha Riggs
Letterbooks; Romulus Riggs Letterbooks, Library of Congress.
J. W. A. Sanford Papers, Alabama Department of Archives and
History.
George W. Stiggins, A Historical Narrative of the Genealogy, Tra-

ditions and Downfall of the Ispocoga, or Creek Tribe of Indians. Draper Collection, State Historical Society of Wisconsin. Photostat, Georgia Department of Archives and History.
John D. Terrell Papers, Alabama Department of Archives and History.
Van Buren Manuscripts, Library of Congress.
Joseph Vidal Papers, Louisiana State University Archives.

3. Government Documents

a. Alabama
Acts of the Legislature of Alabama, 1828–34.
Alabama Reports, 1830–60.
House Journal, 1829–33.
Senate Journal, 1829–33.

b. Georgia
Acts of the Legislature of Georgia, 1828–35.
Georgia Reports, 1830–60.
House Journal, 1825–35.
Senate Journal, 1825–35.

c. Mississippi
Acts of the Legislature of Mississippi, 1828–46.
House Journal, 1825–43.
Senate Journal, 1825–43.
Mississippi Reports, 1830–60.

d. United States
American State Papers: Indian Affairs, 2 vols.
American State Papers: Public Lands, 8 vols.
Congressional Globe, 1835–54.
Court of Claims Reports, Vol. XXI.
House Executive Documents, 1824–60.
Richard Peters, *Reports of Cases Argued and Adjudged in the Supreme Court of the United States,* 1831–32.
Register of Debates in Congress, 1828–34.
Senate Executive Documents, 1824–60.
Statutes at Large, 1814–43.
United States National Resources Board, Land Planning Committee, *Report on Land Planning* (11 vols., Washington, 1935–39),

Vol. IX, *Indian Land Tenure, Economic Status, and Population Trends.*

4. Printed Primary Sources

Adair, James. *The History of the American Indians.* . . . London, 1775.

American Land Company. *First Annual Report of the Trustees of the American Land Company.* . . . New York, 1836.

Anderson, Mrs. W. A. "A Chapter in the Yellow Fever Epidemic of 1878," Mississippi Historical Society *Publication* (Jackson and Oxford), Vol. X (1909).

Baldwin, Joseph G. *The Flush Times of Alabama and Mississippi. A Series of Sketches.* New York, 1865.

Bartram, William. "Observations on the Creek and Cherokee Indians," *Transactions of the American Ethnological Society* (New York), Vol. III (1853), 3–81.

Bensacon's Annual Register of the State of Mississippi for the Year 1838, Compiled from Original Documents and Actual Surveys. Natchez, 1838.

Claiborne, John F. H. *Mississippi as a Province, Territory, and State.* Jackson, 1880.

Davis, Reuben. *Recollections of Mississippi and Mississippians.* Boston and New York, 1889.

[Evarts, Jeremiah.] *Essays on the Present Crisis in the Condition of the American Indians.* Boston, 1829.

Featherstonhaugh, George W. *Excursion through the Slave States, from Washington on the Potomac to the frontier of Mexico; with Sketches of popular Manners and Geological Notices.* 2 vols., London, 1844.

Garrett, William. *Reminiscences of Public Men in Alabama, for Thirty Years.* Atlanta, 1872.

Hawkins, Benjamin. *Sketch of the Creek Country in the Years 1798 and 1799.* (Georgia Historical Society *Publications*, Vol. III.) Americus, Georgia, 1938.

Letters of Benjamin Hawkins, 1796–1806. (Georgia Historical Society *Collections*, Vol. IX.) Savannah, 1916.

Hodgson, Adam. *Letters from North America, Written During a*

Bibliography

Tour in the United States and Canada.... 2 vols. London, 1824.

Hone, Philip. *The Diary of Philip Hone, 1828–1837,* ed. by Allan Nevins. 2 vols. New York, 1927.

Hull, James. "A Brief History of the Mississippi Territory," *Mississippi Historical Society Publications* (Jackson and Oxford), Vol. IX (1906).

[Ingraham, Joseph H.] *The South-West. By a Yankee....* 2 vols., New York, 1835.

Jackson, Andrew. *Correspondence of Andrew Jackson,* ed. by John Spencer Bassett. 6 vols. Washington, 1926–28.

Knight, Lucien Lamar. *Reminiscences of Famous Georgians, Embracing Episodes and Incidents in the Lives of the Great Men of the State....* Atlanta, 1907–1908.

Lynch, James D. *The Bench and Bar of Mississippi.* New York, 1881.

McKenney, Thomas L. *The Indian Tribes of North America, with Biographical Sketches and Anecdotes of the Principal Chiefs.* New ed., Washington, 1933–34.

McKenney, Thomas L. *Memoirs, Official and Personal....* New York, 1846.

Miller, Stephen F. *The Bench and Bar of Georgia: Memoirs and Sketches.* 2 vols. Philadelphia, 1858.

The New York City Directory for 1842 and 1843. New York, 1842.

Olmsted, Frederick Law. *A Journey in the Back Country.* New York, 1860.

Posey, Walter B., ed. *Alabama in the 1830's as Recorded by British Travelers.* Birmingham, 1938.

Richardson, James D., ed. *A Compilation of the Messages and Papers of the Presidents of the United States....* 20 vols. New York, n.d.

Schoolcraft, Henry R. *Archives of Aboriginal Knowledge....* 6 vols. Philadelphia, 1860.

Tuttle, Sarah. *Conversations on the Choctaw Mission.* 2 vols. Boston, 1830.

Woodward, Thomas S. *Woodward's Reminiscences of the Creek, or Muscogee Indians, Contained in Letters to Friends in Georgia and Alabama.* Montgomery, 1859. Republished with introduction by Peter A. Brannon, Tuscaloosa, 1939.

5. Journals and Newspapers

Alabama Journal (Montgomery) 1832.
Columbus Inquirer (Columbus, Ga.) 1842–46.
Daily National Intelligencer (Washington, D. C.) 1828–38.
The Free Press (Hernando, Miss.) 1839.
The Southern Galaxy (Natchez, Miss.) 1830.
The Guard (Holly Springs, Miss.) 1845–46.
The Holly Springs Gazette (Holly Springs, Miss.) 1841, 1845.
Macon Republican (Tuskegee, Ala.) 1851.
Marshall County Republican (Holly Springs, Miss.) 1838.
Missionary Herald (Boston) 1830–35.
Montgomery Advertizer (Montgomery, Ala.) October 9, 1933.
The Natchez (Natchez, Miss.) 1830.
New Orleans Commercial Bulletin 1847–54.
Niles' Register (Baltimore) 1830–38.
Oxford Observer (Oxford, Miss.) 1843.
Southern Tribune (Pontotoc, Miss.) 1843.
Spirit of the Times (Pontotoc, Miss.) 1842.
Flag of the Union (Pontotoc, Miss.) July 4, 1836.
Vicksburg Sentinel (Vicksburg, Miss.) 1844.

6. Unpublished Theses

Chappell, Gordon T. "The Life and Activities of General John Coffee." Vanderbilt University Library, Ph.D., 1941.
Hamilton, William A. "History of Holly Springs, Mississippi, to 1878." Mississippi Department of Archives and History, Ph.D., 1931.
Jones, Dallas L. "The Survey and Sale of the Public Lands in Michigan." Cornell University Library, M.A., 1951.
Neu, Irene. "A Business Biography of Erastus Corning." Cornell University Library, Ph.D., 1950.
Russell, Mattie. "Land Speculation in Tippah County, 1836–1860." Library of the University of Mississippi, M.A., 1940.
Smith, Edwin. "Land Speculation in Tate County, 1836–1860." Library of the University of Mississippi, M.A., 1941.

7. Secondary Sources

Abel, Annie H. "The History of Events Resulting in Indian Consolidation West of the Mississippi," *Annual Report of the American Historical Association for the Year 1906* (2 vols., Washington, 1908), Vol. I, 233–454.

———. "Proposals for an Indian State, 1778–1878," *Annual Report of the American Historical Association for the Year 1907* (2 vols., Washington, 1908), Vol. I, 89–104.

Abernethy, Thomas P. *From Frontier to Plantation in Tennessee: A Study of Frontier Democracy.* Chapel Hill, 1932.

———. *The Formative Period in Alabama, 1815–1828.* Montgomery, 1922.

Bestor, Arthur J. Jr. "Patent Office Models of the Good Society; Relations between Social Reform and Westward Expansion," *American Historical Review,* Vol. LVIII (1953), 505–26.

Caughey, John R. *McGillivray of the Creeks.* Norman, 1938.

Chappell, Gordon T. "Patterns of Land Speculation in the Old Southwest," *Journal of Southern History,* Vol. XV (1949), 463–77.

Cole, Arthur C. "Cyclical and Sectional Variations in the Sale of Public Lands, 1816–1860," *Review of Economic Statistics,* Vol. IX (1927), 44–53.

Cotterill, Robert S. *The Southern Indians: The Story of the Civilized Tribes before Removal.* Norman, 1954.

Crane, Verner W. *The Southern Frontier, 1670–1732.* Philadelphia, 1929.

Cushman, Horatio B. *History of the Choctaw, Chickasaw, and Natchez Indians.* Greenville, Texas, 1899.

Davis, Franklin L. *A Study of the Uniformity of Soil Types and of Fundamental Differences between the Different Soil Series.* n.p., [Alabama], 1936.

Debo, Angie. *The Five Civilized Tribes of Oklahoma: Report on Social and Economic Conditions.* Philadelphia, 1951.

———. *The Rise and Fall of the Choctaw Republic.* Norman, 1934.

———. *The Road to Disappearance.* Norman, 1941.

Dillard, Anthony W. "The Treaty of Dancing Rabbit Creek between the United States and the Choctaw Indians in 1830," *Alabama Historical Society Transactions,* Vol. III (1898–99), 99–106.

Dorfman, Joseph. "A Note on the Interpretation of Anglo-American Finance, 1837–1841," *Journal of Economic History,* Vol. IX (1951), 140–47.

Eichert, Madeleine. "Some Implications Arising from Robert J. Walker's Participation in Land Ventures," *Journal of Mississippi History*, Vol. XIII (1951), 41–46.

Foreman, Grant. *The Five Civilized Tribes*. Norman, 1934.

———. *The Last Trek of the Indians*. Chicago, 1946.

———. *Indian Removal: The Emigration of the Five Civilized Tribes of Indians*. Norman, 1932.

Foreman, Paul B. *Mississippi Population Trends*. Nashville, 1939.

Gates, Paul W. *Fifty Million Acres: Conflicts over Kansas Land Policy, 1854–1900*, Ithaca, 1954.

———. "Introduction," *The John Tipton Papers* (3 vols., Indianapolis, 1942), Vol. I, 3–53.

———. "Land Policy and Tenancy in the Prairie States," *Journal of Economic History*, Vol. I (1941), 60–82.

Gatschet, Albert S. *Towns and Villages of the Creek Confederacy in the XVIII and XIX Centuries*. Washington, 1901.

Gray, Lewis C. *A History of Southern Agriculture to 1860*. 2 vols. Washington, 1933.

Halbert, H. S. "Funeral Customs of the Mississippi Choctaws," Mississippi Historical Society *Publications* (Jackson and Oxford), Vol. III (1900), 353–66.

———. "The Last Indian Council on Noxubee River," *ibid.* (Jackson and Oxford), Vol. IV (1901), 271–80.

———. "The Story of the Treaty of Dancing Rabbit Creek," *ibid.* (Jackson and Oxford), Vol. VI (1903), 373–90.

Hall, Arthur H. "The Red Stick War," *Chronicles of Oklahoma*, Vol. XII (September, 1934), 264–93.

Harmon, George D. *Sixty Years of Indian Affairs, 1789–1850*. Chapel Hill, 1941.

———. "The Indian Trust Funds, 1797–1865,'" *Mississippi Valley Historical Review*, Vol. XXI (1934), 23–30.

Hibbard, Benjamin H. *History of the Public Land Policies*. New York, 1924.

Hidy, Ralph W. *The House of Baring in American Trade and Finance*. Cambridge, 1949.

Hodge, Frederick W. *Handbook of American Indians North of Mexico*. 2 vols. Washington, 1907–10.

Hofstadter, Richard. *The American Political Tradition and the Men Who Made It*. New York, 1954.

Bibliography

James Marquis. *The Life of Andrew Jackson.* Indianapolis, 1938.

Johnson, Charles R. "Railroad Legislation and Building in Mississippi, 1830–1840," *Journal of Mississippi History,* Vol. IV (1942), 195–206.

Kinney, Jay P. *A Continent Lost—a Civilization Won; Indian Land Tenure in America.* Baltimore, 1937.

Kroeber, Alfred L. *Cultural and Natural History of Native North America.* Berkeley and Los Angeles, 1939.

Livermore, Shaw. *Early American Land Companies and their Influence on Corporate Organization.* New York, 1939.

Lowe, Edgar N. *Geology, Soils, and Agriculture of Mississippi.* Jackson, 1915.

Lowry, Albert, and William A. McCardle. *A History of Mississippi from the Discovery of the Great River by Hernando De Soto, Including the Earliest Settlement Made by the French, under Iberville, to the Death of Jefferson Davis.* New York, 1891.

Lumpkin, Wilson. *The Removal of the Cherokee Indians from Georgia.* 2 vols. New York, 1907.

McCorvey, Thomas C. "The Mission of Francis Scott Key to Alabama in 1833," Alabama Historical Society *Transactions,* Vol. IV (1904), 141–65.

McGrane, Reginald C. *Foreign Bondholders and American State Debts.* New York, 1935.

———. *The Panic of 1837: Some Financial Problems of the Jacksonian Era.* Chicago, 1924.

Malone, Henry T. *Cherokees of the Old South: A People in Transition.* Athens, 1956.

Martin, J. H. *Columbus, Georgia.* n.p., 1874–75.

Myers, Marvin. *The Jacksonian Persuasion: Politics and Belief.* Stanford, 1957.

Moore, Albert B. *History of Alabama and her People.* 4 vols. Chicago and New York, 1927.

Owen, Thomas M. *History of Alabama and Dictionary of Alabama Biography.* 4 vols. Chicago, 1921.

Pearce, Roy H. *The Savages of America: a Study of the Indian and the Idea of Civilization.* Baltimore, 1953.

Phillips, Ulrich B. *Georgia and State Rights. A Study of the Political History of Georgia from the Revolution to the Civil War, with Particular Regard to Federal Relations.* Washington, 1902.

Pound, Merritt B. *Benjamin Hawkins, Indian Agent.* Athens, 1951.

Priddy, Richard R. *Pontotoc County Mineral Resources.* (*Mississippi State Geological Survey Bulletin 54.*) University, 1943.

Priest, Loring B. *Uncle Sam's Stepchildren: The Reformation of United States Indian Policy, 1865–1887.* New Brunswick, New Jersey, 1942.

Redlich, Fritz. *The Moulding of American Banking: Men and Ideas.* 2 vols. New York, 1947, 1951.

Riley, Franklin L. "The Choctaw Land Claims," Mississippi Historical Society *Publications* (Jackson and Oxford), Vol. VIII (1904), 370–82.

Robbins, Roy M. *Our Landed Heritage: The Public Domain, 1776–1936.* Princeton, 1941.

Royce, Charles C., comp. *Indian Land Cessions in the United States. Eighteenth Annual Report of the Bureau of American Ethnology.* 2 vols., Washington, 1899. Vol. II.

Sakolski, A. M. *The Great American Land Bubble. . . .* New York, 1932.

Schmeckebeier, Lawrence F. *The Office of Indian Affairs, Its History, Activities and Organization.* Baltimore, 1927.

Scott, John C. *Mississippi Soils: Classification and Use.* New York, 1938.

Sellers, Charles G. Jr. "Andrew Jackson versus the Historians," *Mississippi Valley Historical Review,* Vol. XLIV (1958), 615–34.

Silver, James W. "General Gaines Meets Governor Troup. A State-Federal Clash in 1825," *Georgia Historical Quarterly,* Vol. XXVII (1943), 248–70.

———. "Land Speculation Profits in the Chickasaw Cession," *Journal of Southern History,* Vol. X (1944), 84–92.

Sioussat, St. George F. "Andrew Johnson and the Early Phases of the Homestead Bill," *Mississippi Valley Historical Review.* Vol. V (1918), 253–87.

Smith, Walter B. *Economic Aspects of the Second Bank of the United States.* Cambridge, 1953.

Spoehr, Alexander. "Changing Kinship Systems," Field Museum of Natural History *Anthropological Series,* Vol. XXXIII (1947), 201–30.

Starkey, Marion L. *The Cherokee Nation.* New York, 1946.

Stephenson, George M. *The Political History of the Public Lands from 1840–1862.* Boston, 1917.

Swanton, John R. *Aboriginal Culture of the Southeast.* (Bureau of American Ethnology, *Forty-Second Annual Report.*) Washington, 1928, 673–726.

———. *Indians of the Southeastern United States.* (Bureau of American Ethnology, *Bulletin 137.*) Washington, 1946.

———. *Social and Religious Beliefs and Usages of the Chickasaw Indians.* (Bureau of American Ethnology, *Forty-Fourth Annual Report.*) Washington, 1928, 169–273.

———. *Social Organization and Social Usages of the Indians of the Creek Confederacy.* (Bureau of American Ethnology, *Forty-Second Annual Report.*) Washington, 1928, 23–472.

———. *Source Material for the Social and Ceremonial Life of the Choctaw Indians.* (Bureau of American Ethnology, *Bulletin 103.*) Washington, 1941.

Telfair, Nancy. *A History of Columbus, Georgia, 1828–1928.* Columbus, 1929.

Walker, Anne Kendrick. *Backtracking in Barbour County.* Richmond, 1941.

———. *Russell County in Retrospect: An Epic of the Far Southeast.* Richmond, 1945.

Ward, John W. *Andrew Jackson: Symbol for an Age.* New York, 1955.

Weaver, Herbert B. *Mississippi Farmers, 1850–1860.* Nashville, 1945.

Wellington, Raynor G. *Political and Sectional Influence of the Public Lands, 1828–1842.* Boston, 1914.

Williams, Clanton Ware. "Early Ante-Bellum Montgomery: A Black-Belt Constituency," *Journal of Southern History,* Vol. VII (November, 1941), 495–525.

Zahler, Helen S. *Eastern Workingmen and National Land Policy, 1829–1862.* New York, 1941.

8. Biographical Dictionaries

Biographical Directory of the American Congress.
Dictionary of American Biography.
National Cyclopedia of American Biography.

9. Soil Surveys (Available at the Library of the United States Geological Survey, Washington, D. C.)

N. E. Bell, L. A. Hunt, and J. M. Snyder. *Soil Survey of Russell County, Alabama.* Washington, 1915.

W. E. Hearn and W. J. Geib. *Soil Survey of Lee County, Alabama.* Washington, 1907.

H. G. Lewis, C. S. Waldorp, and F. W. Kolb. *Soil Survey of Cleburne County, Alabama.* Washington, 1915.

Cecil Lounsbury, Robert Wildermoth, G. A. Swanson, M. M. Striker, L. G. Brackeen, Hoyt Sherrod, C. L. McIntyre, and V. O. Callahan. *Soil Survey, Macon County, Alabama.* Washington, 1944.

C. N. Mooney and Charles Nun. *Soil Survey of Talladega County, Alabama.* Washington, 1908.

H. C. Smith and P. H. Avery. *Soil Survey of Chambers County, Alabama.* Washington, 1911.

H. C. Smith, N. Eric Bell, and J. F. Stroud. *Soil Survey of Barbour County, Alabama.* Washington, 1916.

A. E. Taylor, E. S. Vanatta, N. E. Bell, and J. L. Andreas. *Soil Survey of Clay County, Alabama.* Washington, 1916.

R. A. Winston and A. C. McGehee. *Soil Survey of Elmore County, Alabama.* Washington, 1913.

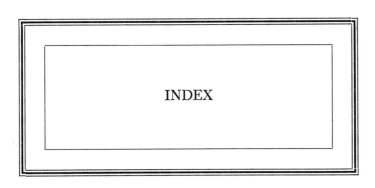

INDEX

Index

213

THE CIVILIZATION OF THE AMERICAN INDIAN SERIES
of which *Redskins, Ruffleshirts, and Rednecks: Indian Allotments in Alabama and Mississippi, 1830–1860* is the sixty-first volume, was inaugurated in 1932 by the University of Oklahoma Press, and has as its purpose the reconstruction of American Indian civilization by presenting aboriginal, historical, and contemporary Indian life. The following list is complete as of the date of publication of this volume:

1. Alfred Barnaby Thomas. *Forgotten Frontiers*: A study of the Spanish Indian Policy of Don Juan Bautista de Anza, Governor of New Mexico, 1777–1787. Out of print.
2. Grant Foreman. *Indian Removal*: The Emigration of the Five Civilized Tribes of Indians.
3. John Joseph Mathews. *Wah'Kon-Tah*: The Osage and the White Man's Road. Out of print.
4. Grant Foreman. *Advancing the Frontier, 1830–1860*. Out of print.
5. John Homer Seger. *Early Days Among the Cheyenne and Arapahoe Indians*. Edited by Stanley Vestal.
6. Angie Debo. *The Rise and Fall of the Choctaw Republic*.
7. Stanley Vestal (ed.). *New Sources of Indian History, 1850–1891*. Out of print.
8. Grant Foreman. *The Five Civilized Tribes*. Out of print.
9. Alfred Barnaby Thomas. *After Coronado*: Spanish Exploration Northeast of New Mexico, 1696–1727. Out of print.
10. Frank B. Speck. *Naskapi*: The Savage Hunters of the Labrador Peninsula. Out of print.
11. Elaine Goodale Eastman. *Pratt*: The Red Man's Moses. Out of print.
12. Althea Bass. *Cherokee Messenger*: A Life of Samuel Austin Worcester. Out of print.
13. Thomas Wildcat Alford. *Civilization*. As told to Florence Drake. Out of print.
14. Grant Foreman. *Indians and Pioneers*: The Story of the American Southwest Before 1830. Out of print.
15. George E. Hyde. *Red Cloud's Folk*: A History of the Oglala Sioux Indians.

16. Grant Foreman. *Sequoyah.*
17. Morris L. Wardell. *A Political History of the Cherokee Nation, 1838–1907.* Out of print.
18. John Walton Caughey. *McGillivray of the Creeks.*
19. Edward Everett Dale and Gaston Litton. *Cherokee Cavaliers*: Forty Years of Cherokee History as Told in the Correspondence of the Ridge-Watie-Boudinot Family. Out of print.
20. Ralph Henry Gabriel. *Elias Boudinot, Cherokee, and His America.*
21. Karl N. Llewellyn and E. Adamson Hoebel. *The Cheyenne Way*: Conflicts and Case Law in Primitive Jurisprudence.
22. Angie Debo. *The Road to Disappearance.* Out of print.
23. Oliver La Farge and others. *The Changing Indian.* Out of print.
24. Carolyn Thomas Foreman. *Indians Abroad.* Out of print.
25. John Adair. *The Navajo and Pueblo Silversmiths.*
26. Alice Marriott. *The Ten Grandmothers.*
27. Alice Marriott. *María*: The Potter of San Ildefonso.
28. Edward Everett Dale. *The Indians of the Southwest*: A Century of Development under the United States. Out of print.
29. Adrián Recinos. *Popol Vuh:* The Sacred Book of the Ancient Quiché Maya. English version by Delia Goetz and Sylvanus G. Morley from the translation of Adrián Recinos.
30. Walter Collins O'Kane. *Sun in the Sky.*
31. Stanley A. Stubbs. *Bird's-Eye View of the Pueblos.*
32. Katharine C. Turner. *Red Men Calling on the Great White Father.*
33. Muriel H. Wright. *A Guide to the Indian Tribes of Oklahoma.*
34. Ernest Wallace and E. Adamson Hoebel. *The Comanches*: Lords of the South Plains.
35. Walter Collins O'Kane. *The Hopis*: Portrait of a Desert People.
36. Joseph Epes Brown. *The Sacred Pipe*: Black Elk's Account of the Seven Rites of the Oglala Sioux.
37. Adrián Recinos and Delia Goetz. *The Annals of the Cakchiquels.* Translated from the Cakchiquel Maya, with *Title of the Lords of Totonicapán*, translated from the Quiché text into Spanish by Dionisio José Chonay, English version by Delia Goetz.
38. R. S. Cotterill. *The Southern Indians*: The Story of the Civilized Tribes Before Removal.
39. J. Eric S. Thompson. *The Rise and Fall of Maya Civilization.*

40. Robert Emmitt. *The Last War Trail*: The Utes and the Settlement of Colorado.
41. Frank Gilbert Roe. *The Indian and the Horse.*
42. Francis Haines. *The Nez Percés*: Tribesmen of the Columbia Plateau. Out of print.
43. Ruth M. Underhill. *The Navajos.*
44. George Bird Grinnell. *The Fighting Cheyennes.*
45. George E. Hyde. *A Sioux Chronicle.*
46. Stanley Vestal. *Sitting Bull*: Champion of the Sioux, A Biography.
47. Edwin C. McReynolds. *The Seminoles.*
48. William T. Hagan. *The Sac and Fox Indians.*
49. John C. Ewers. *The Blackfeet*: Raiders on the Northwestern Plains.
50. Alfonso Caso. *The Aztecs*: People of the Sun. Translated by Lowell Dunham.
51. C. L. Sonnichsen. *The Mescalero Apaches.*
52. Keith A. Murray. *The Modocs and Their War.*
53. Victor W. von Hagen (ed.). *The Incas of Pedro de Cieza de León*. Translated by Harriet de Onis.
54. George E. Hyde. *Indians of the High Plains*: From the Prehistoric Period of the Coming of Europeans.
55. *George Catlin. Episodes from "Life Among the Indians" and "Last Rambles."* Edited by Marvin C. Ross.
56. J. Eric S. Thompson. *Maya Hieroglyphic Writing*: An Introduction.
57. George E. Hyde. *Spotted Tail's Folk*: A History of the Brulé Sioux.
58. James Larpenteur Long. *The Assiniboines*: From the Accounts of the Old Ones Told to First Boy (James Larpenteur Long). Edited and with an introduction by Michael Stephen Kennedy.
59. Edwin Thompson Denig. *Five Indian Tribes of the Upper Missouri*. Edited and with an introduction by John C. Ewers.
60. John Joseph Mathews. *The Osages*: Children of the Middle Waters.
61. Mary Elizabeth Young. *Redskins, Ruffleshirts, and Rednecks*: Indian Allotments in Alabama and Mississippi, 1830–1860.

The text of *Redskins, Ruffleshirts, and Rednecks* has been set on the Linotype in eleven-point Caledonia with two points of leading between lines. W. A. Dwiggins, the American designer of Caledonia, gave this type a name reminiscent of the Scotch face from which he had modified his design. One source of inspiration to Dwiggins in creating Caledonia was a type used by Bulmer around 1790, of which a replica has been used on the title page of this book.

UNIVERSITY OF OKLAHOMA PRESS

NORMAN